Also by Dennis Ford

Red Star

Thinking About Everything

Genealogical Jaunts

Landsman

Eight Generations

Miles of Thoughts

Including Excellent Groaners and Professor Fawcett's Notorious Lecture on Test-Irrelevant Thoughts

Dennis Ford

Miles of Thoughts
Including Excellent Groaners and Professor Fawcett's
Notorious Lecture on Test-Irrelevant Thoughts

iUniverse books may be ordered through booksellers or by contacting:

iUniverse
1663 Liberty Drive
Bloomington, IN 47403
www.iuniverse.com
844-349-9409

ISBN: 978-1-4759-2467-1 (sc)
ISBN: 978-1-4759-2469-5 (hc)
ISBN: 978-1-4759-2468-8 (e)

Library of Congress Control Number: 2012908356

Print information available on the last page.

iUniverse rev. date: 10/29/2020

for my Mother, still here, still reading

for Bluesman Mike Lindner, still here, still working up lyrics

for County Road 539, still my shelter against vehicular madness and

to the memory of my Father and to the roads he drove

TABLE OF CONTENTS

Readers of my earlier book *Thinking About Everything* asked if I would ever write a sequel in the same style of short whimsical musings. I said I never would—when I said this I raised my voice for emphasis. I believe I also used the phrase "Out of the question." But I'm not a virtuous person. I never keep my promises. A sequel was very much *in the question*.

It made all the sense in the world to write a second book of musings. I still drive outlandish distances through the New Jersey Pine Barrens to earn a living at the great Barnes & Noble Distribution Center in Monroe Township. And I still drive the length of the Garden State Parkway to teach General Psychology one day a week at the Borough of Manhattan Community College on Chambers St. By now I've reached the outer rim of the solar system with all the miles I've put on my reliable Saturn *Ion*. I'm sure I'll pass the *Voyager* spacecraft in the near future. I'm a cautious driver and I know the law. I'll be sure to flash the high beams and put the turn signal on when I pass *Voyager*. And I won't cross a solid yellow line even if the oncoming traffic is light.

I'm still on the road and I'm still assailed by *thoughts*—to be exact, by 200 thoughts since October 2008. I can't help myself. It's beyond my power to resist. Whenever I find a thought on the side of the road I pull over and pick it up. If we get along I take the thought home and swaddle it on lined pieces of paper. If we don't get along I let the thought out at the next traffic light. I'm not worried that harm will come to the thought or that it will be left stranded. The tall twisted forest will watch over it like the crossing guards watched over me when I was in grade school and waiting at the curb for the light to turn to green. The thought won't be left alone for long. Another motorist who likes to muse whimsically will pick it up in no time and give the thought a proper paper home.

In addition to these musings I've included for your enjoyment *Excellent Groaners*, a medley of puns, word play, and what I like to believe are witticisms. For your intellectual enjoyment I've included *Prof. Fawcett's Notorious Lecture on Test-Irrelevant Thoughts*. This was a lecture I recorded when I was taking graduate courses at Umatilla University in Lake County, Florida. Told partly in acronyms, Prof. Fawcett's provocative lecture was on the psychological perils of test anxiety. Readers interested in personality functioning will find the lecture stimulating. Anxious readers will find the lecture particularly informative and they don't have to worry—there won't be a test afterward.

MILES OF THOUGHTS

1. Many people are convinced the world is coming to an end. Preachers tell us we are living at the end of time—this is presumably the same as the "end times". This sort of religious prognostication has been going on for centuries—twenty centuries, as a matter of record. The current crop of nigh-sayers with white collars and crosses can be considered diremen in the snooker-and-larder brigade.

They ought to know better, but the scientific crowd has grown equally giddy over the possibility that the end is imminent. The modus operandi for Armageddon is a bit diverse in science compared to that in religion in which Jesus and Satan more or less dook it out amid human cannon fodder. Some scientists claim we are going to suffocate as the greenhouse effect squeezes the collective breath out of us. Other scientists claim we are going to take it on the continental chin when the big asteroid unleashes a cosmic right hook. Still other scientists claim the world will end as humanity incinerates itself in a hailstorm of hydrogen bombs. And there are scientists who put the odds on a little creature called a virus that is presently exchanging feathers for hairy nasal passages.

So the world will end with fire and brimstone. Or with carbon dioxide. Or with a cosmic right hook. Or with H-bombs and nuclear rain. Or with wheezing, sneezing, runny noses, and day trips to the toilet. If it turns out that a virus does the human race in, the *Four Horsemen* will have to be renamed "Sweat", "Pus", "Bile", and "Phlegm".

2. The *Four Horsemen* are not the four guys in the warehouse with stuffy noses and sore throats. According to the *Book of Revelation* they are the apocalyptic figures who usher in the end of the world. In our time the *Four Horsemen* is a sexist term. The modern usage prefers *Four Horsepersons*. To be equitable to half the world's population and balance things out we need to change the gender of two horsepersons. I opt to make Famine and Pestilence female. War and Death can stay male.

The end of the world will come and it will be nonsexist when it arrives.

3. The world is indeed worried about avian flu. Since we have no immunity, the fear is infection could rapidly turn into a pandemic. If a

pandemic breaks out, there won't be any rheum in the ER. As a species we will be in the proverbial "big trouble".

Symptoms of avian flu are similar to that of seasonal flu, with one difference. There are the usual fevers, chills, night sweats, nausea, and trots to the toilet. A symptom unique to avian flu is a fondness for lying in dirt and flapping the arms and legs and dust bathing. If I feel that symptom coming on I intend to buy two bottles of Remy Martin XO. One bottle is for me. The other bottle is for the Ferryman. I prefer a window seat on the boat to the Great Beyond and I hear the Ferryman is susceptible to bribes.

You are welcome to join me if you feel the urge to drop to the ground and dust bathe. Climb up and sit with me on the branch. We can hold hands and reminisce and comfort one another and pass the bottle back and forth.

When it comes to the Ferryman, you'll have to buy your own bottle.

4. The Borough of Manhattan Community College is doing what it can to keep avian flu from the halls of learning in the great building on Chambers St. There are signs in the men's room informing students how to wash. I presume the same information is posted in the ladies' room, but I've never been in the ladies' room.

TO STOP THE GERMS the signs advise students to WET, SOAP, SCRUB, RINSE, DRY, TURN OFF THE WATER. Pictures accompany each step in the process. The pictures are for the students who don't read English.

There is a problem. I don't see how any of this good advice can work. The signs tell students to TURN OFF THE WATER. They don't tell students to TURN ON THE WATER. Students can't proceed to WET unless they TURN ON THE WATER, but they're not told to do that. They will never get to WET.

God keep us from the imminent pan-academic outbreak.

5. The inquiring mind would like to ask, "If the pandemic starts, can we break out of the outbreak?"

6. On summer evenings a Pinelands entrepreneur sells grilled chicken from a flatbed in a parking lot in Warren Grove on County Road 539.

He places advertisements along the road. They are simple wooden signs at fender level that announce "Piney chicken!" in magic marker. This kind of ad produces instant curiosity in drivers going slow enough to read road signs. "Piney chicken? How is that different from chicken that isn't Piney grilled—or is it grilled Piney?" The answer is Piney chicken is the same as grilled chicken in the rest of the state except for the feathers.

7.   If any movie ever came to a decisive conclusion it was James Cameron's *Titanic*. The ship has broken in two and sunk. Jack Dawson has drowned. Rose Dewitt Bukater has survived into old age. She revisits the site of the wreck, tosses the jewels her psycho boyfriend hid in her coat pocket, and quietly slips into the gala going on in the Great Beyond. A sequel didn't appear possible—until now. I've sent the studio an outline tentatively entitled *Titanic Two*.

Here's the story line. Jack won the ticket that got him admission to the doomed liner, but he never got aboard. He was struck by a shillelagh and knocked unconscious by a friend who took the ticket and made the voyage in his place. Jack has been in a coma for days. He's been dreaming he's on board. He's been dreaming the story we saw in *Titanic*.

He awakes from the coma at the exact moment the black and gold stacks blow. A nurse lovingly rubs his forehead with a cool sponge. Of course, the nurse is Rose. Before Jack can lower the hem of his hospital gown, they fall madly in love. Just like they did on the steamship. They spend the middle of the movie cooing over each other and whispering sweet nothings in each other's ears. They also tour the famous sites in London—the film is in 70 mm. and needs panorama.

The story progresses. Jack can't find steady work and Rose has been fired for missing too much work. They decide to use their dwindling funds to buy tickets to America. They book voyage in steerage class on a liner called *Gargantua*, an imaginary sister ship of *Titanic*. (This is literary license on the high seas.) As *Gargantua* sails the North Atlantic it swerves to the starboard to avoid colliding with an iceberg and runs into a debris field filled with *Titanic* flotsam. A sharp-edged object tears a hole in the bow. *Gargantua* promptly fills with water and sinks. There are the requisite scenes of courage and cowardice on the part of the passengers and crew.

The final scene has Jack and Rose afloat on a door. The door can support only one of them. Jack looks at Rose, a last loving look of hope and despair. "Good-by, Rose," he says in a throaty voice. He pushes her off the door and holds on for dear life. Deliciously beautiful though she is, it doesn't have to be Rose in particular. Any woman can make him babies.

Rose drifts into the darkness. Her white dress balloons. Her hair spreads in a black halo. Her fingers curl in a soggy farewell. There's a look of surprise on her face.

I guarantee there won't be a dry eye in the theater.

8. I ask myself what I would have done if I were Jack Dawson and found myself floating on a door in the North Atlantic next to Rose Dewitt Bukater. Would I have let go and slipped into the sea, as in the original? Or would I have shoved Rose off and hugged the door for myself, as in the sequel?

I like to think I would have done the manly—the manful—thing and let Rose stay afloat, but I can't say for sure. We like to flatter ourselves, but we can't know what we'd do until we're in particular situations. By then, it may be too late to salvage our reputations. The urge to life is very strong and, let's face it, the temperature of the water was 40 degrees.

9. My co-workers were talking about food today. They talk about food nearly every day. The topic was jam, as in which kind do they prefer to smear on bread. Two preferred cranberry jam—they don't acknowledge it, but they are Lutherans. One preferred blueberry. Another preferred boysenberry, whatever that tastes like. One opted for raspberry—she's a Libertine and everyone knows it.

I opted for paper jam. There's nothing more delicious than a slice of paper on a mini-baguette with onions, tomatoes, lettuce, and a strip of pickle. I like to soak the insides of the bread with mayo and vinegar. This gives the paper a crinkly taste that tickles the palate.

I prefer lined to unlined paper. The lines give the paper texture. "Al dente," the Italians call it and they ought to know. Sometimes the lines get stuck in my teeth. They can be difficult to floss. If you've ever swallowed a hair in the shower, you know the sensation.

I most definitely prefer blank paper. If I accidentally eat paper that has words written on it, I immediately spit them out. Doing so, I take the words right out of my mouth.

I overdo it on occasion and binge on three-hole lined loose leave paper. I know it sounds déclassé, but I like the cheap paper they sell in the discount stores. The paper gets all stringy in my mouth, but I can crunch on it to my heart's content and give the jaw muscles a workout. It's like eating a ream of celery.

I call this kind of binge a paper jamboree.

10. Apropos of the previous entry, if you and I are *on the same page*, we're sharing dinner.

11. We're broke down in the parking lot in the Orlando International Airport. The tow-truck operator, a good ole boy type, gets the battery charged. (He was in a hurry to get us fixed—he was on his way to the Clay County mud hop.) I show him my Triple-A card and my driver's license. He looks at the license and snickers, "New Jersey, eh."

The remark was bad enough, but the snicker put me out. Does he snicker when people from Montana break down? Or people from Oklahoma? Or people from Texas or from Nebraska? What is it about New Jersey that brings out the snicker in good ole boy types? Is it pity? Is it compassion? Is it a feeling of superiority? Is it a feeling of resentment? It must be resentment. I don't think the snicker expresses a feeling of admiration. If it were admiration he would have said, "New Jersey, wow," instead of "New Jersey, eh."

12. We've had popes named "John". We've had popes named "Paul". We had a pope named "John Paul". We had another pope named "John Paul". We've never had a pope named "John Paul George Ringo." Maybe we ought to. A pope named "John Paul George Ringo" might invigorate the laity and bring lapsed Catholics back into the blue folds of Holy Mother Church.

On second thought the only Catholics who would return to the fold are senior citizens and people nearing retirement.

It's not a bad thing that seniors and people nearing retirement return to the Church before they cross Abbey Road to the concert hall in the clouds.

13. Pope John Paul George Ringo may not work with the new generation, but young people who don't bathe regularly may find spiritual solace in this. I saw an advertisement for the Church of the Holy Turnbuckle, Pastor Modesto Fidelis ministerin'.

"Join us in worshippin' the World Heavyweight Cham-peen, Superstar Jesus Christ!

"Watch as Pastor Fidelis body slams unbelievers! Watch as Pastor Fidelis slaps the sleeper hold on sinners! Watch as Pastor Fidelis drop kicks the angel of darkness out of the ring and clamps the figure-four leg lock on Satan himself!

"Pastor Fidelis teams up with you know who in a no-disqualification, no-holds-barred match and takes on the Brimstone Bulldogs, Baal and Beel-lousy-bub!

"Come early for front row seats and bring the children. And don't let your hands cramp up when the collection plate circulates."

14. It turns out that Desi Arnaz, the beloved television icon, was into voodoo big-time. He sang songs addressed to "Hey, Baba Looba!" These songs were accompanied by soft shoe steps and a full orchestra of guys in white tuxedoes and snappy red bowties. Off camera Desi waved incense sticks and poured shot glasses of rum over statues of Baba Looba. Back stage Desi slaughtered chickens and rodents in ritual sacrifice to Baba Looba.

Desi prayed to Baba Looba that William Frawley never say a funny line or make a funny move on *I Love Lucy*.

It worked. Fred Mertz, the William Frawley character, never said anything funny or did anything funny in all the years the series ran. He wasn't the least bit funny. He wasn't remotely funny. He wasn't in the same universe as funny. He was the inverse of funny.

There may be something to voodoo after all.

15. Imagine this. Desi Arnaz is God. You know who the Devil is. I can hear God exclaiming in the most exasperated Cuban accent, "Lucy-fer, you ja-have es-plainin' to do."

16. Quoting Romans 3:23, the preacher remarked, "We have all sinned and fallen short of the Glory of God." I think he should speak for himself.

17. There are no stupid questions. There are only stupid people who ask questions.

It never fails. Every semester there is always one student who is not part of the program. This student is so far out of the curriculum he doesn't belong in the same building as his peers, still less in the same classroom. This doesn't stop him from asking questions, multitudes of questions, none of which have any relevance to the topic at hand.

This semester the honor of enunciating non sequiturs fell on Edwin C—, a wiry and often wired eighteen-year-old from the borough of Brooklyn. Edwin had the appreciated talent of never knowing what chapter we were covering and of never knowing what was being discussed in class. If we were covering memory, he asked about clinical psychology. (He noticed a neighbor liked to cross dress.) If we were covering clinical psychology, he asked about memory. (He has a relative who remembered being born and he wanted to know if that were possible and how come he didn't remember being born.) If we were covering motivation, he asked about social psychology. (He was bullied growing up and he wanted to know why everyone picked on him.) If we were covering social psychology, he asked about motivation. (He has an aunt who is grossly overweight and what should she do to slim down before she explodes.) This went on all semester long. There was no way to stop Edwin and no way to prevent him from bringing the class to a flustered, if not flabbergasted, stop—a vexcine is not available for his kind of student. He was never in step with the class and he was always speaking out of turn and asking questions that were not only beside the point they were nowhere in the vicinity of the point. The questions couldn't reach the point with the tongs senior citizens use to pick up their socks and panty hose.

The single occasion Edwin asked a question that was on topic produced a memorable question and an equally memorable answer. I was lecturing on brain plasticity, which is the process in which the ever-malleable neurons of the cerebral cortex form new pathways whenever anything new is learned. I explained how dendrites and axons proliferate on the basis of new learning and new experiences and how brain cells connect and interconnect at the synapses. I mentioned that there are billons of neurons in the cortex and trillions of synaptic connections, more connections than there are stars in the Milky Way. At this glorious point in the lecture Edwin raised his hand and asked before he was called on, "Mister"—we were seven weeks into the semester and Edwin didn't know my name—"if my brain is plastic, does that mean it's made of the same material as a soda bottle?" He pronounced the word "soda" as "sodie".

I wasn't mad at the question. I understood he wasn't being provocative. He was serious, insofar as a witless person could be serious. I pointed my zinger at him and answered with a grin, "Yes, Edwin, your brain is made of the same material as a soda bottle." I pronounced the word "soda". "That's why we call it protoplastic."

18. I was picking up pictures at the photography kiosk at the local pharmacy the other day. I had to wait an interminable period of time for an elderly lady who was getting special treatment and having her pictures developed on the spot. When she was done she laid the pictures on the counter for the sales clerk to see. Presumably, they were meant for me to see as well. They were pictures of bulls and cows. The bulls were identifiable by their immense antlers and by straw goatees. The cows—lady bulls—had the goatees but not the antlers. Both bulls and cows wore the same dumb looks, as befit a species who has never wised up to why they are being fattened.

One photograph showed a white object lying in the grass. It was a baby cow recently born and so new to the world it couldn't walk to find sticks of straw to form a goatee. The customer said they had to wait till the cow stood up before they could determine its sex. I got off at that point what I thought was a pretty good joke. I said, "If it turns out to be a male, you can name it Hugh Heifer."

Neither lady laughed. Maybe it wasn't as good a joke as I thought. Maybe they didn't have a sense of humor. Maybe they didn't get the reference. The customer looked like a hick. She was wearing blue jeans and a plaid shirt. I'm sure she had a ten-gallon hat in the pickup parked in the handicapped spot. But the sales clerk was in her early thirties and looked like a sophisticate. Her fingernails were painted purple and she looked a fellow in the eye when she rang him up. She should have gotten the reference.

I got a little embarrassed at this point, having admitted I knew who Hugh Heifer was.

19. Gangsters use the verb "plugged" as a synonym for getting shot, as in "Mother of God, I've been plugged!" It follows that when a gangster goes to the emergency room and the surgeon on call removes the bullet he can accurately say, "I've been unplugged!"

20. This actually happened. I wanted to write it down for posterity's sake—and for memory's.

I'm in Manhattan at the corner of University Place and 13th St. I'm standing over a garbage can. I'm not scavenging for leftovers, I'm finishing the last cold sips of the $3.59 mocha latte I bought at the Bolivian Coffee Bar on Second Ave. The block ahead of me is like any other in the Union Square district. It's dark and dingy and teeming with a conglomeration of natives and tourists rushing to the subway station a block to the north. A homeless person squats Buddha-style near the door of a hardware store in the middle of the block. He's a slim young man about thirty years of age. He has black hair and the scruff of a beard. His clothes are as dark as his hair. It's hot and humid in the middle of summer, but he wears a windbreaker zipped to the neck. A duffel bag is against his leg on the right side. He holds a cardboard sign on his lap. He doesn't have to speak or say a word to beg. The sign says what it needs to, "Please help. I'm homeless and hungry."

A dark dingy street. Teeming masses hurrying on their business. A beggar on the sidewalk in the midst of the chaos. No one pays attention to him or to his sign. The scene is repeated on city blocks from Battery Place to Harlem Heights. But there is one difference. This beggar has placed a plastic cup filled with ice on the sidewalk in front of him.

The cup is immediately kicked over by a pedestrian who rushes by mindlessly making animated conversation with two partners. At first the guy doesn't know what happened. He must have thought he kicked a piece of garbage over. The beggar reaches for his cup. He rights the cup and places it on his lap. His hands gesture palms upward—it's a gesture of hopelessness. If the pedestrian takes another step he is going to stamp the ice into a stain.

When the pedestrian realizes what he did he's mortified. Nothing could be more pathetic. He kicked over a beggar's cup of water. He may as well have spit or trampled on the beggar. His partners stop talking and hurry forward. They don't want to be seen with him. He sputters an apology, takes his wallet out, and drops a few dollars beside the cup. He rushes to join his partners. They disappear into the crush of humanity.

The beggar doesn't say a word. He folds the bills and slips them inside the windbreaker. He wipes the rim of the cup and leans forward to see how far the three men have advanced—they are gone from sight. He opens the duffel bag, takes out a thermos, and fills the cup with water. He returns the thermos inside the duffel and replaces it with a plastic bag packed with ice cubes. He strikes the bag on the sidewalk, opens it, and loosens a few chunks he slips into the cup. He returns the bag of ice to the duffel and places the refreshed cup of water an arm's length in front of him. It's sure to be kicked over in no time by another oblivious pedestrian.

The scam is so clever it melts the hard hearts of New Yorkers. I must remember it in the event that I'm ever homeless and hungry. I might even try it as a second job or when I need extra cash around the holidays. It seems like an easy way to earn a living. All I'll need is a cup, a thermos, a bag of ice, and a good location.

I take the last sip of latte and drop the cup into the can. I'm on my way. I have a train to catch. When I pass the hardware store I'm careful, very careful, to stay on the curbside.

21. Many people speak two languages. In the old days it was English and French or English and German. Those were the languages of commerce and of science. Today English and Spanish are the norm. There's even a version called "Spanglish" in which speakers glide seamlessly between the two languages. For a while English and Japanese were popular,

but this has been nipped since the Japanese economy went *sayounara*. English and Chinese is growing in popularity for the sensible reason that there will always be jobs at Wal-Mart.

I speak only English and that with a bad accent. But I keyboard in two languages. Without sounding immodest, I'm proficient in English and in Typonese, especially the latter.

22. This was overheard on the ferry to the Great Beyond. "There was nothing wrong with the grilled chicken. The feathers tasted fine."

23. Words that refer to pregnancy and to childbirth don't ordinarily relate to men, but there are exceptions, like what happened in the lunch room in the Distribution Center the other day. I walked in behind Leila, one of the merchandise directors. Leila is a prim and proper matronly executive who has been in retail since Barnes bought Noble. She had on the standard gray sweater and green shirt. Her salt-and-pepper hair was kept short. Her half glasses hung on a chain around her neck.

Leila went to the refrigerator to get her container of garlic hummus. I went to the water cooler to get a drink. I grabbed a cup, placed it under the faucet, and poured. I raised the cup to my lips, then thrust it forward before I got wet. The bottom of the Styrofoam was cut. The water poured to the floor in a gush.

I looked at the puddle and at Leila through the hole in the cup. "My water broke," I informed her calmly. "Oh," was all she said.

It was left to me to call maintenance.

24. The West has obviously run out of ideas.

The writer Seth Grahame-Smith is getting a half million dollars to write two novels based on the story line that the sixteenth president of the United States, the Great Emancipator himself, was the Van Helsing of his era. Besides being president, Abraham Lincoln had a second job as a hunter of vampires! What could be more nutty?

The following is more nutty. And more realistic. Abraham Lincoln is not a vampire hunter. He's a vampire—not the pretty boy variety of vampire but the red-eyed, drooling razor-sharp incisor variety. Behind the revered veneer of a writer, orator, military strategist, politician, and moral bastion stands one of the undead. The Civil War was unleashed to abolish slavery. The Civil War was fought to oppose States Rights. The Civil War was fought to maintain the Union. And the Civil War was perpetrated to keep Honest Abe supplied with fresh blood. The Civil War was the perfect cover for vampirism.

General Grant is the Renfield of the saga, routinely forwarding jugs of Federal blood to Washington from the battlefields of Tennessee and Virginia. Occasionally, he forwarded jugs of Secesh blood. Always a Union vampire, Lincoln preferred Federal to Confederal, but drank whatever "The Butcher" sent.

It follows that Lincoln's assassination was staged. A vampire cannot be killed with an ordinary bullet. Everybody knows that—everybody except for the dupe John Wilkes Booth. For his efforts in thinking he rid the world of a vampire Booth got plugged by the Jack Ruby of his time. And he didn't get unplugged. *Sic transit Nosferatu*—not! The crazed Edwin Stanton dug Lincoln up once the period of national mourning passed. A few drops of fresh blood squeezed out of a handkerchief brought Lincoln back to—not exactly to life, but to the kind of wholly unholy existence vampires enjoy.

Stanton told us—he warned us the night Lincoln staged his death—"Now he belongs to the ages." He certainly does. Vampires can never die. Not in the ordinary ways. Maybe not in extraordinary ways. In the Civil War no one believed the President sipped canteens of Bluebelly blood delivered nightly by cavalry officers who would ignite into flame if they rode after daybreak. In our time no one believes that the gaunt, emaciated man in a black suit and stovetop hat lurking in the darkness is the Rail Splitter himself. They think he's just a weirdo in the shadows and not a repulsive creature who intends on ensuring that the government of vampires shall not perish from the earth.

Honest Abe the vampire sounds like a best seller. In the sequel Jefferson Davis is revealed to be a werewolf. We may have a series of books on our hands. We can entitle the series *Ghouls and Generals*.

25. Today is Ash Wednesday and the start of Lent, a time when the devout ponder what to give up in honor of The Savior's suffering. Some people give up meat. Some give up sweets. Some give up caffeine beverages. Some give up carousing. Some give up swearwords. Some give up shopping sprees and the odious habit of collecting tangibles

their survivors auction on-line. Some people give up alcohol—truly, they are the devout ones. I'm going to trump all of them. I'm going to give up sin.

I suppose all this giving up is supposed to represent sacrifice. But it's an odd sacrifice and somewhat lopsided. In exchange for their Savior's suffering on Calvary Christians self-servingly give up bad habits the absence of which can only benefit them. The bad cholesterol breaks off and swims downstream. The calories reduce. Belt sizes shrink. Coffee nerves quiet. Vocabulary improves. Finances improve. Homes are less cluttered. Livers unwrinkle and grow smooth and the neurons that haven't died regenerate. For these selfish gains Jesus had to die on a Cross.

26. A bride-to-be introduces her groom as "My beau". It follows that a groom can introduce his intended as "My tie". As in knot. Rather as in *the* knot.

27. Some people live *storied* lives and careers. I'm not like those people. I live a *short storied* life and career.

28. I was in the local supermarket. A middle-aged lady in a tight pink blouse announcing "Piney Power" and tighter white stretch pants announcing too many late-night binges blocked the frozen foods aisle. She was looking for a product. The product was giving her the slip. She complained loudly, "There are no people around."

I realized she meant, "There are no salespeople around." She was right, of course. Sales help are scarcer than cops on the midnight beat. But I was a little offended. I was in the aisle. I was one carriage removed from her. I count. I'm a people.

29. My great nephews moved back to Florida from a sojourn in snowy Washington State. I reminded them of the perils of life in the Sunshine State—heat, humidity, fire ants, flying roaches, panthers, pythons, not to mention hurricanes, tornadoes, and senior citizens driving Chevy Impalas on the interstates twenty miles blow the posted speed. I reviewed with them the procedure for dealing with unexpected encounters with alligators. I told them to cross the street if they see one

and let the 'gator have the corner—they are bigger than you and they can have the corner if they want it. I told my nephews never to look the 'gator in the eye—that annoys them. If they meet one they should walk backwards slowly and never take their eyes off the 'gator. If all else fails, they should crouch and hold their sunglasses at shin level. The 'gator doesn't know who it's looking at. They don't have identities and are not self-conscious. It'll see two ugly critters reflected in the glass and think it's outnumbered. It'll turn and run. If that happens you can straighten and stand tall. But don't follow it. And whatever you do, don't look like you're gloating. We don't want the 'gators to catch onto the ruse.

There are several million 'gators in Florida and Georgia. The worry is they'll rise up and organize and attack the superior species. They bite with 3,000 pounds of force per square tooth. They cover fifty yards in three seconds—this is major league material. The Army will have to be recalled from the overseas wars. The Navy carriers will have to reverse course and return to port. No human will be safe in the day of the 'gator.

30. I may be overestimating the threat. It appears alligators have been replaced as apex predator in Florida. After millions of years change comes to every species, even to prehistoric reptiles.

The culprit is the Burmese python. I should say the culprit is the species of half-baked rednecks who think they can keep these nasty creatures as pets. When the snakes get too large for the bathtub—the Burmese python can grow to 20 feet and weigh 200 pounds—they are placed in the rears of pickup trucks and driven to the Everglades where they are unceremoniously deposited. Burmese pythons have no predators on land. They have no predators in the water. If they could fly they would have no predators in the air. Established species, alligators included, have no defenses against them. Since pythons are aggressive, feverishly fertile, and in a permanent state of hunger, the worry is native species are headed the way of the Florida panther.

A recent autopsy of a python captured outside Miami showed the risk extends even to the superior species. Found in the belly of this 16-foot beast were rodent bits, ibis carcasses, enough shreds of alligator to sew a purse, and a pair of size 44 Bermuda shorts tagged with a Wal-Mart label.

31.   Once your back goes you're doomed to a life of dorsal misery or so I've been told. There are so many miles of nerves and muscles and vertebra chips in the back, the slightest twist or unintended bad turn can lead to taking out shares in the local pharmacy. The usual expression for this dire state is "My back hurts" coupled with grimaces and alto-soprano sob effects.

We don't have a comparable expression *"My front hurts"* when something goes awry on the ventral side. Surely, there are as many nerves and muscles on our front half to earn an instantly understandable and appreciated catch phrase.

32.   Archeologists announced that they discovered the ruins of a house that existed in Nazareth dating to the time of Jesus. Nazareth is a very large city in our time. In Jesus's time it was a very small place. Maybe a few hundred people lived there. Maybe fewer than a hundred. It was thrilling to consider that Jesus may have walked in the house or visited people there. Maybe the house belonged to a relative. Jesus may have been friends with a kid who lived there. Maybe the house belonged to a client of Joseph. For that matter, the house could have been the Holy Family's. One of the rooms marked off may have been Jesus's. I wonder what the decor was.

33.   *Spartacus* is a classic 1960 movie directed by Stanley Kubrick and starring Kirk Douglas as the rebellious slave and general, Laurence Olivier as the repressive Roman patrician Marcus Licinius Crassus, and literally a cast of thousands. The movie plays a little loose with the facts—Spartacus was not crucified as in the movie, he died in battle in 71 B.C.—but it is truly spartacular in cinemascope and inspiring in its portrayal of an ordinary man taking the courage of his convictions and revolting against the world's first superpower. Spartacus nearly achieved what he set out to accomplish—equality and freedom from servitude are goals all right-minded people have sought. Tragedy lies in the implications of failure—ruthless militarism and slavery for the next two millennia. It's a profound lesson in counterfactual speculation to consider how ancient history would have turned out if Spartacus was successful. Spartacus's noble cause and his noble failure are almost

enough to get me to regret I wasn't with him. "Almost enough" are the operative words.

In the movie's emotional climax Crassus has rounded up the remnant of Spartacus's defeated army. (This does not take place in Appomattox Courthouse, so we know ahead of time there's not going to be a happy ending.) He asks, "Which of you is Spartacus?" Kirk Douglas manfully stands up. "I'm Spartacus," he rasps, twisting his neck in a cervical growl. The Romans prepare to take him away when another slave stands up. "I'm Spartacus," he insists. Another stands up. "I'm Spartacus," he says. And another stands up. And another. And another, until virtually every soldier in the slave army has stood and declared himself to be Spartacus.

I'm not a brave person. If I were there when Kirk Douglas announced he was Spartacus I think I would have stood up and agreed, "Marcus, he is Spartacus." That would have gotten me in good with Crassus. That would have gotten me in bad with my fellow slaves—they were closer than the Romans. I probably would have just sat on the ground and hoped that nobody noticed when the slaves went to their grim fates.

Or maybe I would have shouted, "I'm not Spartacus" and hoped that they'd leave me alone.

34. I wear a large amber ring I got as a present. One of my co-workers happened to notice the swirls in the amber and commented that it looked like a magician's ring. I told her it was. If I touch the amber and say the magic spell demons appear. (Demons don't like to be bothered from tormenting souls in hell, so they are not in good moods when summoned.) She asked what the magic spell was and I told her "The magic spell." She didn't understand and asked again what the magic spell was. I said the magic spell was "The magic spell." She still didn't understand. I was growing impatient and I lost track of what I was doing. "If I say 'The magic spell' at the same time I touch the amber in the ring—oops!"

35. The hungry darkness devours the day and licks clean the plate of light. Evening is not so much a *gloaming* as a *glomming*.

36.   The sloppiest, shabbiest people in Europe live in Slovenia. But "Slovenia?" Couldn't they come up with a better name for a country?

37.   Here's a bilingual pun—the Irishman's pot belly was bolging over his belt buckle.

38.   What the *bleep* is going on with Comedy Central—with Comedy Central so-called?

I was surfing dials around 10:50 PM on Tuesday night when I caught the closing monologue of a stand-up comic—a stand-up comic so-called. He was a short dapper black guy in a zoot suit and derby. He had a tormented look on his face and a dazed look in his eyes. If I didn't know what the station aired, comedy would be the last guess.

The comic strutted on the stage, pointing and pivoting as he cracked jokes. The audience laughed hysterically, but I didn't get the jokes. He didn't speak in an ordinary language of words, so much as in sound effects.

The guy peppered his monologue with a profusion of *bleeps*—the monologue was all pepper and no salt. Usually I can identify what lies under the *bleeps*—there are only a few unsavory swearwords in the lexicon—but this guy was speaking so rapidly and using so many swearwords the monologue was gibberish. I've done graduate work in gibberish, but that didn't help. The monologue must have been at the postdoctoral level. I couldn't identify the parts of speech the *bleeps* represented, whether they were nouns, verbs, adjectives or adverbs. Even the *–ing* at the end of a *bleep* wasn't much help. The only parts of speech I identified were prepositions and they weren't much use in getting the gist of the jokes. "The *bleeping bleep* in the *bleep* on the *bleeping bleep bleep bleeped* a *bleep* at the *bleepily bleep bleep*."

The camera cut between this slinging song of *bleeps* and showed members of the audience. They looked to be mostly young people of college age. They were howling in laughter, clapping the tables, and rubbing their wet faces raw. I was lost at sea without a swearword to guide me, but the audience heard the parts of speech that got *bleeped* out. The hysterical laughter had more to do with the collections of beer bottles on the tables than with the litany of jokes. A person needs to be drunk to laugh at this kind of monologue.

The only thing odder than what went on in the club was the fact that Comedy Central televised a monologue awash with untranslated *bleeps*. There is something stupendously unfunny—something laughable—listening to a profane progression of *bleeps*. I don't know, maybe that's the joke. If it is, I don't *bleeping* get it. I should say for good measure that I don't *bleeping bleep* get it.

39. The *lap of luxury* is a place most people want to occupy. If money is the root of all evil, we should refer to this place as the *crotch of luxury*. Only vulgarians live there. We call them the *filthy rich*.

40. Here's a question you can never get wrong.

New Jersey:
a) sucks
b) rots
c) blows
d) all of the above choices are correct

41. Push comes to shove, frequently. We know the brawl that erupts. But does shove ever come to push? If it did, maybe something terrible would break out. Push has to—well, push back when shove shoves. On the other hand, maybe shove never comes to push because shove is a scaredy-cat verb. Maybe shove is a coward. But that's harsh. Maybe shove is an amicable verb. Maybe it's a pacifist verb. Who knows? Maybe they'd hit it off if shove comes to push rather than the other way around.

42. I believe it was the philosopher Nietzsche who wrote about the "eternal return." I don't think it was the linebacker Nietzsche. Whoever it was, we don't know if the idea of the "eternal return" is true, referring to some barely graspable concept of cosmic boomerangs, or whether it is another hokey idea espoused by intellectual dilettantes with too much time on their hands and too much paper in their inkjets.

Nietzsche hasn't returned.

If he came back as the philosopher Nietzsche—even if he came back as the linebacker Nietzsche—we certainly would have heard about it.

If he came back as someone else I suppose we wouldn't know about it. Nor would he.

43. San Antonio is rated the "friendliest city" in the United States. It really is.

Recently I was in the Balcones Heights section at the corner of Hillcrest Drive and Crestview. I needed to go to Laredo St. a few miles distant. I had tickets for a production *Of Mice and Men* put on by the Sam Houston Dramatic Society. I boarded a bus on the 522 Babcock Line and realized I didn't have change for the $1.25 exact fare.

I told the driver I didn't have the change and needed to get off. I started to back down to the sidewalk, thinking I needed to find a store to break a ten. He said I'll do no such thing. He insisted I stay on board and that I could pay double on the return trip. The passenger on the driver's right said that he'd cover the fare. The passenger on the driver's left immediately contradicted him. "No, I'll cover the fare." Someone in the back of the bus said that he'd cover the fare and the return fare as well. A lady seated in the middle of the bus said she would buy me a coupon book good for a week of fares. Another lady shouted that she would buy me a month's worth of fares. Someone else yelled that he would cover me with a coupon book good for a year. An elderly guy seated near the rear exit—he was wearing the shoe laces they wore as neckties in the Old West—said that he would buy me a coupon book good for a year and airline tickets in and out of San Antonio. A passenger across from him said he would buy me a year's worth of airline tickets in and out of San Antonio. Someone else said he would buy me a year's worth of airline tickets "good anywhere in the world."

In no time everyone on the bus was shouting what they would buy me for the trouble of not having $1.25 in exact fare. People were getting agitated and I was becoming afraid. This was the Lone Star state, after all, where people were known to carry firearms. I didn't know which offer to accept and which to turn down. I was tempted to accept all the offers, but I didn't want to take advantage of these generous people.

I discreetly stepped off the bus. Not a moment too soon. A tall hombre in a tan ten-gallon hat punched the passenger to his right. Another passenger—he looked to be Mexican—clocked the man seated in front of him. An elderly lady in a blue skirt, white sweater, and a

Texas tiara, struck a man with an umbrella. Another lady threw her bag of groceries at a man. The driver reached in the ditty bag next to the brake pedal. I think he pulled a wrench out. It could have been a six-shooter.

I walked away as quickly as possible and hiked to the playhouse. I missed the opening act, but I knew the story, so it was no great deal. As I proceeded I heard the wail of police cars. I knew where they were going and I felt very bad. I didn't want to get anyone in trouble and I didn't want to get into trouble. San Antonio was the friendliest city in the United States, only in trying to outdo one another the passengers on the bus screamed and cursed and struck one another. I had no doubt they would start to plug one another with buckshot in the rush to show just how friendly they were.

I hated to think they killed themselves on account of kindness.

44. I understand they're meant to advance the story lines, but sometimes characters make decisions that are so ridiculously bad you want to scream, "What the heck!"

Consider the Gothic horror film *Horror of Dracula* made by Hammer Studios in 1958. The film is considered a classic of the genre. It spawned a number of sequels and unleashed the careers of Christopher Lee as the unconquerable Count and Peter Cushing as his nemesis Van Helsing. The movie also contains one of the dumbest decisions ever seen on the big screen.

Posing as an archivist, Jonathan Harker has traveled to an unnamed Central European country to exact revenge on the Count. He searches the Count's spotlessly clean castle—the cleaning service is not named—and locates Dracula and his bride asleep in the basement in lidless coffins. (They sleep in separate coffins—the horror is rated PG-13.) It's late in the day. The light is rapidly draining from the sky. The Prince of Darkness will soon walk among us. Harker hasn't much time. He opens his valise, pulls out the hammer and stake and impales the bride. Huh? I mean—duh. Everyone in Central Europe, not to mention everyone in the rest of the world, knows you have to impale the Count first. The bride is not in his league. She'll melt to genomic goo when the Count is nailed. But no. Harker goes for the lesser menace first and saves the stronger Count for second.

If it existed that far back, Harker would be the recipient of a Darwin Award. He stakes the bride and gets his comeuppance before the commercial break. He turns to stake the Count—not entirely to our surprise, the Count is out of his coffin and standing at the head of the stairs. He is not amused—we can tell this by the flames in his eye sockets. The Count would be dust if Harker had used the least smidgen of intelligence. Harker appeared to be a competent guy, but at the crucial moment he chose to do the dumbest thing.

The wish is that movies could be interactive, so the audience could advise, "The Count, stupid, stake the Count first." Because he didn't, the Count continues to roam the countryside picking panicked peasants off at will. And poor Harker gets teeth marks in the carotids and a chance to pass the days sleeping in the bride's recycled coffin. Let's hope for his sake the Count is a straight vampire and not bent sinister.

45. Texas had the chainsaw massacre. That's nothing. We have the New Jersey forklift massacre.

There have been buckets of bloody movies about vampires. To my knowledge there has never been a movie about a monster forklift. That thought occurred as I tramped from my cube to the ticketing office in the far distant corner of the warehouse. This is a 15-minute trek in a generally northwestern direction. I wear loafers and business casual attire. I need helmet, flak-jacket, and a forklift-sniffing dog to make my advance. Actually, I don't need a dog. I can see the forklifts plain enough. The important question is whether the drivers can see me.

I counted 23 forklifts in the northwestern quadrant of the warehouse.

Three golf carts passed me. So did one guy on a bicycle. Golf carts and a guy on a bicycle don't scare me. Forklifts scare me. Some of the forklifts were light machines with short blades going out three or four feet. Some were low and squat in design with blades that extended ten feet and longer. Others were monsters the size and height of tractors. They could reach the upper racks five stories above ground—I don't doubt they could poke through the roof if they had to. The drivers to these behemoths stand on platforms and wear safety chains like window washers. Regardless of their size or shape, the forklifts flew about the receiving floor like sedans on the interstates. I'm not sure these machines come with brakes. If they do, the drivers mustn't like to use them.

I thought of a horror movie about killer forklifts after a near run in with one—it wasn't so much a run in as a near *run over*. I was trying to spot the ticketing office in the distance when one of the low and squat varieties of forklift roared by between pallets. The body of the forklift was too low to be seen. The body of the forklift driver was too short to be seen. If I wasn't able to stop on a dime my once intact body would have been protoplasmic pennies on the receiving dock. My foot was an inch from the blade as it passed. My belt was an inch from the corner boards of a pallet of a new printing of Shirer's *Inside the Third Reich*. If I didn't keep my balance I'd be abstract art on the dining room wall in Berchtesgaden.

Once the forklift passed the driver blew the horn to warn of his approach. The horn roused me from the state of shock that descended— it took longer for the sympathetic nervous system to grow quiescent. I started to walk again. This time, I kept my gaze in a near-sighted radius—this doesn't take much effort given the state of my eyes. I thought about my life and about all the things I had and had not done. And I thought about the fact that there has never been a horror film featuring forklifts as the monsters.

The mind reels at the havoc these mechanized monsters can inflict on the bodies of the warehouse crew. The possibilities of evisceration are endless. I almost got creamed. The entire second shift will finish the night like cow patties on the open range—flat and wet and runny with guts oozing out the dermal flaps the blades tore open. The morning shift will have to duck under the bodies of the drivers hanging by their safety chains from the platforms of the behemoths. Made of metal inches thick, the blades of the forklifts run through booksellers with no more difficulty than knives run through logs of wet butter. The short arms of the light machines impale booksellers at a hectic rate that would make the primal Vlad pluck his chin whiskers with envy. The long arms of the heavy machines run through rows of booksellers standing back to back. Pierced hearts and brown slabs of chopped livers dangle at the end of the prongs. Blood-glued nametags adhere on the metal like strips of onions pasted on a greasy pan. The blades remove a man's head with a glancing blow. The machines aren't sexist—women's heads detach with equal ease. Arms and legs and necks and the visceral organs are ripped to shreds like pastrami through a deli slicer. The rags of flesh are deposited on conveyors and poured into insulated cartons for UPS ground delivery to the zombies who relish the disembowels. Samples are forwarded to vampires in a show of creature solidarity.

By closing time the second shift will have checked out in hideously gory ways. The morning shift will get theirs first thing at daybreak. So will the clerical staff—they'll have more to bandage than paper cuts.

The set is in place—I hiked it on my way to the ticketing office. Makeup artists and computer geeks can generate the special effects imagination visualizes. Writers' conferences can enhance the death and destruction in specific scenes. I'm just not sure of the story line. I'm not sure whether a single ferocious forklift or a fleet of forklifts should deliver the carnage. And I'm not sure who should stand in the driver's seat—a sociopath or a demon—or whether we even need a driver. The story may work best if a machine gets possessed by the soul of a disgruntled employee dead set on revenge.

46. This is what is called a "near miss".

This past term I had a pretty good run as a substitute teacher at the General Kearney Regional High School in Essex County. English Lit and Pre-algebra were my specialties. I got assignments nearly every school day. The administration liked me, so they kept asking me back. The kids liked me, too. I never gave homework and I never turned anyone into the office for discipline. No one failed. In fact, no one got less than an "A".

I was in the faculty dining room one afternoon. Miss Geismar, chair of the English Dept., was seated across from me. We were discussing how we could better structure the curriculum to include modern works of fiction. Novels like *A Separate Peace* and *Mansfield Park* just don't cut it with the modern urban teenager. There's no violence, no sex, and no swearwords in these classics. There's nothing to hold their interest. I had just finished my peanut butter and jelly sandwich and started to peel an orange. It was a thick-skinned orange the size of a softball. Since I was in a public place I couldn't use my teeth and bite my way to the pulp like I do in private. I don't have long fingernails and the plastic knives the school supplies couldn't cut through a rind that had the corrugated texture of burlap. After a few minutes of turning the orange in circles and digging with my thumbs I had the peel off and the naked white interior exposed. I poked my index fingers in the groove on the top and pulled the orange apart.

A spray of juice shot across the table as I split the orange. It was like a squirt from a water gun, only the stream was citrean and on the acidic side. The stream struck Miss Geismar on the upper cheek a few fake eyelashes from the pupil of her left eye. The juice slid down her cheek, wiping an orange trail on her makeup and anti-oxidant aging cream before it dripped off her chin to the essay she had been grading in between bites of melon squares. I was mortified. I was never so embarrassed in my life, not even when I tore a hole in the seat of my trousers bending to pick up a playbill during the intermission of the General Kearney Dramatic Society's matinee performance of *Long Day's Journey into Night*. Here I was sharing lunch and exchanging shop talk with the chair of the English Dept. and a spray from my orange nearly struck her in the eye. I was sure the blade of juice killed my career as a substitute teacher of English Lit and Pre-algebra. No more early morning phone calls begging me to arrive at home room before first period. No more sophomore classes uninterested in the story lines of *A Separate Peace* and *Mansfield Park*. No more inquisitive juniors busily trying to figure out how to move the X from one side of the equation to the other. No more fat paychecks every two weeks for enlightening the young people of Essex County about English and math.

And it was worse than that. A hose of orange juice nearly destroyed Miss Geismar's eyesight. She had only recently returned to school after recuperating from an eye transplant—a left eye transplant. Her right eye was too far gone to be restored—it wasn't any good, but the surgeons left it in so she wouldn't scare the students or get called "one-eye". Her left cornea had been re-stitched. The clouds had been drained from the lens. The rips in the retina had been repaired, their frayed tissue patched like the shredded threads of a macula carpet. And I nearly ruined everything just by peeling an orange. I can live without the early morning phone calls. I can live without the adulation of urban teens. I can almost live without a fat paycheck. I could never live with the thought that a squirt from my orange blinded Miss Geismar in her one good eye. We were seated three feet apart, but that squirt was traveling so rapidly it would have punched a hole in the bulletin board behind her if she didn't intercept it. I hate to think what damage it could have done if it punched the visual purple in her left eye to the visual black and blue.

If I'm ever again in the faculty dining room in General Kearney Regional High, I'll eat a banana.

47. This is not a near miss.

Robert Jones of Woodstock, GA, was killed this summer when a small plane struck him from behind while making an emergency landing on the beach at Hilton Head Island in South Carolina. The plane had lost power and was gliding downward from 13,000 feet. The pilot's view was obscured by a mat of oil that covered the windshield. Jones was jogging and listening to his iPod. He was oblivious of what was zeroing in from behind at several hundred miles an hour.

Some people make an entrance. Jones made an exit. We can only hope he was listening to something soft and soothing when he got run over by a plane.

48. In genealogy there's an old-fashioned term for offspring or progeny—now, "progeny", that's a vulgar-sounding word if there ever was one. The term is *issue*. It follows that parents who have problem children may be said to have *issues* with their *issue*.

49. I spoke with a fellow genealogist about the possibility that our beloved ancestors have an inkling that their names are spoken or written down a century and better after their passing. I like to think the dear departed get a chill or some psychic sensation whenever their names are mentioned. The living do whenever anyone walks on our graves. Why not the departed? It might be something as simple as ghostly goose bumps. It might be something like a call forwarded, "Hello, a living person is speaking about you at this moment." It might be a neutral sensation like a hit on an ethereal cow-web site. The departed don't know who spoke about them—the afterlife is a timeless place, but I can't believe my ancestors know who I am. They know only that a living person said their names. The more often the names are repeated, the higher the digital count on the astral screen. "Welcome living visitor number—."

I should have spoken with a more optimistic person. This genealogist discounted the possibility that the dead know when the living speak about them. Quoting the *King James*, he cited Ecclesiastes 9:5, "The dead know not anything." The verse was originally, "The dead know not nothing," but that aggravated grammarian rabbis, so it was improved.

"The dead know not anything." This means I'll be less bright in the Great Beyond than I am now. That's nothing to look forward to.

50. There's a made-for-television movie in which Jon Voight plays John Paul II. In one scene the Pope is with Mother Teresa in a hospice in India. He's so moved by her work among the sick and dying he says to the effect, "I want more than anything to resign the papacy and work with you among these people." Mother Teresa replies to the effect, "I want more than anything to assume the papacy once you relinquish it." I think that's what she said. It might have been something different—I was peeling a can of Pabst *Blue Ribbon* at the moment and wasn't paying close attention.

It never occurred, of course, but John Paul's resignation would have been a magnificent gesture. The world would have noted that a pope rejected the pontifical seat and all the pomp and circumstance that attend to it to minister to souls who were beneath "the least of the brethren". Many individuals would have been inspired to follow his example. A worldwide revolution of charity would have commenced. Even atheists would have joined in.

We like to think that the Great Pope was sincere and not just placing his light atop a barrel for all the faithful to admire. Of course, the Church hierarchy would never allow this radical career shift from pontiff to bedpan orderly. Lose the most charismatic Roman Catholic since St. Francis just so the homeless can receive shelter? Lose the person responsible for toppling communism and liberating Eastern Europe from the tyranny of Marxist-Leninism just so the sick can get a sponge bath? Lose the great defender of the Militant Catholic Church just so dying people can receive solace in their final hours? Not on your life. They'd never let John Paul resign.

If John Paul took this seriously and snuck out of the Vatican while the Swiss Guard were distracted, they'd have to bump him off like they did his predecessor. The Italian Navy might have to torpedo the ship he sailed on. A corrupt altar boy might have to sprinkle poison in the sacramental wine. A renegade cleric might have to jab him with a tainted needle while he knelt for evening prayer. They'd have to get rid of him one way or another. They couldn't have a new pope in Rome and an ex-pope in the back wards of Calcutta. Two popes at the same time just doesn't go, even if one of them was incommunicado in a hovel.

Bumping off a pope sounds like a bad thing, but it's not necessarily so. Everything would turn out for the best if John Paul II absconded to India. They'd have a new pope and John Paul would be an instant saint and martyr—he'd be a double saint and martyr dying while doing good works for the sorely oppressed. He'd ascend to heaven with no stops in purgatory along the way and the Church would have an icon of staggering importance. In this eventuality the Church hierarchy might be said to eat their host and have it too.

51. The blessed *host* is the body and blood of our Lord Jesus. If the Savior had been a woman, her body and blood would be called the blessed *hostess*.

52. There's a saying in common usage, "to come undone." It happens to beds and to articles of clothing. It also happens to people. Usually, "She's come undone." Less frequently, "He's come undone." When I come undone I immediately summon the Head Man, "Good Lord, I've come undone."

The term *come undone* means to fall apart and to lose one's focus and self-control. This happens to people who are upset, overwhelmed by events, and knocked off their strides by unexpected and unmanageable developments. The result is that people lose their grips and become unglued—I suppose *untied* is a better description.

It follows that we can be said "*to come done*" when we maintain our grips on things and when the strings hold on the frangible ends of our beings no matter how events assail us. Her stride hasn't been broken, "She's come done." He's kept his focus, "He's come done." When I come done I keep it a private matter—God needs to be in the loop only when it starts to fray.

53. Some people don't mind, but I have an aversion to visiting fortune tellers. It's not so much that I'll hear the usual blather about coming into riches and living a long and productive life. And it's not even that the cards will turn out badly or that the psychic will advise against my making plans for the weekend.

My fear is that the fortune teller will excuse herself, reach behind the drapes, and grab a steak knife. "You son of Satan!" she'd scream frothing at the mouth and trying to carve me for some clairvoyant or precognitive reason. I haven't done anything really bad in this life, but we never know what will happen in the future.

Even worse, my fear is that she'd gaze into the mad ball and suddenly throw herself to the floor and grovel at my feet. "My lord and my master!" she'd exclaim, peeling open the Velcro flaps of my loafers with her kisses. I'm a good person, or so I life to believe, but I'm not that good. If she started to worship me for some unknown future reason, I'd be lucky to squeeze my inflated ego out the door.

54. It's Saturday afternoon two weeks before Christmas and I'm on my way to meet Bluesman Mike for our biannual powwow at Bull McNabe's tavern on St. Mark's Place. Unfortunately for us, this Saturday the bars in the neighborhood sponsored a promotion. Anyone dressed in a Santa Claus outfit can drink for half price. What a swell idea! The promotion drummed up business in a slack season. It also resulted in hundreds of drunken men in Santa Claus outfits hopping—staggering, rather—from tavern to tavern.

Some of the Santas were in bad shape. Their suits were disheveled, their caps were crooked, their eyes were red and squinty. Some held plastic cups full to the brim and white with foam. Some held plastic cups half full with foamless flat beer. Others gripped squashed cups in pinched and pointed fingers. They followed their hands in hopes of a refill. They tried to coordinate vision with geography and find the next watering hole. They looked as if they could use a reindeer to guide them. They were lucky to find a traffic cop.

I came across a Santa passed out at the corner of 4th and Broadway. His head was chocked at an awkward angle against the side of the building. The fuzzy brim of his cap was pulled low on his forehead. His eyes were half open. He was snoring loudly. The tassel of his cap was blowing up and down with his erratic breaths. A few feet away a boy of four or five years of age was standing with his mother at the corner. They waited for the light to change. The boy wasn't looking at the Walk / Don't Walk message. He had a pained expression on his face one micro muscle short of a cry. I knew his life was ruined seeing Santa on the sidewalk. I felt so sorry for the little boy. Instead of thinking of Jolly St. Nick hauling sacks of toys up fire escapes, he will think of Santa sprawled on the sidewalk in front of *El Reno Tex Mex Restaurant, Chili a Specialty.*

I thought of a way to santatize the boy's mind. I stepped to his side as the light turned to green and whispered, "Hey, Sonny, Santa's not dead, he's dead drunk." I hope that helped.

55. On the surface a Santa Claus impersonator lying drunk at 4th and Broadway doesn't appear to be indicative of anything other than the common vice of gluttony, but the sight of Old Nick in his cups signifies a portentous rift in our society.

America is a deeply divided society. I don't think we have been so divided since the Civil War. There are seemingly unbridgeable divisions between the rich and the poor, between the have's and the have not's, between theists and atheists, between Democrats and Republicans, between native-born people and immigrants, between colorless people and people of various complexions, and, most ominously, between the military and the civilian population. The last rift—between people in and out of uniform—ruptures the moral fabric of our society and threatens democracy.

The decision was made in 1973 to convert from a conscription military to a volunteer military. The pointless Vietnam War exposed fundamental problems and inequalities in the draft. The Federal draft began in the Civil War with the "call up" of individuals regardless of the state in which they lived. (Earlier drafts, such as in the Revolutionary War, involved the establishment of militias run by states.) The draft was unpopular in the Civil War—witness the savage "draft riots" in New York City in July 1863—but men joined the armies Blue and Gray in enormous numbers. In the Civil War "Billy Yank" and "Johnny Reb" blindly obeyed the most idiotic death-dealing orders, as at Marye's Heights in Fredericksburg and at Cemetery Ridge in Gettysburg. In the 1960s things had changed. The leadership threw a war and for the first time men did not want to join the party. Men did not want to go to war in Southeast Asia. Their families and peers supported the decision to avoid military service. The home front did not support the war or the soldiers who fought it. People started to refrain from asking what they could do for their country. Instead, they asked how they could give their country the slip.

In the Civil War civilians who were well off could avoid serving by paying a "substitute" to take their places. This sounds like a strange career choice, but the motivation for being a substitute was strictly financial. The going rate was a few hundred dollars. Many substitutes worked scams in which they deserted after being paid to serve. They promptly found a different sponsor in a different city and repeated the act. There were no substitutes in the 1960s, but middle-and-upper-class young men could avoid serving by obtaining medical deferments for ailments serious and trivial. They could also stay in school and receive a college deferment. The massive state college system now in place originated in providing men of draft age a place of refuge. Poor men and uneducated men couldn't afford doctors and they weren't college material. When the bad news came in the mail that they were "called up", they had no option but to go.

The burdens of war have not been shared equally across social classes. Social scientists Douglas Kriner and Francis Shen documented a "death gap" between servicemen at the top and bottom rungs of the socioeconomic ladder. In the Vietnam War the three lowest social classes suffered 37% of the deaths compared to 26% in the three highest social classes. The death gap has grown since then. In the ongoing Iraq War the three lowest classes have suffered 38% of the deaths compared with 23% in the three highest classes.

The concept of a volunteer military looked good on paper. Unmotivated men did not have to serve. The military would be staffed with motivated men and women. Richer elements in society could serve if they chose. Poorer elements would not receive notices in the mail merely on account of their income. A lot of things look good on paper that turn out not to be so good in practice. The volunteer service demonstrated Merton's "law of unintended consequences", one of which was a drunken Santa passed out on a public sidewalk.

The burden of "defending democracy" as it's often deceitfully called—American democracy hasn't been imperiled by an outside power since the 1940s—has fallen on an excessively brutalized segment of people. This burden has fallen on a million or so people out of a population of 300 million. It has been the same million for a long time. The United States has been at war for ten straight years. In fact, it has been at multiple wars for ten straight years. Before 1973 the terrible burden of war—Kennedy's "pay any price, bear any burden" strategy—was spread, however unfairly, among the general population. Since 1973 the burden has fallen on a smaller and self-selected group.

This burden has been a grievous one. Since 2001 more than 6,000 service members have been killed in combat. Traumatic brain injuries and loss of limbs have afflicted thousands—loss of limbs have occurred in such numbers new medical specialties have arisen to treat the disability. Suicide rates in the military have skyrocketed by 70% in the decade. Currently the suicide rate for Marines and for soldiers is double that of the civilian population. Since 2001 more than 300,000 service members have developed depression or post-traumatic stress disorder—this is 18% of the total deployment. Prescriptions for painkillers exceed three million yearly.

Service members are maimed in the body. They are also maimed in the mind. Men who have experienced combat and perpetrated violence often become unhinged. Stress and anxiety flow from the war zones and produce consequences in the civilian world that are sometimes not perceived as cause and effect. Addictions to alcohol and to painkillers increase. Self-control and anger management become problematical. A state of sensitization ensues in which insignificant events produce convulsive reactions. Families rip apart. Husbands and wives become estranged. The stress and anxiety experienced in the conflict between spouses flow into the offspring. Children become estranged from their parents. Children become nervous and hostile. Children become disobedient to their elders. Siblings become aggressive toward one another. Sensitization ensues. Immersion of children into the mainstream culture—so important in the grade-school years—becomes uncertain.

One million have borne the price of volunteering. The rest of society gets a pass without so much as a word of gratitude. The attitude of civilians toward the requirements inherent in American culture reverses Kennedy's pledge. "Pay any price, bear any burden"—"Pay it yourself," the response is, "bear it yourself." The attitude of civilians toward the military is "You chose to volunteer, you didn't have to volunteer."

Being a citizen imposes a few obligations on the members of society. At a minimum citizens are expected to obey the law, to vote, to pitch in and contribute in times of need, and to share in the common defense. Citizens in and out of the military have pretty much ignored the first three. The fourth was sidetracked in the civilian world by the instigation of a volunteer army.

Civilians are relieved of their obligations. They are let off the hook. They are not discomforted. They are not in danger. Their lives are not interrupted. They are not inconvenienced. It's business as usual on the home front. Civilians are told to go and shop. Someone else will do the fighting. The commander-in-chief doesn't advise it, but for a segment of the population business as usual means partying. Sometimes partying hard. Santa partied till he passed out.

Thomas Paine wrote during the Revolutionary War that "Those who expect to reap the blessings of freedom must, like men, undergo the fatigues of supporting it." This is precisely what is not happening. Civilians are not undergoing fatigue in the sense Paine meant it. They're not undergoing anything other than credit card debt and hangovers.

On the surface it appears everyone gets what they want. Men who want to fight, fight. They suffer the consequences, accordingly. Men who don't want to fight, don't. They suffer consequences, too. It may appear that civilians reap all the benefits and get off lightly, but it is not possible to cheat in the moral sphere. It is not possible to be excused. Civilians suffer the consequences of whatever goes on in the wars volunteers fight and they suffer a moral degeneration for letting other people carry their share.

The civilian world in America has degenerated into what John Paul II called "the culture of death". Ironically, this has resulted not from military service but from the avoidance of military service. Relieved of this fundamental obligation civilians are free to self-actualize and to engage in self-aggrandizement. The society has degenerated into the crassest consumerism. Their peers are fighting overseas and civilians throw hissy fits if the latest electronic toy isn't available. The attitude has become "The best things in life are available on-line, shipping and handling included." The society has degenerated into the darkest slough of narcissism and self-absorption. Their peers are losing limbs on dirt roads potted with mines and civilians are getting massages in mall store fronts in order to relieve the stress of shopping. The society has degenerated into a pandemic of lawlessness and incivility. Their peers are losing grip of their minds as a result of combat and civilians knock each other's brains out for the slightest, most inane, reason.

A century ago the psychologist Alfred Adler conjectured that mental disorder resulted from a morbid self-preoccupation. Individuals who contribute nothing and who are told they don't have to contribute anything descend into selfishness. They become obsessed with their own situations—with what Adler called "private interest" rather than with "social interest". Anxiety, anger, resentment, social isolation, obsessions and compulsions follow private interest. People who are not challenged to contribute are never led outside their closed situations into a consideration of the larger society and the greater good.

In the Civil War men walked across fields to certain death to preserve the Union. In the Second World War men who could not swim jumped into the surf to defeat Hitler and Hirohito. In our time "patriotism" has become a dirty word. The civilian world has lost the virtue of patriotism for the good reason they are asked to contribute nothing— they are actively encouraged to contribute nothing. "Go and shop." "Go and party." These are different instructions than "Go and share in the common defense." And they have very different consequences for the people who follow each.

There are additional unintended consequences of a volunteer military. A volunteer force leads to an entrenched society of soldiers and sailors who have different values than the world outside gates manned by military police. Since volunteers are likely to serve for longer periods than conscripted soldiers, the military society becomes further removed from the concerns of civilians. It also comes into conflict with the civilian society over political orientation—the military society is much more conservative than the civilian world—and over economic issues—dependent on civilian funding, the military society sees any reduction in defense spending as perilous.

A volunteer military leads to excessive militarism and to the privatization of war—the reinstatement of service by conscription would end these consequences in a season of parental rioting. Presidents use a volunteer force for any reason they choose and to fight whatever undeclared war they see fit to engage in. President George W. Bush used the volunteer force to do what the Nazis used to do—invade a country under false pretenses. President Lyndon Baines Obama is fighting four undeclared wars. He continues the wars in Iraq and in Afghanistan. He unleashed a bombing campaign in Libya and a quasi-secret bombing campaign in Yemen. Since World War Two the United States has dropped a lot of bombs on a lot of people. And we wonder why the world hates us. There are hundreds of American bases worldwide. The United States spends ten times the amount defending democracy than China, its nearest competitor, spends on vanquishing democracy. The difference is 600 billion annually to 65 billion.

The president can do this because the public is disengaged. The media is also disengaged—they're savvy to what their subscribers want to read. On Sunday, August 7, 2011, the *Press of Atlantic City* reported on page three that 38 soldiers and Navy Seals died in a helicopter attack in Afghanistan. The lead story on page one of the paper was that beachgoers on the Jersey Shore are inconvenienced by poor cell phone reception. The civilian world has lost interest in what the military world is doing. Wars are fought and no one in the civilian world notices. Wars are fought and no one in the civilian world cares. Everyone is busy shopping. Everyone is busy partying.

The best-case scenario is that this rift between the military and civilian societies continues as the status quo. The homeland is not attacked. Wars are fought in obscure places and with enemies everyone loathes. The worst-case scenario is a *Seven Days in May* complication in which a mentally unhinged general or admiral wrests control of the government and dictates terms to the president. For that matter the general or admiral might be mentally hinged but full of ferocious resentment of how the volunteers are used. The military world wouldn't mind this outcome. It would be business as usual for the men and women in uniform. And the civilian world wouldn't notice what happened and who took over and to what purpose. The stores stay open late. The bars serve drinks at half-price. And Santa lies drunk on the sidewalk. All's well with the world.

56. Every president comes into office with an agenda. Sometimes the agenda is all pabulum and preachy make-America-feel-good-about-itself sermons he has no intention of keeping. Sometimes the agenda bespeaks the candidate's core beliefs and seeps from his heart and soul—in this case America is in trouble. But the agenda the president enters office with rarely matches the accomplishments of his term. The lessons the electorate derives when the president leaves office are seldom the same as the ones the president intended to teach while in office.

President Kennedy's New Frontier was not the ultimate lesson of "the thousand days". President Carter entered office espousing efficiency and management. He left office the exemplar of inefficiency and micro-mismanagement. President Obama entered office with an ambitious list of progressive goals. Health care reform, environmental protection, expanded civil and personal rights. The lesson he teaches in the third year in office is not among the ones he started with. It's the lesson that, just like White Americans, Black Americans can fail as president.

57. We say "God bless you" when a person in earshot sneezes. Let's hope they use good hygiene and not forget to cover their mouths—I'd hate to be at the ground coop when avian flu starts to fly. Why don't we say "God bless me" after we sneeze when we're alone and no other person is nearby to express the good thought? For that matter, why don't we say "God bless me" after we sneeze and other people are present? It's not in bad taste to wish ourselves well and to join in the exchange of blessings. We need all the blessings we can get.

Of course, if we say "God bless me" we're not obligated to answer, "I'm welcome."

58. Inspired by the Lenape Indians who lived in the neighborhood in the long ago I set out on a spiritual vision quest when I was fourteen. I didn't get past the backyard gate. A greenhead fly went for my shin like a wolf goes for the jugular. I immediately hurried back inside. I was in the most profound despair. What kind of deplorable loser was I that I failed in my spiritual quest? I would not be *pilsit*—chosen by The

Great Spirit. I would be among the lost and rejected ones. I would not be a tribesman in full standing. I would be like a bachelor in a peasant society.

I considered atheism. Freud was right. Religion is a mass delusion and obsession forced on children by corrupt powers who hypocritically repress our wholesome human urges. Chasing visions in the great outdoors is a foolish endeavor. I'm not an outdoorsman. I'm an indoors man and one of the intellectual elite. I would be a Vulcan if I lived in *Star Trek* times. Why wander around the housing complex cold, hungry, and clueless when I could be inside a warm and cozy living room? Then it struck me. I didn't have to convert to atheism. I wasn't a loser. I wasn't a reject. I was a tribesman in full feather.

I had found my totem and it was a worthy creature. The greenhead that took a chunk out of my shin was my totem. I was *pilsit*, after all, and a member in full manhood. I had paid in blood to join. True, the totem at the end of my vision quest wasn't as beautiful or as majestic as a bear or an eagle, but it was a mighty creature nevertheless. The greenhead causes grown men to run indoors. It causes grown women to scamper for the swatter and to bop and swing like they suffered St.Vitus Dance. It breaks up parties more quickly than thunderstorms and sends human beings scurrying for cover. It scatters crowds of swimmers at the clubhouse pool and propels children to dive into the deep end without their arm floats on. It causes greater havoc than any predator on the ground.

Yes, the Jersey greenhead was the kind of creature a fellow could be proud to call his own.

59. Atheists claim religion is for the birds. This can be literally true in a Lenape vision quest. I wouldn't mind having a bird for a totem, unless it was a pigeon.

60. I've heard that the origin of Irish step dancing lies in the Penal Times of the eighteenth century when the peasants were forbidden to enjoy life and party, but I have me doubts about this explanation. The British imperialist bastards could not have been so dense that they failed to notice peasants hopping up and down in a rhythmic manner. (This being Ireland, we can call it a *rhythmick* manner.) Even if they saw only

the top half of the peasants' bodies they would certainly interpret this type of coordinated movement as a form of dance. An odd form, true enough, but dancing nevertheless.

For their part the Irish might have explained that they were not dancing on the barn door but stepping on coals that spilled from the hearth. This explanation might have sufficed given the untidy state of Irish cottages. Or they might have exclaimed that they stepped out of the way of a rascally child. Or out of the way of a rascally pig.

The following explanation is anachronistic, but the Irish of that period might have explained that they suffered as a race from restless leg syndrome.

61.   Properly used, restless leg syndrome might have provided an alternative explanation for the suspicious behavior of a senator in a public rest room. (In his case it was a *restless* room.)

Larry Craig of Idaho had an illustrious career. He was a representative for ten years and a senator for eighteen years. He was a member of the United States Senate barbershop quartet. He was a member of the Idaho hall of fame. In short, he was a credit to his species. Glory came to an ignominious end on 7 June 2007 when Craig got snared in a sting operation in the men's room of the Minneapolis - St. Paul Intl. Airport. He promptly joined the parade of former representatives and senators who demonstrate the timeless practice of hypocrisy.

While in a stall Craig tapped his foot and moved his foot closer to the guy in the next stall. Unfortunately for him, the guy in the next stall was an undercover cop placed there precisely for the purpose of catching leg tappers—tapping the leg appears to be the signal for a tryst in Minnesota – St. Paul airport toilets. Craig was arrested and charged with disorderly conduct.

Craig announced he would resign from the Senate, but changed his mind. (He served out his term and did not run for reelection.) Craig denied the charge that he was signaling a tryst. And he claimed that his leg tap was innocuous and without lewd intent—he sits rather wide on the throne and needs a lot of leg room. He noted there was no touching and no exchange of words. The leg tap never became a love tap.

Restless leg syndrome would have been a better explanation for what happened in the toilet. Restless leg syndrome is a recognized medical malady suffered by an estimated seven percent of the American population. Many of Craig's constituents in Idaho are sufferers. Pleading restless leg syndrome would have provided an honorable explanation of his behavior and it would have done a good deed shedding light on this obscure condition.

Restless leg syndrome involves motor restlessness and uncomfortable feelings when the legs are at rest. Described like "pins and needles" and like an itchy or tingling sensation, the condition worsens when the person is inactive for a period of time, such as when lying in bed or sitting on a toilet. No cause is known with certainty. Culprits include diminished dopamine levels in the brain, iron deficiency, and vein disorders. Treatment involves boosting dopamine levels and monitoring iron levels in the blood. Non-drug treatments include exercise and stretching routines.

Craig appears to be *having a Foley* rather than *having a Bennett* in the terminology of *Thinking About Everything*, since he condemned the same act he was accused of procuring. Senator Craig opposed same-sex marriage. And he opposed extending penalties for hate speech to gender orientation. This means he could have been called "queer" and "fag" in the men's room and no one would be held tongue to task.

62. To paraphrase the Holy Gospel (John 9:2), I often ask myself, "Who did sin, me or my parents, that I was born in New Jersey?"

63. There's an unusual practice in the South in which people eat dirt. The technical term in case you're taking the SAT is *geophagia*. I wish I could report the practice is limited to backwards people of an earlier generation, but I can't. The practice is currently found among school age children and young adults. The dictionary relates it to extreme poverty. Doctors relate it to extreme nutritional deficiencies.

People who engage in *geophagia* apparently like the practice. Many carry pouches that they raid throughout the day, like it was chewing gum or tobacco dip. Some are reputed to have favorite plots where they stoop and swoop. Some walk the proverbial mile for a handful of the finest dirt. Some say, "It's finger-licking good" and they mean it. Dirt that's finger-licking good must be mud. Maybe it comes in pies.

Geophagia gives special meaning to the term *bites the dust*. But dust is like diet dirt or dirt light.

64. On 12 September 1609 the Delaware Indians who happened to be standing on the cliffs of the Palisades saw a unique sight on the Ma-hi-can-ittuck River below. Henry Hudson's sloop, the *Half Moon*, sailed up the gray waters and dropped anchor mid-river. The Indians were surprised. They had never seen so large a ship before. They had never seen Europeans before. They didn't know what to make of it. Some were thrilled—these were the adventurous ones and the sensation-seekers. The general mood on shore must have been upbeat. The following morning they rowed out in hollowed tree trunks of rafts to offer the visitors gifts of beans and oysters.

Some of the braves and squaws lingered on the cliffs—these were the insecure and bashful Indians and the frightened ones. They didn't know it, but they were wise to be frightened. Their tribe was in the same predicament as the herd of T-Rex's who looked up from dinner and watched the big asteroid singe the prehistoric sky.

65. It is widely believed that Josef Cardinal Ratzinger chose the name Benedict XVI in honor of Benedict XV. He said so himself, but that was just the old soft slipper on the papal spin—you might call it papal *bull*, but that would be sending the wrong message.

Pope Benedict XV was one of those individuals who history has undeservingly passed by. He ought to be widely known, but he isn't. He reigned in the turbulent years 1914 – 1922. By all accounts he was a noteworthy pope in a critical time period. He actively sought to broker peace at the outset of the War to End Wars and he engaged in humanitarian efforts throughout the course of the war, notably on behalf of children and POWs. His reign saw the emergence of the Soviet Union and the commencement of religious persecution in the Slavic world. And the Fatima apparition occurred in his reign.

He appears to have been a shrew observer of events. He saw the inevitable outcome of the Versailles Treaty—another World War once Germany rearmed. He also appears to have been a genuine man-of-conscience. He was horrified by the development of aerial warfare and he begged that it be banned from the conflict—nine decades later his successor faces the same issue with the development of aerial drone warfare.

Back to Josef Cardinal Ratzinger. Contrary to the received reports of the origin of the name, Cardinal Ratzinger chose the name to honor his favorite breakfast—*eggs benedict.*

The cardinals in the conclave were appalled when they heard this. They thought they had their man and a worthy successor to The Great Pope and he goes and names himself after a breakfast. On closer consideration the Curia transformed great upsetment into great relief when they realized Cardinal Ratzinger might have named himself *Pope Eggs I.*

66. Speaking of names, here's a wonderful coincidence. The world's first outboard motor was created by Cameron Waterman around 1904.

Two bad Cameron didn't have the family name *Rocketman.* We might have gone to the moon sooner.

67. *Mothman* was a mysterious creature seen in and around Point Pleasant, West Virginia, in the fall of 1966. The creature was described as human-shaped, six or seven feet tall, with wings and glowing red eyes. The original sighting was by two young married couples in the woods near an abandoned munitions factory. Spotted, the creature pursued their car in a high-speed chase into town. Whatever happened at the factory, the townspeople took the story seriously. An armed posse went in search of the creature the next day. The creature was not captured and was observed a few more times in the vicinity. Sightings ended after the Silver Bridge collapsed in the Ohio River in December 1967, killing 46 people.

No one knows who *Mothman* was—in fact, the creature's gender isn't known for certain. It's an assumption that the creature was male. For all we know the creature should have been named *Mothwoman.* Devout people took the creature as a harbinger of the bridge's collapse. In the parapsychological literature there are reports of other sightings of *Mothman*-like creatures before disasters occur. Fanatical skeptics—the kind who delight in telling children there is no Santa Claus—suggested the entire incident was a hoax. Less fanatical skeptics suggested that the creature was an ordinary animal misinterpreted by panicky eyewitnesses as something extraordinary. The likeliest candidate for the animal explanation of the events in Point Pleasant is the Sandhill Crane, which can grow to three feet and have a wingspan of five feet. With retelling the original story grew feathers and soared among a gullible and superstitious public. Once the animal transmogrified into a supernatural *creature* additional sightings were inevitable, as happened in 1910 with the Jersey Devil who, without ordinary means of public transportation, was observed bounding from one watery side of New Jersey to the other.

Some years ago I had an unexpectedly close encounter with a mysterious flying creature. I was driving on Route 524 near the Reed sod farm in Allentown minding my own business and thinking about something when a huge black creature glided across the road and into the woods. I was taken completely by surprise. For a moment I thought a man in a tuxedo was coming in for a landing. I expected to see a parachute or some sort of hang-gliding apparatus behind him. I don't know how I managed to maintain control of the car.

I was told by naturalists who work in the Distribution Center that the creature that flew over the hood of my Saturn *Ion* was most likely a turkey buzzard. The largest bird in New Jersey, the turkey buzzard is black, ugly, and has a wingspan of five feet. Buzzards can often be seen on the side of roads performing their biological function of eating carrion. They are less often observed in flight, so they can be impressive on take off and landing. The bird I saw may have been zeroing in on a dead deer or groundhog. Buzzards are generally not hostile to people. Their only defenses are flight and an intimidating appearance. We're warned not to get too close—buzzards use vomit as a defense mechanism. The rumor is people who suffer a spray of buzzard vomit turn into zombies and disappear into the Pine Barrens where they soil themselves and compete for road kill. No one knows if this is true and no one wants to find out.

There are paranormal explanations for the appearance of *Mothman*. In certain circles these are the preferred explanations. The late John A. Keel documented that sightings of *Mothman* occurred amid a flurry of strange events—poltergeist activities, bizarre phone calls, and the arrival of the mysterious men in black. Keel himself was subject to harassment by these occult forces. I don't know if these phenomena are on the beam or off the beam and I don't doubt there were strange lights seen in the West Virginia woods. As with *Mothman*, no one knows what poltergeists really are or who the men in black were. Keel called them "ultra-terrestrials", but that doesn't nail it down.

The term *Mothman* was coined by a reporter, but this must have been a joke. Ladybugs might object, but moths are about the least offensive creatures on the planet. They certainly don't have glowing red eyes and they can't bound along the road in high-speed pursuit of fleeing humans. The creature that terrorized Point Pleasant flew in need of a better title. It should have been called *Dragon Man* or *Red-eyed Devil Man*. If the term "moth" had to be retained, better descriptions were *Behemoth Man* or *Mammoth Man*.

68. Next time you eat a mussel say "Thank you" before you swallow.

Modern humans originated in Africa around 195,000 BC. A long glacial period began around 123,000 BC that seriously threatened the existence of *Homo sapiens*. Much of Africa became uninhabitable. Numbers of humans decreased from an estimated 10,000 to a few hundred. This population catastrophe is reflected in the DNA record— humans show little genetic diversity compared to other species, suggesting the billions of people alive today derive from a very small ancestral pool.

We don't know where these humans lived in the glacial period, but the archeologist Curtis Marean and his colleagues have located a strong candidate in a series of caves on the coast of South Africa, specifically at a place called Pinnacle Point near the town of Mosel Bay. Excavations show that caves were intermittently occupied between 164,000 and 35,000 BC. People who lived there survived on shellfish—a source of protein—and on tubers from the fynbos vegetation—a source of carbohydrates.

This area of South Africa has always been rich in vegetation and in shellfish—shellfish thrive in cold water and occur year round. Excavations have found mussel and snail shells in the caves dating back 164,000 years. Limpet shells date to 110,000 years.

The caves provide tantalizing hints that these ancient people possessed cognitive skills comparable to our own. Cognitive skills such as language and mental mapping of geography may have arisen with modern humans rather than developed later as an evolutionary result of slow brain growth.

Shellfish harvesting by hand is perilous, as the beds grow on rocks pounded by the tides. Safe harvesting is possible only at certain times when the tides recede. The cave dwellers must have had knowledge of the tides and of the lunar cycle—if they didn't, genetic diversity would be less than it is now. Since the drift of the coastline changes over the years, these people would have had to develop cognitive maps of the coast to find the mussel beds. And they would have had to communicate this information to their successors. The obvious candidate is the spoken word. Similarly, they would have had to cognitively map and communicate the locations of the vegetable patches.

There is evidence that the cave dwellers used fire in a controlled manner to create stone tools. To cut these tools a stone called silcrete was used. In the cave silcrete remnants are red and gray, colors that never occur in nature. Silcrete assumes these colors only when exposed to fire and not just to any fire, but to a controlled heating and cooling process. This process was in use by 72,000 years and possibly long before.

Finally, there are collections of seashells in the cave whose contents would not have been eaten. These shells drifted to the beach like shells do all along the Atlantic and Pacific coasts. Someone carried the shells back to the cave. Perhaps they were seen as having symbolic or artistic value. Perhaps they were used as toys or as decorations. However they were used, the ancient cave dwellers were doing exactly what the day trippers of today do the world over.

69. Allen Ginsberg was an acclaimed poet who came out of the mid-twentieth century Beat tradition. He was widely admired by East Coast glitterati types. Gay people reveled in a genius who shared their orientation. Liberal straight people reveled in their open-mindedness in appreciating a gay poet. Closed-minded conservative types thought his claim to wearing the "Poesy Laurels" was his ability to scan the word "penis" into his poems.

In one of his poems Ginsberg used the phrase "the Negro night". I heard him say this in a dramatic voice—I was driving home from school and listening to National Public Radio. I couldn't believe what I was hearing. I wrote the phrase at the next traffic light. I'm sure

Dennis Ford

Ginsberg took the image seriously. I'm sure his many admirers did. To the contrary, I thought the phrase was a howler.

If the night is Negro, the day must be Caucasian. "The Caucasian morning." "The Caucasian afternoon." "The Caucasian evening." At some point the evening must become "Mulatto".

The image of the day as Caucasian has been in common parlance for as long as I've been around and, probably, for a lot longer. The image may have inspired Ginsberg. We often use the expression *"Crack 'er dawn"* to indicate the moment when the night loses its pigmentation.

70. Speaking of Negroes, young black people sure do talk funny.

I was on the PATH train coming home one Saturday evening from Manhattan Community College. Four brothers in their early twenties boarded the train at Exchange Place. I was intimidated at first and hugged my brief case tighter, but then I remembered my social psychology. They were examples of the concept of conformity and walking stereotypes from the ghet-go. They wore hoods under bright football jackets—I don't know the names of modern athletes, but I assume the names emblazoned on the jackets belonged to prominent players. Their trousers were five sizes too big and their sneakers, sky blue in color and double laced, looked like they cost a hundred dollars. They carried cell phones that they referred to frequently and they talked exceptionally loud. They sat side by side and across the aisle, but they shouted at the tops of their voices, as if they sat at opposite ends of the car. Every second word out of their mouths was the "N-word". "N-word this." "N-word that." "N-word something else."

There is a lot of controversy over the use of the N-word. Serious people believe it should be banned from the lexicon and never used. Other serious people believe the use of the N-word should be restricted to African-Americans. Other serious people believe African-Americans should never use it and that the N-word should be restricted to redneck types and Caucasian lowlives. The four brothers on the train had no interest in political or social debates over the use of words. They were going to use the N-word whenever they wanted. I should say they were going to use the N-word whenever they opened their mouths. They used it as often as they used prepositions.

46

This is all to be expected. Like a swearword, the N-word is banned from civilized discourse. Like a swearword, it is used all the time. I hear it in the all-white taverns in Ocean County and I hear it in the all-black cafeteria of Manhattan Community College.

What was unusual was their use of the word "Negro". One brother made a comment about which contestant was going to win a boxing match in Atlantic City. The brother sitting across from him shouted, "This Negro thinks he knows boxing!" A few minutes later one of them started talking about a girlfriend—he didn't use the word "girlfriend", but I knew what he meant. The brother sitting to his side slapped his thigh and shouted, "Would you listen to this Negro!" A little later they started arguing about the quickest way to get to the Montgomery Gardens projects. One of them suggested they should take a cab. Another shouted, "What cabbie is going to pick up this Negro?" I had never heard this use of the word "Negro" before, but then I'm not often in earshot of young black guys in their twenties.

Their use of the word "Negro" occurred whenever a speaker was accused of not knowing what he talked about or of making a foolish statement. The concept seems useful, but I doubt that this particular detonation of the word is going to enter general usage. I suppose it was considered a friendly slur. It was always said with loud laughter and in an animated manner. The laughter sounded spontaneous. We don't hear "Would you listen to this Caucasian!" Or "to this Slav" or "to this Balt" or "to this Spaniard" or "to this Peruvian", but "Negro" in the sense the brothers were using the word might be analogous to one redneck shouting to another, "Would you listen to this redneck!" or to one hillbilly insisting about another, "This hillbilly doesn't know what he's talking about!"

The usage struck me as representative of what members of a fringe group might say to one another in friendly derision. In the case of the four youths it might be a back-derivation from the N-word. Everyone in the world outside their clique was described by the N-word. Inside their clique the N-word was too odious to use. In a weird round-about way their use of "Negro" was a sign of friendship and respect.

71. In the never-ending quest to prevent the outbreak of avian flu Manhattan Community College has introduced high-pressure hand

dryers in the men's rooms. I suppose they've also introduced high-pressure hand dryers in the ladies' rooms, but I don't know that to be a fact. If students can figure out how to wash their hands, they can dry off by inserting their wet hands inside these machines. Activated by movement, a high-pressure blast of warm air dries the hands within a few seconds. Students can dry off without having to touch a single scrap of tissue paper. Students don't even have to rub their hands together. They merely have to stand and wait. Presumably, they can rehearse the next class's quiz while they're waiting.

There is a problem, however. It's the door. Students can dry off without touching anything, but they have to grip the door handle and turn it to get out of the washrooms.

So, students are sterile for all of two seconds.

72. This was overheard on the ferry to the Great Beyond, "I don't know what could have happened. I followed the recipe for fried fillet of *fugu* liver to the letter."

73. And this was text-messaged on the ferry, "Next time I'll shut the cell phone off while crossing the express train tracks."

74. Hans Holzer, the legendary ghost hunter of yore, has died. We like to think he floated through the tunnel and proceeded directly into the light. He did a lot of good in life, helping the departed as an expert in paranormal logistics and ministering to the living as a high priest of Wicca. We hate to think he became a ghost and stayed behind as an unhappy soul wandering in the astral regions. He can't exorcise himself. He can't lay himself. It's tragic to consider that the man who sent so many souls to their eternal homes may himself be bound to this plane and in need of a ghost hunt.

75. Even the most odd-dent fan has to admit there have been some strange sports in the Olympics. In the Summer Olympics there have been such sports as synchronized swimming, badminton, handball, speed walking and table tennis—this is also known as Ping-Pong. Some of these sports sounded like what we played in Mr. Gaynor's gym class in high school. I'm surprised dodge ball or touch Frisbee hasn't been

included. There is one sport that is conspicuous by its absence. It is the universal sport.

In the Winter Olympics there have been such sports as skeleton bobsleighing, snowboarding, curling, and the luge. What is a luge and did I ever play with one? No one on the East Coast or in the former Confederate States of America knows what these events are. Maybe they do in Michigan or in Wisconsin or in Russia or in the Baltic Republics. We don't in tepid New Jersey. The universal sport that everyone watches throughout the year and in every country and clime remains conspicuously absent.

Even if the swimmers continue to wear those skimpy trace-through trunks I won't watch the Olympics, Summer or Winter, until they include Professional Wrestling as an event.

76. I heard a word today I haven't heard since the fifth grade. The word is *spitball*. The thought immediately occurred—why isn't spitball an Olympic sport? An armed and aimed spitball requires exquisite mouth – eye coordination. Directing a spitball to its destination requires as much skill as shooting a basketball through a hoop or drilling a puck between a goalie's knee pads. Spitball is certainly as skillful as table tennis or speed walking.

There are any number of spitball contests. There's spitballing for distance—the gold goes to the farthest spit. There's spitballing for stickability—the gold goes to the spitball that adheres to a surface longest. There's spitballing for accuracy—the spitballer who hits the most targets brings home the gold. There's a combination of distance and accuracy—the spitballer who hits the most targets at the greatest distance wins the gold. And, of course, there's speed spitballing—the winner of the gold gets off the most spits in an allotted period of time.

The United States is competitive in most Olympic sports, especially in the Summer Olympics. We can be certain that the United States will always bring home the gold in spitball. America is a nation of spitballers. We spitball from preschool into college and beyond. We spitball from the playground to the nursing home. We spitball from when we cut our baby teeth to when we get false teeth—some playful seniors spitball without teeth. Our Olympic ranks will never be depleted. When it comes to spitball our competitive advantage will never dry up.

77. The Lion's Mane jellyfish (*Cyanea capillata*) is the largest jellyfish. It varies in size from 20 inches to seven feet in diameter. Three feet is average. The trailing clusters of tentacles also vary in length, ranging from a few feet to hundreds of feet. The longest trail on record was 120 feet. There are about 150 tentacles on an average size specimen. This adds up to a lot of stingers even in length-deprived jellies.

The Lion's Mane prefers cold water, so it rarely puts in an appearance on the Jersey Shore. It feeds on plankton, small fish, and moon jellies. Encounters with humans are by inadvertence. Ring the Lion's Mane bell and you hear funeral chimes—it's *cyounara* for you. I don't exaggerate. The sting is not painful, it's excruciatingly painful. The emphasis is on "excruciating".

The usual encounter happens when a swimmer brushes the tentacles that drift in the tides. On occasion, mass encounters result in pandemoanium. This summer in Wallis Sands State Park in Rye, New Hampshire, as many as 100 people were stung by a single 40-pound Lion's Mane that broke into pieces when lifeguards raked it. The lifeguards tried to be helpful, but as in so many things, the best laid plans oft lead to excruciating pain. The number of people stung by this jelly set a world's record. If he were alive, Mr. Ripley would slap himself in startlement.

Firemen from six communities had to be called to calm the panic. Local supermarkets quickly ran out of bottles of vinegar. I don't doubt aspiring screenwriters powered up their lapboards to pound out a movie with the working title *Tentacles*.

The jellyfish accomplished all this dead. We hate to think the mayhem that would have ensued in Rye if the creature were alive. It's a lucky thing phylum *Coelenterata* never evolved intelligence.

78. There was a strange noise in the house around 2:30 AM. These kinds of noises never happen at 2:30 PM, only at 2:30 in the AM. It sounded like the splatter of water, as if someone were rhythmically spraying water against a hard surface. I tossed the blanket off, got out of bed, put my snuggly slippers on, and went to investigate. I couldn't find the source of the noise. There was no tap left on, no leak under the toilet, no drip in the shower. (The only drip in the shower is when

I take one.) I went back to bed. I decided the noise was either the lawn sprinklers turned on at the wrong time and in the wrong direction or a paranormal manifestation. If it is the former I intend to write a letter of complaint to the homeowners association. If it is the latter I intend to find a reputable priest to bless the house. Given the state of Holy Mother Church, this is not an easy task.

79. This actually happened.

It's a Monday evening in the spring of 1994, give or take a year. I'm working in the Barnes & Noble Sale Annex that once stood at the southwest corner of 18th St. and Fifth Ave. in Manhattan. We were transitioning from a full service bookstore to a strictly used bookstore. We sold new books, gift items, and magazines at the entrance of the store near the cash wrap. I was in the rear section with the used books. If I wasn't doing resort or filing books off a V-cart, then I was goofing off.

The loudspeaker flipped on with a gargle and Lincoln Vallee, the stringy assistant manager, asked in an excited voice, "Is there a doctor in the store?"

"That can't be good," I thought. I looked around. The customers in the used book section looked in good health—in health, anyway. Alfred, the book scout and kleptomaniac, perused a table of scholarly remainders. He stood stooped over the selection, as his eyes were going bad. The top of his head was as bald as an un-inscribed bookpate. No sickness is going to deter him from finding a book he can peddle to the Strand for a few dollars.

Captain Textbook, a short white-haired man with various facial tics, drooled over an analytical geometry textbook. Maybe he discovered a formula he never saw before. He'd have to memorize the formula, as he had a lock on his wallet and never bought anything. Like Alfred, he was another book person who wasn't going to let a medical emergency distract him from finding an out-of-print gem. If the *Titanic* had a bookstore, they wouldn't leave it, not even for an iceberg.

Josh Linx, the Friedrich Nietzsche aficionado, was in the N section of the philosophy stacks. Josh was a short man and on the slim side, rather an *undermensch* in stature. If he found anything new, he'd have to fetch a stool to reach it.

I let a half hour pass and strolled toward the front of the store. Everything looked normal in the Lit Crit section. Kip, the Jack Kerouac want-to-be, was loading up a basket before hitting the road. Thanks to Kip, we'll make a few sales this evening.

There was nothing amiss at the mass market dump table. Mrs. Bauer had a stack of paperbacks set aside. She was fingering the titles placed spines up in the table. If she found a book placed spine down or with its title out of sequence, she turned it right side up for the convenience of other customers. One time we caught her changing retail price stickers. We banished her for a month and then let her back inside. She promised she'd behave and not switch prices again.

Lincoln hadn't come back on the loudspeaker and asked if there was a nurse in the store. Maybe there was a doctor in the house. We had a small selection of out-of-print medical texts and the Annex attracted a lot of professional people. Things must be all right.

Unfortunately, I was premature. When I reached the entrance of the Annex I found out things were not all right. I told myself I have to stop being an optimist.

Lincoln was standing in the aisle. He had a worried look on his face. He liked to go clubbing once the Annex closed and he hated to dally. He must have thought he'd have to stay past closing and fill out reports. Tanya, the cashier girl, was counting coins to save time at closing. I don't know where she went after-hours, but she was another bookseller who mad-dashed out of the store. Once she counted coins she refused to make change. If customers wanted to buy books they had to have exact change. A policeman was reviewing the sports-and-fitness section of the magazine rack. He wore long sleeves, but I could tell from the ripples that he was flexing his forearms and comparing his build to the chiseled specimens featured on the covers. Two paramedics from the ambulance corps stood at the opposite end of the magazine rack. I could tell they were paramedics—the word was emblazoned in white lettering on their blue pullovers.

An elderly man was on the floor. His head rested on a Stephen King bestseller that served as a pillow. His hair was thin at the top, but so exceptionally long on the sides it extended like a halo around his pale skull. A luxurious gray beard folded like a drop clothe in the nape of his neck. His wire-rim glasses were on the floor beside him. His face was bluish-gray in color. His eyes were open and staring unmovingly upward. He looked bad—I didn't think he was going to make it.

And it was worse than that. He was lying face up in front of the sophisticated magazine section of the rack—"sophisticated magazine" is corporate double-talk for pornography. He eyes were fixed on breasts the size of potato sacks and at rotors of butt cheeks that were as large and as round as the breasts and a good deal firmer. I hate to think the last image this customer had of the world was the lesbian action on the cover of the spring issue of *Biker Bitches* and that he went to the Particular Judgment with air-brushed nipples glowing in his eyes. That could get him in big trouble at the pearly gates.

He led a blameless life until he landed on the floor of the Sale Annex. It's a shame that a few prurient thoughts at the last moments sent him on the down escalator to a bookstore where a fire sale is in permanent progress. Of course, if he took ill and died shopping his favorite section of the magazine rack, then he made a rather happy check out from life.

80. If our lives are books, when we die we can be said to go out of print.

81. And this actually happened in the Sale Annex.

It was near closing on a quiet night. The usual characters were in place. Lincoln Vallee was ensconced in the manager's office. Tanya had started to count the loose change so she could make a quick get-away. I could hear the clink of coins all the way in the back of the store. Alfred and Captain Textbook were stalking the stacks looking for rare pieces. Josh was at attention in front of the philosophy section. He touched every book with his index finger, but there was nothing new by his main man. Kip looked ecstatic. He had found an early edition collection of Beat poetry. He better get to the register before Tanya closed the drawer or he wasn't buying that book tonight. Mrs. Bauer had raised a wall of mass markets on the dump table. She moved her hands in a suspicious manner behind the books. I hope she hasn't fallen back into her evil ways of changing retail price stickers. If it were earlier in the day I'd stroll by and check what she was up to.

I happened to notice a new customer wandering in front of the Literature section. He was a tall man with black hair and a receding hairline. He wore white slacks and a slightly oversized auburn blazer with black elbow patches. He ran his hand through his hair and pressed his black-framed glasses to his nose. He could be no more obvious than if he held a poster aloft with the notice, "I need help." I didn't ordinarily ask customers if they needed help, but I made an exception in his case. I must have been in a happy mood.

"Hello. Can I help you with anything?"

"I—I don't know," he answered in an unidentifiable accent that may have been Italian. "I was here last night and I saw a book with a bright red cover. I don't see it tonight."

"Do you remember the title?"

"That's just it. I don't remember the title. I remember it was in this section." He pointed toward a wall of books.

"Who was the author? The books are in alphabetical order, sort of."

"I don't know." He touched both hands to the top of his glass frames and shrugged. "All I remember was the book had a red cover. I knew I should have bought it when I saw it."

"I know the feeling—that's the story of my life." I stared at the shelves. There were a lot of red-spined books to sample. I was going to suggest that he take a chance and pull a few books out, but he didn't look like he was in a hunting mood and I wasn't about to hunt for him. I thought the cords of memory might be untied if I suggested a few titles.

"Maybe it was *Mein Kampf* by A. Hitler."

"No, that wasn't it."

"Was it *War and Peace* by L. Tolstoy? Maybe in the original Russian?"

He shook his head. "I don't read Russian."

"Was it *Fear and Trembling* by S. Kierkegaard?"

The agonized look on his face proclaimed it wasn't.

"Well, I don't know what else to suggest. Maybe if you walk around you'd spot the book."

He nodded and stepped away.

I tried to be upbeat and to end the encounter on a positive note. "Maybe you'd spot a better book in a different color. We sell books in all kinds of colors."

He wandered toward the exit. His walk was halting and indecisive, as if he debated whether to make an attempt and peruse the shelves. He paused for a moment at a stack of scholarly remainders. *Show Trials of the Soviet Presidium* by N. Mironowicz was the first book on the table. The book had a red cover, but he wasn't interested.

"Thanks for the business," I whispered as he stepped outside.

82. The latest health craze making the rounds is the simplest one of all—sunshine. It seems every miserable ailment can be cast off just by standing outdoors and letting Old Man Sun shower your pores with the good vitamin D. The guy who collapsed in the Annex should have spent more time in the sunlight than indoors in front of girlie magazines.

This lunch break I got my daily dose of life-promoting sunshine by walking around the empty end of the parking lot in the Distribution Center. In all my born days I never felt better. I feel perfectly healthy. All my sicknesses are transpiring through my skin—that's not sweat you see glistening but sickness. Every nugget of cholesterol is dissolving—I hear the swish of blood racing through unblocked arteries, I hear the clots shattering on the pavement. Every chromosomal mutation is untying itself genomic strand-by-strand. Every heinous malady is evaporating into thin air. Every germ in draining out of me. The bacteria are in full flight and they're carrying the viruses piggyback. I'm no George Gordon Meade when it comes to my microbial enemies. I'm going to be in full pursuit till they regroup in the next county.

I'm a citizen of the state of wellness, but you better not come too close. Stay at arm's length. Better still, stay at double-arm's length. Cover your mouth and hold your breath. Once they leave me, this nasty slough of sicknesses and germs have to go someplace. They don't disintegrate and pass into nothingness. They linger at ground level and look for someone new to infiltrate. If you're in the vicinity, they may find you an agreeable host and rush inside. They don't care who they sicken—you'll do nicely. I'd hate for that to happen.

Believe me, you don't want my illnesses.

83. One of the most inane things grownups do is to walk up to babies and ask questions. I saw this happen in the entrance of Wal-Mart the other day. I'm sure it happens in entrances in stores all over the world. A lady rushed up to her baby niece, pressed noses, and gushed, "How are you, lovely thing? Are you being a good little girl for Mommy?" The baby frowned, chewed her pacifier at an increased rate, and dribbled.

This kind of behavior is comparable to people asking their pets questions. "How are you feeling today, Fido?" "Is my baby Fido warm this morning?" "Is this a good place for Fido to do his business?" "Does Fido want to walk another block?"

When I hear this inanity I wish I could hide in the bushes and throw my voice. "Cold hard concrete is as good a place as any to do my business and, no, I do not want to walk another block."

84. This is the proof that Jesus was divine—he healed Peter's mother-in-law. Only God would be so accommodating to heal another man's mother-in-law.

85. It's summertime and the living is greasy. The politicians have slithered from their hiding places under the marshland's sooty mat. It has recently come to their attention that Atlantic City is going the way of South Jersey's Revolutionary War-era forges. Thirty years of gaming have resulted in thirty years of blight, corruption, and desolation. Atlantic City is unchanged from before the casinos were erected—it's a dark, dirty, and decayed stretch of middle-and-lower-middle class homes occupied by people born and bred in the unbreakable chains of poverty.

The politicians are not concerned with the citizens of Atlantic City. What concerns them is that the casinos are themselves joining the cascade into oblivion. Their fear is the cash cow will become a cash goat. Some of the casinos may go out of business—odds are being placed on which will survive and which will go extinct. The ones that survive will need to downsize. This means the loss of much needed revenue and patronage. The once glamorous strip will come to look like the boarded-up gas stations and strip malls that dot the countryside since the Great Recession robbed them of customers.

There's been a proliferation of conjectures about what caused the decline in gaming. One theory is that there is too much competition from casinos and slot parlors in Pennsylvania, Delaware, and New England, not to mention from nearly everywhere else. Another theory is that too little competition over the thirty years caused the casinos to grow flabby in the customer service department. Another theory is that there is competition from horse racing in North Jersey. Or that there has not been enough competition from horse racing. Or that there is competition from NASCAR and from Jai Lai. Or that there has not been enough competition from NASCAR and from Jai Lai. Or that there are too few rooms in the hotels. Or that there are too many rooms. Or that there are too few family attractions in Atlantic City. Or that there are too many family attractions in Atlantic City and not enough sleaze. Or that there are too many concerts that compete for too few fans. Or that the geriatric groups who appear in the concert halls attract fans who start to snore during the performances. (There is only so much space in the aisles for wheelchairs before the fire wardens turn the house lights on.) Or that there are too few high rollers and too many people at the penny slots. Or that there are too many high rollers and not enough people at the penny slots. Or that there are too many access roads feeding into too many choke points. Or that there is too much local traffic and too many stop lights as local residents go about the homespun business of dropping letters in the post office and dirty clothes in the laundries. Or that there are too many distractions on the Boardwalk. Or that there are too few distractions on the Boardwalk. Or that there are too many hand-drawn rolling chairs on the boards. Or that the rolling chairs resemble some coolie system out of The Third World—self-reliant Americans from the heartland prefer to walk than to sit in chairs and be pushed by local people.

Jon Hanson chaired Governor Christie's "Advisory Commission on Gaming, Sports and Entertainment." He came up with a novel conjecture why Atlantic City has hit the skids. His conjecture was seconded by Assemblyman John Amodeo (R., Atlantic County). Hanson perceived that the view of the ocean is an "asset that has not properly been utilized." That explains everything—the sand dunes are to blame for the drop in revenue.

It's not the competition. It's not the number of hotel rooms. It's not the number of family attractions. It's not the sleaze. It's not the age of the entertainers. It's not the age of the audience. It's not the income level of the gamblers. It's not the Boardwalk. It's not the traffic. It's not the rolling chairs pushed by local people. It's the sand dunes.

The solution is obvious. Raze the dunes. The gray ocean will be visible and gamblers will flock to Atlantic City like the laughing gulls in season. Because they can see the ocean, gamblers will come from all over. They'll desert tables in Pennsylvania, Delaware, and New England, not to mention tables from everywhere else. They'll leave the bleachers in NASCAR tracks and in Jai Lai arenas and rush to New Jersey. They don't care how many rooms are for rent or where they'll stay—they might even sleep on the beach so they can catch the royal rays of dawn. They don't want to be in the theaters listening to aging rock stars, they want to be on the boards admiring the view. They don't care about finding places at the gaming tables, they want to be outside and wondering whether that slice beyond the breakwater is the crest of a wave or the fin of a porpoise. They don't care about shops on the Boardwalk or about the amusements. All they care about is the view of the ocean, a view that's enticing, beautiful, and deadly. They don't care about sitting in traffic at choke points backed up to the Parkway tolls—the view of the ocean is just over the hood of the SUV parked ahead of them. They don't even care about the propriety of the rolling chairs. They're not going to move out of the way—the view beyond the leveled sand is too wonderful to forsake. They prefer to get run over than to give up the view, even for a moment. This is Atlantic City—they gamble on the driving skills of the men pushing the chairs.

This is New Jersey where nothing is done right and where nothing turns out for the better. It's clear what's going to happen. Today, the dunes get flattened. Tomorrow, a chunk of Gibraltar the size of Atlantic County slides into the ocean.

86. It's Powerball madness in the Gangster State. The prize is now 360 million dollars. I splurged and bought a ticket. Just one ticket, but who needs a second when it's the winning ticket? Three hundred sixty million dollars for a one-dollar investment. Not a bad return. People ask what I could do with 360 million dollars. I can think of a few things. And they ask if I'll remember my friends when I hit. Of course, I'll remember my friends. What kind of person do they think I am? When I hit the big one every one of my friends is getting $25.00.

87. The inquiring mind would like to know—if you own a *pet peeve*, does that make you its master? What do you feed a *pet peeve*? And does a *pet peeve* need grooming?

Does a *peeve* need to be walked daily? If you walk a *peeve* do you have to drop its business inside a plastic bag and deposit the bag in the community dumpster so Barnegat Bay doesn't get polluted? What does my *peeve* think seeing me bend down and bag its business? Does it think I'm a weirdo of the worst order? Does it think I'm demonstrating a specific-specific behavior unique to *Homo sapiens*?

And can we circumvent the entire business of bagging by house training the *peeve*?

88.   There is so much development along Barnegat Bay in Southern Jersey the water is polluted. Things have gotten so bad, dead zones have developed where algae proliferate and prevent other species from prospering.

Similar dead zones are found on the scalps of the middle-age men who reside along Barnegat Bay.

89.   A gruesome discovery was made recently in the woods near the famous *Hollywood* sign in Los Angeles. A human head was found wrapped in a bag. Police canvassed the woods and found severed hands and feet in the vicinity. The appendages were not wrapped. The headline blazed on the television, *"Hands, Feet Found Near Head!"* I thought, *"What?"* and looked at myself in the mirror. Hands? Feet? Found near a head? Isn't that where they're always found?

90.   We often use the expression, "He knew it like the back of his hand." But does he really know *it* like the back of his hand? A more fundamental question is does he know the *back of his hand*? Because if he doesn't know the back of his hand, then he can't know it, whatever it might be. Could he recognize the back of his hand if it were detached from the rest of his arm?

I'm not aware of any experiment testing the hypothesis that people know the back of their hands with the certainty they claim they do. It would be interesting to conduct such an experiment. The procedure is straightforward. We'd have to photograph the back of a person's hand from the wrists to the knuckles, but not above the knuckles. I suspect most people would recognize the backs of their hands if they saw their fingers attached—this is a topic for a second experiment. The photograph would then be placed in an array of photographs of the backs of hands of strangers. Probably, we would need seven or more photographs to make a fair test. Participants would attempt to choose the photographs that in their estimation match the backs of their hands. The procedure resembles what eyewitnesses to crimes do when presented with an array of mug shots. Participants would have to wear gloves when making the selection in order not to be able to compare the backs of their hands with the photographs. We might need to deceive the participants by elaborating a cover story for the experiment—perhaps the participants could be told the experiment had to do with identifying the hands of models. To control for experimenter bias the person conducting the experiment would have to be blind as to which photograph from the show of hands is correct. This person could not see the ungloved hands of participants. Overall sample size would number approximately 100.

Many research proposals come to mind. We can examine the relationship between personality type and back-of-hand recognition. It may be that extraverts recognize the backs of their hands with greater accuracy than introverts—introverts frequently sit with their palms pressed to their foreheads as they think, so they have less opportunity to see the backs of their hands. We can explore the relationship of psychological disorders to back-of-hand recognition. We can hypothesize that, compared to a control group of normal participants, schizophrenics and psychotic individuals would be less familiar with the backs of their hands, as they may perceive their hands as disembodied rather than as integral components of an intact body image. Compared to a control group, individuals afflicted with anxiety disorders may be more familiar with the backs of their hands, as they often engage in hang-wringing. If successful in differentiating between groups, the back-of-hand recognition task may come to serve as an adjunct to differential diagnosis.

We can examine developmental issues when it comes to recognizing the back of the hand. Following traditional views of developmental capabilities, we can expect the very young and the very old to do poorer at back-of-hand recognition than young adult and middle-aged samples. We can expect the accuracy of back-of-hand recognition to peak in the late teen years and remain fairly stable into old age. The back-of-hand recognition procedure might be employed to discover the development of personal identity and individuality. It can assess when children became aware of themselves as individual entities and thereby supplement the dot-on-the-head technique in comparative psychology. The back-of-hand recognition procedure can also be employed to assess when, at the opposite spectrum of life, seniors lose awareness of parts of their bodies.

Finally, the issue of gender differences can be explored using the back-of-hand recognition procedure. Females are generally superior at nonverbal tasks and they may be more familiar with the hand in general, as they apply nail polish and wear jewelry, so they may out-perform males on the back-of-the hand procedure. However, males may have an advantage, since they engage in sports such as baseball and billiards that involve manual dexterity and they frequently give one another a slap of the hand in jest and in jostle.

The back-of-the hand recognition procedure can be used in every subject domain in psychology. It can keep master's level students busy for years. It can keep doctoral candidates equally busy. Entire departments of psychology at reputable universities can be organized around it. A division of the American Psychological Association can be built on it. The possibilities are limitless.

91. I'm at Thanksgiving dinner thinking about having to go to work on Friday—that's a thankless task. It's a grind to have to go to work the day after I pig out in honor of God and country. I recommend that we change Thanksgiving to the last Friday in the month of November. That way, we can celebrate a three-day weekend and honor God and country in the gluttonous way they deserve. I don't know how Thanksgiving got to be celebrated on the last Thursday in November. What were people thinking of?

While we're changing holidays, we can make Christmas the next to last Monday in December—this gives us another three-day weekend. We have religious feast days pegged to particular days in the week. The Crucifixion always occurs on a Friday, the Resurrection on a Sunday, and the Ascension on a Thursday. There's no reason Christmas can't be moved to a Monday. It's merely a convention that we celebrate Christmas on December 25 whichever day of the week it falls on. No one knows when Jesus was born. I once read that Jesus was born in the spring rather than in the winter—this had something to do with the season in Israel when shepherds tended their flocks—and that December 25 was chosen to coincide with a Roman feast of Apollo. If this is true, that's reason to change the day we celebrate Christmas. It's in poor taste that the Savior's birth is associated with a pagan deity. I wonder if the Pope knows this.

If we change Christmas we need to change New Year's Day to the first Friday in January irrespective of the actual day it falls on. It may seem like we'd want to balance things out and make New Year's Day the first Monday in January, like Christmas is the next to last Monday in December, but Friday is definitely a superior choice. Making Friday New Year's Day gives us two whole days to sleep the partying off.

92. I happened to be looking up a word starting with the letters "ma" when my eyes fell on the word "mambo". I read the definition, "A Latin dance originating in Cuba related to the rumba." I looked up the word "rumba". The definition was, "A Latin dance originating in Cuba related to the mambo." Well, that's not very helpful.

If I'm dancing to Salsa music in the Copa, how do I know which one I'm doing?

93. Here's a tip for terrorists—hire appearance-challenged people to carry your bombs on board planes.

Homeland Security is starting to use full-body scans to avoid another incident like the one in which a terrorist stored explosives in his underwear. Agents are going to view passengers in the altogether and fully nude—they are allowed to scan individuals for as long as thirty seconds. They will need to pay special attention when good-looking people step in front of the screen. "What's that bulge hiding?" "What's on the other side of that curve?" "What's in-between those mounds?" The agents are just following procedure and giving selected people, chosen randomly it goes without saying, the full thirty-second treatment. In the interest of national security they're just dotting their jocks and tittling their eyes. It's human nature to want to look at good-looking people in the altogether and fully nude and it's homeland security as well. Agents can never be sure what death-dealing devices are hidden in the body orifices of beautiful people, so they need to take an in-depth and prolonged view.

Security agents may not be as diligent when it comes to appearance-challenged people. Obese individuals, individuals with deformities, ugly people, and the just plain bland may earn less than the thirty-second treatment. Their scans may last no more than a few seconds. They'll get a quick once over and a brisk, "Step away from the screen." This is perfectly understandable. It's human nature not to want to look at sagging body parts or at hepatic moles when there is so much beauty standing in line to scan and cherish.

94. I was streaming tsunami style to arrive at the end of the lecture before we arrived at the end of the class. I needed to get all the information in the lecture, as there was a quiz coming up and I don't like to test students on what I don't cover in class. (Many of the students do not read the book, so the lecture is the only chance they get to hear what's on the quiz.) Little caring whether their writing hands could keep up, I rushed through the variables that intensify the deleterious effects of stress—in class I used "negative" in place of "deleterious". Social isolation, the lack of coping skills, a failure to provide a rationale for the stress, and an inability to predict the duration of the stress—these exacerbate the situation. In class I used the word "worsen" in place of "exacerbate". Blowing harder than a squall in the Bermuda Triangle I covered the variables that reduce the effects of stress. Having a shoulder to cry on, the availability of coping skills, identifying the causes of stress, and predicting the outcome of the stress—these mitigate the psychological and physiological effects. In class I used the word "detensify" rather than "mitigate". I didn't mean to say "detensify". It just came out, like all the other words flowing in a flood tide of coherence.

The end of class was fast approaching, but I paused. I realized that detensify is not a word. But it should be a word. It has a place in the lexicon and can be used when a speaker is in a hurry. It means the same and it works a lot better than "de-intensify".

95. Everyone has one of those unguarded moments when we say what we should have kept to ourselves and express statements we can't take back or withdraw the way we can recall an unread e-mail. This kind

of moment happened to Bradley Byrne, a Republican candidate for governor of the state of Alabama, when he slipped and said out loud in the hearing of an audience that parts of the Bible are not literally true. (This was in reference to the outlandish ages the Old Testament patriarchs reached.) The statement immediately led to gasping and to the sounds of open palms slapping foreheads. It also led to a television commercial pegging Bradley as a "liberal" who believes the theory of evolution "best explains the origin of life." A political action committee called True Republicans, based in Linden, Alabama, paid for the commercial. It appears the Alabama Education Association is a major contributor to the True Republicans. The largest association of educators in Alabama, "an advocate organization that leads the movement for excellence in education", according to their website, sponsors a political action committee that does not believe in the theory of evolution.

Bradley Byrne was Chancellor of Alabama's community colleges and presumably responsible for excellence in education in the two year-college system. But he is running for office in the state of Alabama. He did what we expect of a candidate in the state of Alabama. He immediately caved into the True Republicans, declaring in an official statement that he was misunderstood and that he was the victim of "spewing lies"—I don't think Peter the Apostle took less time setting the record straight. Challenged by his fellow Republicans, he wanted everyone to know that "I have never wavered in my belief that this world and everyone in it is a masterpiece created by the hands of God" and that "every single word" of the Bible is true. Furthermore, he insisted that "The record clearly shows that I fought to ensure the teaching of creationism in our school textbooks."

Let's be clear what's involved in this case. Every person is free to hold whatever religious beliefs they want. Every person is free to hold their beliefs unwaveringly or to waver in those beliefs, as the case may be. But no one, including an educated man who was a former college Chancellor and an organization that touts itself as promoting "excellence in education", is free to force the religious belief of creationism onto others or to insist that creationism be treated as an equal of scientific beliefs. This is not to imply that scientific thinking is superior to religious thinking. It is to imply that they are different. They have different objectives, they fulfill different human needs, and they have different internal standards of proof and disproof. Scientific beliefs are changeable, for example, whereas religious beliefs are not.

Bradley may have slapped himself around and knocked some sense into himself while gasping, "What I just said and people were listening", but he promptly validated the stereotype of the rubes and the rednecks as hay-chawing illiterates. He's done what I thought was impossible—the people of Alabama are making the people of Tennessee look sophisticated. Henceforward, the *state of Alabama* shall be congruent with the *state of Ignorance*.

I wonder why we didn't let the South secede when we had the chance.

96. I was in the driest patch of e-mails I had ever experienced in the workplace. One vendor sent an e-mail asking whether pallets needed to be made of wood or of plastic. (They have to be made of wood.) Another vendor e-mailed asking whether pallets had to be open on four sides or on two sides. (Pallets have to be open on four sides.) Another vendor asked whether they could ship a week early. (They could.) Another vendor asked whether they could ship a week late. (They could.) Another vendor asked whether they needed to seal the cartons with clear tape or with brown tape. (The color of carton-sealing tape doesn't matter.)

All of the sudden a gem of an e-mail arrived into this yawning chasm of boredom to light up the computer screen with prurient glee. The e-mail came across the ether like a green patch in the desert to a parched caravan with empty canteens. It came like a tropical beach to shipwrecked sailors on a leaky life raft. It came like a comfy cabin to winter sojourners after a trek across a frozen lake. I think it was Oscar Wilde who said that "Gossip is the lifeblood of a nation"—maybe the old guy who used to sit on the porch and wave to the traffic said it. Whoever said it, the e-mail instantly renewed my passport into the land of rumor and innuendo. I felt invigorated. I was overjoyed. I was no longer a man without a country. I could carry on for the rest of the day.

Melody J.—a third-shift supervisor—had unintentionally copied me on an e-mail describing the peccadilloes, proclivities, and perversions of her staff. (She used paragraphs rather than bullet points.) Leave it to Melody to detail what went on in the lunchroom and behind the racks of stacked books. The e-mail explained in so many words why her crew has not been especially productive. They've been goofing off in ways that will never make the company's annual report. It's amazing what can be done with duct tape. It's equally amazing what can be done on the raised blades of a forklift. Talk about balancing acts. It was extremely risky what they tried on the conveyors. I doubt that our medical plan covers the contortions Melody referred to. I know I would never try what they did, not even if I were in my cups and delirious.

Melody not only described practices, she also named names. I never realized Luis and Annabelle were an item. And Jacinta—I had heard the rumors and never believed them. If Melody didn't include them in the fourth paragraph I still wouldn't believe the rumors. Poor Jorge, I was sad to read about what they did to him. I was happy for Rose. She got what she wanted, although not with the person she intended. And Harold—I didn't think he was that kind of a person.

Melody's e-mail was six paragraphs long. I read the first five seated. I reread them standing so as not to drool on the keyboard. And then I came to the sixth paragraph. I didn't know what to do after I read it.

"The information contained in this message is privileged and intended only for the recipients indicated. If the reader is not an intended recipient, any review or copying of the information it contains is forbidden. If you are not an intended recipient, please notify the sender and immediately delete the message."

I was stuck. I didn't want to get into trouble for reading something I was not supposed to. I clearly wasn't an "intended recipient". I couldn't even pretend that I was. I couldn't notify Melody that I got her gossipy e-mail. I couldn't notify her that I got it and didn't read it. She would never believe that, not after writing the opening line, "Guys, wait till you hear about the incident in the locker room!" I couldn't go back and un-read the e-mail. I couldn't force myself to forget what I read. Memory doesn't work that way—you can't force yourself to forget something. The images about their after-hours hanky-panky were indelibly implanted in my mind, especially the images of Jacinta. (If you knew Jacinta, the images would be ir-erasably implanted in your mind, too.) I couldn't excise the parts of the brain responsible for creating long-term memories. I certainly didn't want to mess with the cortices of the temporal lobes. I've always lived with the motto, "Take care of your brain and your brain will take care of you."

There's a *Twilight Zone* episode in which a bookworm survives a nuclear blast. He's the last man alive in New York City. For once and forever he's free of the bane of people bothering him and keeping him from reading. He can read every book in the public library without interruption. And then he trips and falls and breaks his glasses on the rubble. He can't see a thing. I'm like that bookworm. I was in residence in the capitol city of the country of gossip and I couldn't say a thing— not a single word—else I betray the fact that I read an e-mail I wasn't supposed to. Though I dearly wanted to, I couldn't click on the forward icon, open the address book to "Everyone", and send the gossip back into the electronic ether.

97. This is the tragedy of Segundo.

Segundo H— was a native of Mexico and an eight-year company man. His position was in maintenance, trash a specialty. Segundo stood four-foot nine and weighed 140 pounds. He had black hair, thinning on the top and tied in a fashionably long tail in the back. He was anywhere from 50 – 70 years of age. He had a pleasant personality and greeted everyone by holding his broom aloft and proclaiming, "Beby!" He called everyone "Beby" from his maintenance co-workers to the suits in upper management. He said "Beby!" in the same tone of voice other people shouted, "Arriba!"

Segundo had an outstanding work record, the kind of record anyone would be proud of. But in the last year of his employment Segundo developed a fondness for *the drink*. Segundo was able to control this fondness at first, but the drink soon became master of the man, rather than Segundo master of the drink. It started with a pint of rum after work while he watched professional wrestling … and progressed with fatal rapidity to drinking before punching the time clock in the morning … and then to drinking on the job all hours of the shift.

The first time Segundo went blotto in the Distribution Center he was found fast asleep, broom in hand, behind an assortment gaylord. The supervisor who found Segundo was a kindly man—he was rumored to be friends with Dr. Bob, so he knew what drink can do to the best of employees. He sent Segundo home with a stern warning never to come to work with his sheets unfurled. Segundo obeyed the supervisor for several weeks, but couldn't resist the *demon rum* forever.

The second and last time Segundo was caught in his cups on the job could not be overlooked, since it happened in plain view of the warehouse crew. Segundo was bent over, sweeping packing rice with a flattened box and half a broom, when he suddenly tumbled to the ground. It's unclear whether Segundo turned a cartwheel or just plain collapsed forehead first. Eyewitness testimony is divided on this point. Be that as it may, Segundo could not get back to his feet, which became wobbly and like unto jelly. A different supervisor was on duty, a well-known authoritarian type. Segundo was fired on the spot and he fired back.

This supervisor decided to test Segundo's blood-alcohol level through the torch technique, just to be sure that Segundo was *once* sheets to the wind and not diabetic or epileptic. (The company could get sued firing him for a medical condition.) He held his cigarette lighter in front of Segundo's mouth and had Segundo blow—and blow Segundo did, 90 proof rum at twice the legal limit. *Ay dios mio!* The flame traveled at the speed of light and ignited the shrink wrap pasted to a pallet of *Cracking the Da Vinci Code*.

Segundo was sent home and instructed never to come back. Rumors are he went home to Mexico City, but no one knows for sure. Wherever he went we never heard "Beby" again. The supervisor was revived and kept his job, since no books were set on fire—quick-thinking employees extinguished the flames before they reached the spines of the books. The warehouse crew had a jolly good time reviewing events of that day and telling stories about Segundo. The clerical staff shook their heads and wondered just who was going to clean the office trash now that Segundo was gone. The Bargain department pondered the situation and drew the lesson never to come to work in their cups or, if they do, to hide in their cubes and pretend they're bent in the deepest perusal of Excel spreadsheets.

98. It's said that most people use ten percent of their brains. I'm different than most people. I use eleven percent.

99. The Summer/Fall issue of *Salesian* magazine arrived in the mail. This is a slim magazine put out by the Salesian order of priests. I'm not sure why we get it. Someone must have made a contribution in our name.

The Salesians were founded by Don John Bosco, who was born in the Piedmont region of Italy in 1815. Don John was by every account a kindly man. He dedicated his order to educating children born into poverty. In pursuit of this noble task he came up with an innovation in nineteenth—indeed, in twentieth—century Catholic education. He used tenderness and kindness in dealing with children rather than the usual meanness and brutality. This kind of approach must have seemed incomprehensible to the raptors in collars and full-body habits.

Don John knew the psychology of children better than his peers in the priesthood. Rather than threats of hellfire and damnation he used fun and games to grab the attention of children. He learned to juggle and to perform magic acts to entice children to religion class. He subsequently became the patron saint of magicians.

Right from the outset the Salesians have been a missionary order. The magazine demonstrated the missionary zeal has not abated. It featured articles on a hospice in South America, on a school built for Cambodian children, and on relief efforts in earthquake-devastated Haiti. True to its roots, the magazine had an article about counseling troubled Italian teens. The good work continues long after Don John ascended into sainthood.

The odor of sanctity is colossally soured by an advertisement that runs on the last page of the magazine. For $12.00 readers can be the proud owners of a Don John Bosco coffee mug. The mug bears Don John's portrait—a mug on a mug—and an unspecified inspirational quote, possibly, "As you send a suggested offering to the least of the brethren, you send a suggested offering unto me, shipping and handling included." It's very dispiriting to see this tacky ad after reading so many uplifting accounts of spiritual heroism in a blighted world.

What's in the Winter/Spring issue, a Don John Bosco bobble-head doll for sale-sian?

100. Our department in the great Distribution Center recently got a digital camera. This is for use when books come in damaged or when

pallets are not built to specification—when pallets wobble or tilt or when the books leak out from the bottom layers owing to insufficient shrink wrap and cardboard corner boards. I was so happy seeing the camera I started to sing, "I ought to be in pictures!" This surprised the crew. Usually I sing as I work "I'm just a teenager in love."

I went on to explain that, really, I ought to be in pictures. A lot of people think I'm a dead ringer for Cary Grant. It frequently happens that strangers walk up and ask, "Hey, aren't you Cary Grant and didn't you die?" I don't answer. I smile and leave them guessing. Other, less assertive, strangers walk up and comment, nervously looking me over, "Nah, it can't be." I don't say anything to them. The bashful strangers don't walk up. They don't say anything. But I know what they're thinking. "There goes Cary Grant and how can that be?" I nod and throw my head back and wink. I know how good that makes them feel. "I just saw a movie star and doesn't he look great for being dead?"

I can understand how easy it is to get confused. The resemblance is there, definitely. Both of us are tall and in relatively good shape. We wear glasses. We have full heads of hair—we're lucky in having maternal grandfathers who didn't go bald. My hair is turning gray—I'm not as gray as Cary was, but I'm getting there. We have a self-deprecating sense of humor. We're amicable and inoffensive. Both of us walk fast. I'm not half the egomaniac Cary was—I'm not one tenth the egomaniac Cary was. But people don't know that. The see the cool self-confidence and they hear the witticisms directed against my supposed foibles and they think, "This guy is full of himself." Sometimes I hear them snicker, "Married to a cowboy, hey?" but that doesn't bother me. I'm a grown up and a sophisticate. None of us can speak to the mysterious ways of love.

Rumor had it that Cary was such an egomaniac he refused to have mirrors or any reflective surfaces in his mansion—even the silverware was scuffed to keep him from catching a glimpse of the wrinkled advance of age. The rumor was that his long hermitage and absence from Hollywood was due to his vanity. He couldn't bear the thought people whispered, "Wow, has that guy aged."

Cary started appearing in public again only when he turned 80. It bothered him that people saw him at 60 and 70. But at 80 people could only think, "He looks great for being 80." It pleased him no end that people thought he looked great at 80. Every octogenarian should look so good, in shape and svelte and with wits intact and a full head of snow-white hair.

Cary's last public performance was in a one-man show entitled, "An Evening with Cary Grant." Mostly, he toured college campuses and small venues where there was an intimacy between the man and his admirers. Cary sat on stage and did what he did best—talk about himself. He answered unrehearsed questions about his life and career and showed collegians that he was as sharp at 80 as they were at 20.

Cary died on stage in one of these sessions—this one could aptly be called "The Last Evening with Cary Grant." A film school major asked if Sam Jaffe was difficult to work with. Cary fielded the question, adjusted his black glasses, and keeled over. The audience stared for a while—it may have been for as long as two minutes—before someone had the sense to ask, "Is there a doctor in the house?" the moment before the curtain dropped.

Cary was gone, but it would have gratified him to know what the audience was thinking. "That guy can play dead better than anyone."

101. I met B.F. Skinner, the notorious behaviorist, one time. Actually, I was in the same room with him along with 500 other people. And it wasn't a room. It was a ballroom in a New York hotel during the 1987 American Psychological Convention. The occasion was a presentation called "an Evening with B.F. Skinner", which it was, sort of. The idea was for Skinner to stand on stage and field questions fired at him from members of the audience, some of whom were admirers, others of whom were critics. The critics did the firing. With the admirers it was more like lobbing.

The problem was Skinner, who was in his mid-80s, was deaf as a clam. He couldn't hear anything. A member of the audience called out, "Dr. Skinner, what is love in a behavioral analysis?" Skinner cupped his hand to his ear, bent over the lectern, and asked, "What?" Dr. Sexton, the hostess of the evening, was standing next to Skinner. She followed up and asked with her mouth nearly over his ear, "The questioner wants to know what love is in a behavioral analysis." Skinner cupped his hand over his ear, bent forward, and asked, "What?" This wasn't getting very far. After a few rounds of hand-cupped ears and "Whats?" Skinner gave an off-the-cuff speech about books he was reading on Behaviorism—

Dennis Ford

probably, he was reading the sections that referred to him. The evening broke up early.

The trouble started the next morning. I woke up blind. I couldn't see the darkness in front of my eyes. Specialists with strings of letters after their names couldn't find anything wrong with my eyes. The macula was fine. So was the fovea. The retina was properly attached. The visual purple was royally stained. They suggested I see a psychotherapist. They thought the blindness might be hysterical in nature and the kind of conversion disorder women suffered in nineteenth-century Vienna. I was insulted by the comparison, but took their advice. I consulted an analyst with an European accent. I learned things about myself, unsavory things, but I didn't get my eyesight back. Next I tried folk remedies. I tried the kinds of remedies they practice in the back woods and bayous south of Mason-Dixon. I tried the remedies they practice in the evergreen forests of Eastern Europe. Nothing worked. No one could figure out what happened.

One dark day I put two and two together. I saw B.F. Skinner, the number-one rated psychologist of all time, in the evening. The next morning I woke up blind. It was obvious—I was blinded by his brilliance. That had to be the explanation. I supposed I could wait till the brilliance wore off—it does eventually—but the disability money was running out and a Braille keyboard doesn't work well with the pick-and-hunt technique of typing. The blindness didn't look like it was going to lift anytime soon—we are talking about the number-one rated psychologist of all time. I thought I should sue Skinner or the American Psychological Association, but this kind of lawsuit would be costly and difficult to prove.

Things were getting desperate—I was looking to supplement my cane with canine eyes—when I heard about a holy man of God who had extraordinary healing powers. I'm a man of science and I don't believe in extraordinary healing powers, but I had run out of options. There was nothing left for me in the rational world. I bought a train ticket and went to visit this holy man. He lived in a suburb of Buffalo.

Things worked out for me, but not as well as they could. This holy man laid me backward in a chair—backward was the direction proprioception told me I was going. Once I was settled with my head against a pillow, he spit at me, aiming for my eyes. His eyesight was

72

almost as bad as mine. The pellet of spit missed my eyes and hit the middle of my forehead in the place where occultists say we have a third eye. Fortunately, the force of the spit was great enough to cause a downward splatter over my eyelids and onto the corneas. That's the reason I wear glasses and don't have perfect eyesight like I had before I attended an evening with B.F. Skinner. If that holy man had aimed his spit properly, I would have 20/20 vision instead of 20/40.

Still, I took whatever I could get in the way of eyesight. 20/40 vision was better than 20/0. I caught the express train back to New Jersey. I couldn't get home fast enough. I wanted to tell everyone about this holy man and his healing saliva. I wanted to tell my cousin Arlene who has eczema bad on her elbows and my buddy Benjamin who's bald as a melon that they should take the train to Buffalo and have the holy man spit on them just like he spit on me.

102. When it comes to famous people I've lived a sheltered life.

B.F. Skinner was the most famous psychologist I ever saw. I've seen a few other famous psychologists, but not many. I haven't seen many famous authors—there weren't book signings in the used bookstore I worked in. I haven't seen many famous singers or musicians. And I haven't seen many famous actors. I did have drinks with Lee Marvin one night in a tavern in Hoboken. The only thing I remember is that Lee kept complaining they didn't wash his glass before they refilled his drink. At the rate he was going they would have needed to hire a second dishwasher.

I haven't seen many famous politicians. The only president I ever saw was Richard Nixon and that was by inadvertence. I was in college and worked for the brokerage house of Merrill Lynch, Pierce, Fenner, and Smith. My job entailed running to brokerage houses to pick up and deliver preliminary prospectuses. I knew the financial district inside and out—I knew where all the short cuts were. Like many buildings, 20 Broad St. has two entrances—this is the building that houses the New York Stock Exchange. I rushed in the back door to save time on the return trip. To my surprise, the lobby was packed. No cutting through that day. Just as I was about to back out and leave, President Nixon emerged from an elevator. I recognized him immediately—I was certain he didn't recognize me. He looked exactly like he did on television, only he was taller, heavier, and pastier. He disappeared into the crowd at the front entrance.

I immediately ran back to the office at 70 Pine St., rushed into the men's room, and washed my eyes out with soap and water.

103.   Behaviorism was the perspective that insisted that the subject matter of psychology was to be restricted to observable behavior and that internal variables, whether psychological or physiological, were to be excluded from consideration. Behaviorism became the dominant force in American academic psychology, notably in the area of learning, from 1920 – 1970. It was so dominant it led to the exclusion of such topics as cognition, emotion, personality, and creativity.

The origins of this radical approach existed in the state of psychology in the early decades of the twentieth century. At that time psychology was thoroughly speculative and thoroughly non-observational. Psychologists derived their theories the old-fashioned way—by sitting in lounge chairs and thinking them up. John Watson, the father of Behaviorism, became the vocal spear that slashed at the heart of the inert practices of his time. Watson asserted that psychology was a natural science that relied on observation and experimentation. Watson practiced what he preached and did some of the experimenting himself, famously in the case of Little Albert and the white rat.

Behaviorism was an advance in the light of the profitless pastimes that preceded it. Behaviorists like Watson and, later, B.F. Skinner made deadly accurate criticisms of psychology and they offered productive methodologies based on learning principles and procedures. In Watson's case the principles involved classical conditioning. In Skinner's case the principles involved operant conditioning. Both these principles saturate our lives. Examples of classical conditioning—of associationism—abound in our lives and there is no question we are motivated to maximize reinforcement and to minimize punishment.

Inspired by Watson's aggressive personality and evangelical energy the early behaviorists crushed opposing viewpoints and occupied American universities. Unfortunately for everyone, they held onto power for too long. The old theorists had been overthrown, but the behaviorists overstayed their allotted time, like the decrepit East European dictators in the Cold War era. The party line became too strident and too narrow.

Too many vital topics had been overlooked. Too many important themes had been left unexplored.

Behaviorism offered trenchant criticisms and magisterial concepts, but it was a deeply flawed development. It worked as an orientation only by chopping off fundamental components of our human experience. Cognition, emotion, personality, creativity—these were amputated and tossed like scraps in the slop tank. If these components were considered at all, it was only through the torturous application of inadequate operational definitions.

Performed in the interests of parsimony and the need for experimental control, the procrustean disregard of these components had serious consequences. It set the study of cognition, emotion, personality, and creativity back by decades. And it provided an amazingly warped view of human nature. Human beings were construed as lab rats and as pigeons—control the environment, control the consequences of behavior, drop a pellet of food in, and people will jump through loops at the experimenter's bidding. There was a nod toward complexity, but the nod never became a bow and little progress was made incorporating human complexity into behavioral theories. Behaviorists never specified how people are more complex than rats and pigeons, and they couldn't. Cognition and emotion and personality and creativity make us complex—these were the topics behaviorists refused to consider.

Behaviorism was criticized from the outset. It continued to be criticized through the long lean years. Critics pointed out that Behaviorism was an overly simplistic orientation that worked in laboratories where total environmental control was possible but not in "real-life" situations where control—still less total control—is rarely possible. Die-hard dust-bowlers might believe otherwise, but the world is more complex than a "Skinner box". We need only compare a solitary rat pressing a bar to get food with a teacher trying to control a rowdy seventh-grade classroom to appreciate that more principles than reinforcement and punishment are needed.

Critics of Behaviorism also pointed out what is obvious to any semi-conscious being. Never mind complex social situations like classrooms. The categories of stimulus – response – reinforcement can neither describe nor explain the simplest situation. Consider walking into a church. We see the pews, the altar, the stained glass windows—these serve as stimuli. We place our hands in the font and bless ourselves with the holy water—this serves as the response on entering a church and, yes, we have been conditioned to do such. But there is a lot more going on than observable stimuli and responses. There are memories of religion and of experiences in churches. There's motivation—maybe we've lapsed into doubt and disbelief and are yearning to find our way back to the faith. There are emotions—we feel awe and fear and reverence. There's cognition and there's meaning—the words in the missal and the images in the glass carry a lot of information beyond what we see in the aisles and along the walls.

Other critics noted that behaviorists neglected the exquisitely important topic of *reactance*. People don't like to be punished—maybe they like what they do. People don't necessarily like to be reinforced—maybe they don't want to do what the experimenter wants. On a historical scale we saw the tragedies when the Soviet Union tried to convert people to the state religion. Sure, many converted. But many didn't want to convert. Whether it meant getting reinforcements for changing or punishments for not changing, people resisted. The cost was murderous, but people didn't give in. On a homely scale we have the child who doesn't want to eat the vegetables on the dinner table. The threat of punishment doesn't work. Nor does the promise of reinforcement. "Eat your vegetables and I'll give you five dollars," the father says. The child thinks, "Five dollars? The vegetables must taste really horrible."

I'd like to add a slightly different criticism of Behaviorism and one that presents a more flattering image of humanity. An explicit objective of Behaviorism has been the *prediction* of behavior. This was Watson's objective from the get-go. This was Skinner's objective throughout his long career. This was Edward Tolman's objective—he wanted to predict behavior at a choice point in a maze. And this was also Clark Hull's objective—Hull's grandiose scheme resulted in "reaction potential", which was a high-brow term for the prediction of behavior.

We are creatures of habit. Much of what we do on a daily basis is predictable. Everyday for decades I've performed my toiletries in the same order—I'm not going to tell you the order because I don't want you to lose respect for me. Everyday for years I've driven to work in exactly the same way. I change lanes in the same places. I slow down at the same intersections. I switch radio stations at the same mile markers. I park in the same space even when closer ones are available. When I arrive home from work I eat dinner in the same manner and watch the same television programs in the same order. I go to bed at the same time and wake up the next morning at the same time. I read the sections of the newspaper in the same order. Probably, I have the same dreams, but I don't know about them.

These ordinary behaviors are nicely explained by the principles of classical and operant conditioning. They are predicted by these principles—unless something really bad happens, you know what I am going to do tomorrow if you know what I'm doing today. But these predictable behaviors are the least interesting and least important of my life. To study these behaviors is to study the most trivial elements in my life. You can reliably predict the order of my toiletries and my driving and my dining and my newspaper reading, but you wouldn't be saying anything relevant. To study these predictable behaviors is to stay at a peripheral level and at a level that doesn't much matter to me or to anyone else. I really don't define my existence as the sum of my toiletries or as my driving habits or as my dining habits or as the habit of reading the newspaper in a particular order.

The most important events of our lives are the events that emerge unexpectedly and cannot be predicted. I define myself through the unpredictable and the unpredicted events that happen. They are the ones that matter. They are the ones that I talk about—maybe they are the ones I go out of my way to conceal. The unpredictable events are the ones that are going into the memoir—the exceptional ones may take up entire chapters. The routine, trivial, and altogether predictable events are going to be left out.

So I start to perform my toiletries in the usual order and a clot breaks off and makes a left turn at the aorta. I never predicted that when I entered the bathroom, but my life is going to be changed in a moment. And I'm driving to work and a deer leaps out when I'm changing dials and I wind up parked between pine trees. I never predicted that when I left the house in the morning, but my life is completely changed. And I walk into the local pharmacy to play the lottery and a gunman barges in and announces that this is a stickup. I never predicted that when I walked in, but my life has just been unpredictably changed and a new chapter has been added to the memoir.

Examples of the importance of unpredictable events need not be negative. Maybe it happens the gunman picks a different pharmacy and I buy the winning lottery ticket—actually, I predict this everyday. And maybe I find true love when I swap glances with the cashier girl who rings up my purchase. I never predicted that when I stepped inside.

Behaviorists missed what is fundamentally important by focusing on predictable events. The little events can be predicted, but they hardly matter. The big events that surprise us and intrude into our lives for better and worse can't be predicted. These big events matter in the most crucial ways. They don't often happen—it's not everyday I drive off the road and get pinned in the pines and it's not everyday I find a soul mate at the checkout counter—but when they do they change our lives decisively and they define us and re-define us in ways the predictable events do not.

There is an irony in this. Behaviorists define learning as a *change* in behavior due to practice or experience. Restricting their program to predictable behaviors leads to a study of behaviors that do not change, certainly not in a fundamental way. By disregarding unpredictable events behaviorists ignored fundamental changes in behavior. The fact that I perform my toiletry and drive to work successfully can be predicted, but these behaviors change nothing. The possibility that I can go off the road or fall in love cannot be predicted, but when these events occur they change everything.

104. Consideration of the importance of unpredictable events opens up a slightly different—and slightly expanded—view of our existence and it challenges the capacity of science to capture a valid image of human beings. B.F. Skinner repeatedly claimed that psychology cannot be the science of mind. If the key word in that phrase is "science", he may well have been right.

Events have consequences. Most consequences are predictable—these are the inconsequential consequences. I've purchased innumerable lottery tickets at pharmacy checkouts. I think I've stayed poor purchasing lottery tickets at pharmacy checkouts. I can never know when the next purchase will be the jackpot I've been waiting for all my life. Tomorrow's ticket usually winds up in the waste can, but a fellow can hope.

In my driving career I've run innumerable yellow lights. I've never gotten a ticket for reckless driving. I've never gotten into an accident. I can never predict that the next time I run a yellow light will cost me severely. It usually doesn't, but it may. A fellow can pray it doesn't.

Science requires predictable events. Theories describe reliable and repeatable relationships between events. If I do X, then Y will happen. If I change A, then B will change. These statements are true the vast majority of times. The world is an orderly and predictable place. But these statements are not true all the time. The next time I buy a lottery ticket something wonderful may happen. The next time I run a yellow light something terrible may happen. I can never know ahead-of-time when X leads to Z or A to C.

Karl Popper wrote about the importance of the "horizon of expectations" in science. Certainly, this horizon is vital for predictable events. But there is a no less important "horizon of *unexpectations*" that is central to our existence. There is a built-in and prefabricated unpredictability in our lives. This unpredictability comes with the cellular matter of our bodies and with the creative expressions of our thoughts. We can never know when the next consequence of a reliable and repeated action will have profound consequences. We can never know when events become terribly important. And we can never know when something original might emerge from the ceaseless flow of our thoughts.

Right from the outset critics recognized that the stimulus-response psychology of the kind Watson and Skinner preached had severe limitations that precluded an understanding of our human existence. Every response is more than the history of its pairing with particular stimuli. The emission of a response depends on the meaning of the stimulus—meaning is a cognitive construct. The emission of a response also depends on motivation and on personality. There are occasions when we withhold a well-learned response. There are social factors that cause us to withhold a response—I don't respond because I don't like the person or perceive that the person doesn't like me. And there is simple variability in making a response—I know how to throw a curveball, but for whatever reason I don't throw it well every time.

And there is an inscrutably creative factor inherent in our existence. I suppose every response is a creative act of some kind, but I'm thinking more of the order of a joke or a pun or a creative idea or observation. In Chapter Seven of *Landsman* this pun appears—"A ghost of a sailor ought to go up to [Jamie] Drake and say 'buoy'." I admit this is a pun that needs crutches, but it is a pun nevertheless. Something new appears, a combination of words that did not exist before but now exists on paper. The combination of "buoy" and "boo" could not be predicted. I thought it up—more accurately, it occurred to me—but I couldn't predict its occurrence the moment before I wrote it. This pun *came to me—from where* is a question that can never be answered.

Consider the limitations of the scientific and Behaviorist emphasis on predictability. If you knew my history with the words "buoy" and "boo", you could not predict that they would come together or how they would come together. If you knew the precise moments I learned how to spell and write the words and what the words meant, you could not predict how they would be used in Chapter Seven of the novel. If you knew my entire learning history you could not predict that these words would come together. For that matter, if you mapped every neuron and synapse in my brain you could not predict that this pun would occur at the moment it did. There is always something extra, something creative, something creatively unpredictable, that eludes a thorough understanding.

The Behaviorist rejection of internal variables was a tragic and benumbing development. The lack of interest in the *from where* set psychology back half a century. The unpredictable and creative use of words and experiences is not a fringe or unusual characteristic of our personalities, but the central and defining characteristic of what it means to be human. The failure to consider what Alfred Wallace called, "Those grand mysterious phenomena of the mind" is to remain at the most superficial and least interesting level of understanding.

105. A neighbor's child swallowed a quarter. The wonder was he passed two dimes and a nickel. That was small change to pay for such a unique experience.

106. Passing two dimes and a nickel is nothing. Lawyers have to pass the bar. Ouch.

107. We had a vendor manager in the Distribution Center named Melinda C—. She was a short and somewhat stocky lady of around 35 years of age. She had a most attractive face, distinctively Swedish with blond hair cut short and steel-gray eyes. I saw her in the corridor any number of times, but we seldom exchanged greetings. I was a little intimidated by her classic good looks—it would be like addressing an advertisement in *Vanity Fair*—and, truth to tell, she was not a friendly person. The first few times I said "Hello" she never responded, so that was a turn off. One time she did say "Hello", but she was looking over my shoulder and past me toward a manager approaching in her direction.

One morning Human Resources called us into the office and said that Melinda had died that night. Hearing that shook me up mightily. I wished I had been friendlier—I wished she had been friendlier. And I wondered what had happened. I saw her the day she died. She looked the picture of health. Possibilities clouded my mind. I thought of an accident. I thought of suicide. I thought of murder. I thought of salacious motives. The company should have told us the entire truth than to fob us off when it came to the cause of death. Whatever happened couldn't be worse than the rumors that started brewing in the lunch room.

Melinda's death saddened me in a deeply disturbing way. She spent her last day on earth in the office and on the job. Her last day in life was passed attending to the most trivial and inconsequential details of dealing with book vendors and warehouse supervisors. I made up my mind that I was not going to spend my last day on earth in the office and on the job. My last day is going to be spent knocking back cognacs with my family and friends. My last day is going to be passed tidying up details and letting my survivors know what was important. My last day is going to be spent on my knees beseeching Almighty God for forgiveness—I do not want to swim into the darkness encumbered with sins mortal and venial. If the weather's agreeable I'm going to spend my last day at the beach. Like the dying peasant lady Asenath Nicolson saw in Ireland in the 1840s, I'm going to spend my last day dancing on the shoreline. One foot will be on the sand, the other in the shallow water. When the time comes I won't hesitate. I'll step in and go under. I won't forget to say "Thank you."

Of course, none of this is possible. I suffer the direst, most distressing, poverty. I just can't get up and leave the job and go. On my last day I'll be at the desk busily doing vertical lookups between Excel spreadsheets and checking bad barcodes and preparing overseas stickering requests to our newest vendor in Outer Mongolia. I'll look up at the shadow that crosses my desk. It won't be Larry the mailman. It'll be the Grim Reaper.

"Am I interrupting something?" he'll ask.

"Only the rest of my life."

"Do you have a second?"

"Not any more. Should I take a few print screens of my life for reference?"

"That won't be necessary."

"Just let me power down and close the computer and put out the light in my work station. I better make a pit stop in the men's room before we go. We don't know how long these things take."

"Oh, not very long.'

"Do I need to bring a jacket?"

"Not where you're going."

108. The longer I stayed on the job, the more likely I was going to expire on the job, but I just couldn't resign and walk off. My nest egg was laid by a finch. I was afflicted by the awful burden of poverty—how could something as light as my bank account become so heavy a burden? I tried everything to make a financial killing. I purchased lottery tickets by the sack. I took a second job. I took a third job. I put all my books for sale at a local flea market. I peddled story lines to Hollywood agents. Nothing lifted the burden. I had exhausted every option—except one. In my genealogical jaunts to Ireland I encountered a North Kerry man who claimed he knew the whereabouts of a leprechaun. With leprechauns come pots of gold. I made my mind up—my ticket out of the office would be a leprechaun's pot of gold.

I booked passage on an Aer Lingus flight to Shannon Airport. I took the train to Tarbert in Kerry and hitched the rest of the way. I met my informant at the same spot I left him a few years previously, standing roadside at Dooneen Point in Kilconly Parish at the mouth of the Shannon River. He was a study man with broad shoulders and a broad face, jowly at the jaw and cheeks. His black hair was thick and gray at the sides. In age he was anywhere from fifty to seventy. He wore a thick black sweater and black trousers and a bronze-colored coat that was a little lighter than the complexion of his face. His work shoes were muddy—the portions without mud stains were roughly the same tawny hide as his coat and face. He held a black cane that came up nearly to shoulder level. I don't know why he needed a cane. I had never seen him take a step in any direction. Rather than use the cane to walk, he screwed tiny ruts in the soil.

The view from Dooneen Point was scenic—"grand", as the Irish say. The water was dark and gray—it was ocean at this point and not river. In the distance County Clare was a blue landmass a shade darker than the sky. Petted by gravity, the branches of nearby blackthorn trees bent in elliptical fashion over tall grass that had never felt blade or scythe. A path no wider than the human foot had been flattened in the field that led to the water. Green to the brim of the Emerald Island, the field ended abruptly at the water's edge. There was neither beach nor sand below. The strand consisted of rocks that varied in size from billfolds to suitcases.

"That's where the bugger lives," my informant said, pointing with a gnarled hand to the openings in the seawall that curved to the south.

I thought at first that he was pulling my leg, but I could tell by his expression that he was serious. A North Kerry man and a devout Catholic, he would never lie about one of the *good people*.

I asked why he didn't avail himself of the opportunity to grab the leprechaun's pot of gold. He said that age and infirmity prevented him from making the attempt. He also said something about wealth being a sin, but that couldn't be true. Even if it were, I didn't want wealth for any perverse or ravenous reason. I simply didn't want to die on the job.

I asked if he was going to stay and help me bag the leprechaun. He responded with a frown—actually, his usual expression was a frown, but the fissures in his forehead deepened and the corners of his mouth tightened in an unspoken, "Are you crazy?" He made the Sign of the

Cross—he made it so deliberately I could hear the joints in his shoulders crack—and then he turned and looked in the opposite direction.

I positioned myself behind a blackthorn and waited—and waited and waited. I waited for four days and didn't see anything supernatural. Except for a few stationary bovines in the distance I hardly saw anything natural. I wondered whether St. Patrick ran all the animals out of Ireland when he deported the snakes. I wondered whether the people went with the snakes.

I had one more day's lodging at the bed-and-breakfast, so I waited a fifth and final day. I didn't crouch in the grass for more than a half hour when I heard off-key whistling. It sounded like *Kathleen Mavourneen*, but I couldn't tell for sure. I saw the ripple of the tall grass and the brim of a top hat bobbing like a skipjack on the green surf. I waited a few moments and pounced. I covered in two what it took the leprechaun ten steps to traverse. I swooped and snatched him at the start of the second refrain. He yelped, grabbed his hat in a startle, and clicked his heels in preparation to disappear, but it was too late.

"Got you, you bug—er, leprechaun."

"Put me down, Yank."

"Not on my life." He wasn't hard to hold. He was about the size and weight of a preschooler. His stubby arms were trapped between our bodies and he couldn't summon any force to hit me. His stumpy legs extended too far behind me to do any damage with the points of his shoes. He was squirmy and he smelled bad, but I wasn't letting go. "Give me your pot of gold and I'll put you down."

"I'll pour a pot of bricks ov'r your brash Yankee head before I give up me gold." He started to speak in a foreign tongue. I wasn't sure whether it was Irish or a fairy dialect. I was sure he was cursing me out, but I wasn't intimidated.

"You know the rules. I caught you fair and square. The pot of gold is mine and rightfully won."

" 'Tis, 'tis," he said in a low sad voice. "But why would ye be pickin' a poor leprechaun's pot of gold?"

He tried to appeal to my pity, but I wasn't showing any. I had what I came to get and I wasn't leaving without the gold. He could keep the pot if he loved it so much. I had deep pockets, well sown and sturdy, and I brought along an insulated shopping bag for the occasion.

I hurried to the edge of the grass and stepped to the rocks. The tide had been out for a while and the rocks had dried and grown warm in the sun. I worried how I could identify his cave—I suspected he wouldn't willingly point it out—but that proved a baseless concern. He had unfurled a rope ladder to descend to the rocks. The entrance to his cave was at the level of my shoulders. It was a small distance to drop, but I supposed the leprechaun's bones had grown brittle from centuries of wear.

I pushed him in ahead of me and hoisted myself up and in. I barely fit—if I didn't get a haircut before leaving the States my head would be mopping the ceiling. The reflection of the sea behind us provided the only light to the interior. A few pellets of turf, white with age, laid on the stone floor of a makeshift hearth against the back wall. A tiny table no larger than the miniature kind girls play dolls on was to the right. Two dusty bottles of Hennessy cognac stood on the table. I almost had a generous thought about the leprechaun. He had a hard life and was entitled to a belt every now and again. Too bad he didn't have any to share. I broke into a thought phrased in stage Irish—'tis a poor sight to behold empty Hennessy bottles and me not having partaken in emptying them.

Another table was to the left. This table held a number of tools and what looked to be wallets. Closer inspection revealed they were soles. A puddle of shoes was in front of the table. Every variety of footwear from the daintiest high heels to furry boots that reached above the knees laid in the pile.

"I'd have thought a leprechaun would own a hut or a hovel of some kind and not have to live in a cave."

"Ye be insultin' a leprechaun in his own home."

"It wasn't meant as an insult."

"The woeful economic situation has affected even leprechauns."

I stared at the leprechaun. Thankfully, the light was inadequate or I should die looking on ugliness. He wasn't so much a leprechaun as a leperchaun. He wore a top hat with a white smear in the rim. The smear had once been a feather. His clothes were dishabille. They had started out a red flannel but had turned a sooty brown for want of washing. His face was thickly crinkled and resembled the composition of a frequently thumbed book. If his face was a book, it was a leather-bound. The boards of his ears were oversized and thick with hair and his eyes were small and reptilian. I remembered he wasn't human but took on the semblance of a human for public show. Only God and the Devil know what his true form was.

It didn't matter what he looked like. The pot of gold was mine.

He knew what I was thinking.

"The pot of gold is yours, but gold slips away more quickly than the years. I can give ye sum-tin better than gold. I can give ye three wishes that can keep ye in gold forever."

I was tempted, but I remembered that leprechauns were the sociopaths of the fairy world. I couldn't let myself be tricked.

"Do ye want six wishes then? Twice three makes six, hey."

"I want my pot of gold."

"Is it nine wishes ye desire? Thrice three makes—"

"Nine, but no, I want me—my—pot of gold. Tell me where it is."

"I won't. Not for a tow-sand years will I tell."

"Then don't. I'll find it on my own."

I knew it had to be close. Leprechauns always keep the pot within hand's reach—within a short walk's reach, anyway. They liked the security of keeping it near and they liked to look at the gold and count it and rub it between their dirty fingers. If they could fit in, I had no doubt they would take baths in the pot. I looked around the cave. There were no cabinets. The walls were smooth. The floor was bare rock. I walked over and picked up the Hennessy bottles. I wiped a streak of dust off each bottle and peeked inside. The bottles were empty. I walked to the table on the left and sifted the soles. The smell of leather was strong. Still no pot. There was only one spot left that could serve as a hiding place. I bent and scattered the pile of shoes.

"Noooooooooooooooooooooooooooooooooooooooooooooooooooooooo!" the leprechaun screamed, hopping up and down and punching his tiny hands together.

There it was. The pot of gold stood like a statue of a king atop a rubber pedestal. The pot was black and thick and shaped roughly like a vase. Gold coins filled the pot to the brim. They twinkled even in the foamy glow of the ocean's reflected light. I didn't know how many coins there were or what their value was, but the possibility that I would expire on the job evaporated on the instant.

"Why would ye take a leprechaun's hard-earned gold?" he cried, wiping his eyes with a black rag that had started as a white handkerchief. I thought at first the leprechaun was going to attack me, but that was against the rules. He was sliding into the weakness of grief. That didn't make him any less dangerous. "Oh, me poor gold. 'Tis not right, 'tis not right. Taken by a foreigner. What will become of me poor gold in Amerikay?"

I bent and lifted the pot. It was so heavy I almost threw my back out straightening. I cuddled the pot against my left side and stroked the coins. I couldn't identify them with certainty, but they looked like doubloons. Probably, they had been salvaged from the Spanish Armada. Whatever their origin, I had become fabulously rich.

"Ah, poor me. What's to become of me wit-out me gold?"

"Don't worry. I'll leave you enough to live on." Wealth made me generous. "I'll leave you enough to get decent quarters." In the spirit of the moment I pronounced the word "daycent".

I wanted to bite one of the coins just to be certain they were real. I wanted to kiss one. If I could fit, I wanted to take a bath in the pot. I started to slobber.

" 'Tis yours and far-ly won," the leprechaun said, wiping his eyes and sniffling. "But a fine Catholic lad like yourself coming into this great wealth and not givin' tanks to the Good Lurd above. For shame, for shame. Greed is a more-tal sin, harven't ye been taught?"

I told myself that my greed was for a good cause, but I felt uneasy. It's going to take time to learn how to think selfishly like a rich man. I remembered what Jesus said about a camel and a needle and I started to feel a tad regretful. The leprechaun was right. I should be thankful. God led me to the North Kerry man and to his stories of the leprechaun. The low tide led me to this cave. To make amends for my greed I intended to donate a handful of coins to the parish.

I raised my eyes heavenward. "Dear God, thank you for making me rich," I started to pray, but I stopped in mid-sentence. There was a jolt on my left side and a loud swishing sound led from my hands to the entrance of the cave and then to the turmoil of the gray sea. I was stroking empty space. I was holding vacant air—the air felt much heavier than the pot of gold that vanished.

I had been tricked by that awful little creature. I was determined not to let it happen, but it did. I had made up my mind—much good that did. He was the epitome of greed and he made me feel guilty about my righteous motive for desiring wealth. In my rush to square accounts with conscience I had forgotten a fundamental rule in dealing with a leprechaun—if you want his pot of gold, you must never take your eyes off him. I looked heavenward and I lost sight of the leprechaun for a moment and I lost the pot of gold.

They say all things happen for good and that the things that actually happen are the things that are supposed to happen, but I can't accept the fact that I'm destined to stay poor. And they say all things happen according to God's plan, but I can't accept the possibility that I'll don wings and a halo leaning over a keyboard.

I'm back at the desk powerless and penniless. I can't escape the risk that the janitors are going to find me one evening stiff as a clipboard. If they do I'm not leaving the building with the recyclables. The thought horrifies me. To paraphrase President Clinton, "I feel my pain."

I'm going back to Dooneen Point someday and I'm going to bag a leprechaun. If not the wretch who tricked me, then another. I'm preparing myself for the encounter. I'm getting in shape to grab that soulless miser. I'm working out in the company gym. I've dropped snacks from the groceries. I'm consuming fish oil tablets and baby aspirins daily. I'm eating only unprocessed foods. I'm going light with the Hennessy. These habits have paid off. I've lost a few pounds. I've gained a few notches on my belt. I don't have to suck my gut in when I pass the ladies at the water cooler—it stays sucked in on its own. I had to buy a new wardrobe that matched my slimmed down contour. I didn't need new shoes. Ever since my trip to North Kerry I have the greatest collection of shoes. I would have had more shoes, too, enough to open a store, only the tide rolled in and put a stop to my patent-leather pilfery.

109. Old Man Winter turned into Old Superman Winter. We've had over 50 inches of snow in Ocean County, including two mammoth snowfalls of twenty inches apiece. We had any number of Nor-easters, including one that dropped four inches of rain. For the first time in ten years sections of County Road 539 flooded. There were lakes in the

ditches beside the road. Swollen with rainwater, trees toppled. Other trees came down in forty mile wind shears. Branches landed on lawns. Branches landed on windshields. Branches landed on pedestrians. One poor soul was killed in Central Park when a branch landed on him. When it came to trees, gravity ruled. On the ground ice ruled—so did mud and porous earth and soupy soil with the composition and sound effects of sponges.

Contrary to our reputation as whiners and milksops, we're hardy folk in New Jersey. Whatever the weather, we commuted to our jobs. We kept the celebrations marked on the calendars. We left our umbrellas in the closets and ventured bareheaded into the pouring rain. We strolled on the ice fields. Some people even danced on the ice. We stood tall—sideways, anyway—no matter how hard the wind blew. Fifty inches of snow might send Midwestern Lutherans to hunker down in 'fraidy cellars. Fifty inches of snow didn't keep us indoors. Four inches of rain might cause Texans sitting tall on the range to slide over and ride sidesaddle. Four inches of rain didn't stop us. Lakes in ditches on the sides of the county roads might cause cowboy types to pack up the griddles and head for the barns. Lakes in ditches on the sides of the county roads didn't keep us from driving where we were going. Howling gales snapping branches at the trunks might inspire mountain men to find refuge inside caves. Howling gales didn't stop us from heading to the great and stormy outdoors.

I drove through one storm where it rained so hard I couldn't see the taillights of the car ahead of me. Hail belted the roof of the car incessantly. The wet white gauze of atmosphere turned whiter when lightning dropped in explosive crackles. Peels of thunder rattled the exhaust pipe. The wind was so fierce I had all to do keeping the car in the lane, wherever that was. For some strange reason I thought that driving through the storm was how it must have been for the Rebs in Pickett's charge the afternoon of July 3, 1863. I couldn't veer to the side—I couldn't see the shoulder of the road to find refuge there. I couldn't back up. The hail on the roof was the hail of Minie balls on bayonets pointed toward a clump of trees. The lightning was the spray of canister. The thunder was the cannonade of a line of howitzers. I couldn't stop in the midst of the watery chaos—I would get hit by the soldier behind me. There was nothing to do but go forward and hope that the man holding his hat on a sword was a character in an overactive imagination and not a pedestrian foolishly crossing against the light.

I made it across the Cemetery Ridge of my fantasy and New Jersey made it through the worst winter on record. You might say we weathered the weather. Which is more than we can say for the beaches.

The storms have devastated the beaches. The north end at Sunset Beach in Cape May got cut in half. The stream that runs outland at the northern boundary was pinched off by a wall of sand pushed ashore— the stream no longer connects with the sea. Even the great beach at Wildwood was shaved by the relentless gales. In an unprecedented development sunken patches of the beach flooded and formed lakes near the Boardwalk. The miniscule beaches at Long Beach Island took such a pounding they considered changing the name of the resort to Long Island—unfortunately for them, the name was taken and can't be used again. In the interest of tourism they couldn't consider *Short Beach Island.*

In the best and calmest of seasons the Long Beach Island beaches were never wide. People paid good money for the opportunity to press shoulders on a dwarfish beachface barely wider than a healthy-sized lawn in suburbia. After the malicious winter the beaches are shorter than lawns—they're about the width of a suburban sidewalk. It is going to be hard for six-footers to stretch out. They'll cover the entire beach from sidewalk to shallow water with no room to spare. They may even be longer than the beach. Sunbathers of every height are going to have to lie parallel with the water rather than the usual perpendicular. In the worst eventuality people may have to sun bathe standing up.

It's going to be difficult for late arrivals to get to the water without stepping on human mats—visitors will be lucky to find sand and not skin slick with sunscreen. Space is going to be so precious the forty-seven towns on this twig of an island may need to assign sunbathers into two-or-three hour shifts to accommodate all the day trippers. Anyone caught in a different shift than the assigned one will be fined and have their beach tags rescinded—this is a surefire revenue enhancer. Or the towns may need to hold raffles. Winners earn the chance to loll at the water's edge before the sand permanently washes away in the next big storm.

110. There was a mat of wet snow an inch thick adhering to the rear window of my Saturn *Ion*. It was the kind of snow that stays melded together no matter how it's moved. I was tempted to write a swearword on the snow so the neighbors could see what I thought of Old Superman Winter, but I couldn't think of any.

111. There are typos and there are typos.

A scandal rocked the Barnes & Noble publishing world recently. An extra "t" was inadvertently added to the word "its" in a book for first graders entitled *Encyclopedia of Sharks*. You can imagine which side of "its" the extra "t" appeared on.

The mistake was noticed by customers. It was not noticed by the editors. This is referred to as a failure of proofreading. Four thousand books were promptly ruined, not to mention the lives of the children who saw the extra "t" and asked their parents what the word meant.

112. Some words do not have plurals—but ought to.

I realized this at the check-in counter at the Atlantic City Airport. The agent at the counter asked how many *pieces of luggage* we had. I looked to my left—there was one piece of luggage. I looked to my right— there was a second piece of luggage. I looked in front of me—there was a small carry-on that could fit under the seat. I looked behind me—there was a second carry-on that could fit in the overhead compartment. I decided the words deserved plurals.

"I have two *luggages* and two *baggages*."

The agent looked at me. Formerly, she practiced customer service with a fac-smile. She ceased practicing customer service. Her expression altered to a frown and she asked in an annoyed tone of voice, "What country are you from?"

"I'm from New Jersey," I said with a glare.

"I understand, sir." She bent and lifted the luggages and baggages onto the conveyor. Her expression portrayed what she was thinking, "He's from New Jersey. That explains it."

113. While I'm offering syntactical suggestions I'd like to make the following proposal—we should replace the word "and" with the ampersand "&". This doesn't shorten saying the word, but it saves two

strokes on the keyboard. Since "and" is one of the most frequently typed words, this adds up to a lot of saved strokes.

Americans who type "and" are at a disadvantage compared to keyboarders in other languages. There are languages that use two letters for their version of the word "and". Afrikaans has "en", French and Latin have "et", Lithuanian has "ir", Turkish has "ve", and Swahili has "na". There are languages that use a single letter for "and". Polish has "i", Italian has "e", and Welsh has "a". There are no known languages that use no letters for "and"—that could present a problem identifying whether "and" was indicated or an extra space was typed by accident. Compared to these efficient languages poor English has three whole letters for "and". German also has three letters for "and", but who cares about them.

The problem in English is that the letters in the word "and" are not available. "A" is taken. "An" is taken. That leaves "nd" and "d". The latter two could stand for "and". So could twenty three other letters, singly and in combination. But this would take considerable relearning. The proactive interference factor would be enormous. So would the pronunciation factor if "nd" is selected. The ampersand is available. It is widely used in corporate America and in informal writing. Everyone knows what the ampersand means and where it is on the keyboard. No one will have to learn anything.

Business can proceed as usual & no one will be discomforted.

114. We commonly say "It *dawned on* me" when we realize something vital or remember a thought previously unformed. It follows that we can say "It *dusked on* me" when we fail to realize something important or when a thought is left unformed and forgotten.

115. I'm looking at a bowl of Halloween candy. The thought has crossed my mind—has *Baby Ruth* ever grown up?

116. There's a first time for everything. The air conditioning broke in Manhattan Community College and the heat in N771 became so intense I conducted the class seated. I had never done that before. We formed a circle and I sat at the center and started lecturing. The students took notes as best they were able. Heat exhaustion was a risk if they

moved their arms too eagerly and their notebooks soon became soggy with sweat. Mostly, they sat and fanned themselves, as if they were at a revival and listening to a homily on social psychology. They leaned back and looked at me with blank stares. Some students make the same faces when I conduct the class standing and the air conditioning is functioning at its usual Arctic efficiency.

I was stuck once I sat. I couldn't write notes on the chalkboard and I didn't want to for fear of passing out. I could hardly conduct class flat on the floor. For that matter I couldn't stand and proceed to the board. I was so sweated the back of my clothing adhered to the chair as if fixed by booger glue. If I stood I'd tear the back of my clothing off. It would be most embarrassing walking to the front of the class with the back of my shirt torn off and with my boxer shorts showing.

And it would be a long walk to the PATH train station. I'd have to walk backwards for five blocks and that could be dangerous. I might trip over a leash—some dog owners use leashes as long as fly-fishing reels. Or I might get run over by yuppie fathers wheeling their baby carriages. I rather think I'm a peer of the yuppies. I would hate for them to see me on the sidewalk. Or I might step off a curb and twist an ankle. Limping would call additional attention to my predicament.

If I walked backward I wouldn't be able to see the traffic or the traffic signal, whether it flashed Walk or Don't Walk. I'd hate to get sent heavenward over the fender of a yellow cab. It's bad form and disrespectful to enter Paradise wearing half your clothing.

117. There's a story they tell about Robert E. Lee when he was president of Washington College after the Civil War. We like to think the story portrays real events and is not in the category of phonifying tale. The story may have been the basis for the fictional dialogue in Ted Turner's *Gettysburg* between Lee and Jeb Stuart the night of the second day's battle. Lee at first severely chastises Stuart for the cavalry's absence at a crucial moment. He then flatters Stuart, telling him that, like the quality officer he is, he will learn from his mistake and never repeat it.

The story has it that a few Washington College students failed an exam miserably. Lee called them into his office—it must have been a terrifying moment for them to walk into the office of a man who sent thousands of their peers to death. But Lee didn't flunk them. He didn't dismiss them from school. He didn't berate them—or not that they ever told anyone. He tore up the exams and told them the grades were not acceptable. He told them they must study and take the exam over. They did and aced the exam with near perfect grades. Lee's confidence in them gave them confidence in themselves. They could succeed if they applied themselves.

In the fall semester I had a student in General Psychology named Martin S—. Martin was a mediocre student, scoring in the C range throughout the semester. He missed the final quiz, which is mandatory. I had the option to fail him, but out of the goodness of my heart I chose to give him the benefit of the doubt. He was, after all, a college kid in his twenties. This isn't the time of the Civil War. The young people of today don't have to be mature until later in life. I gave Martin the grade of "Incomplete". He could come in and take a makeup exam. In all honesty I wasn't confident that he would. To my surprise he took the makeup at the start of the Spring semester. He failed it miserably. I don't recall that his grade cracked 50.

At this point I decided to emulate Robert E. Lee. I didn't type the letter "F" in the Web grading roster. I mailed Martin the quiz with a note saying. "You can do better. Come in and take a makeup of a makeup." He never showed. He never answered the note. I had no choice. I typed "F" in the Web roster.

There are a few lessons we can draw from this sorry episode. I'm no Robert E. Lee. Martin wasn't impressed with my authority. He certainly wasn't impressed with my generosity. And Martin is no Jeb Stuart. He's not even a Washington College student. He didn't study the first time. He didn't study the second time. He wasn't prepared to study the third time. I had more confidence in him than he had in himself. Sad to say, some people can't do right no matter how many opportunities they get.

118. Martin S— is proof that a teacher can lead a student to the stream of knowledge, but can't make him drink.

In recent years there have been two faulty developments in education. They're particularly noteworthy in the state of New Jersey, but they must occur in other states as well—New Jersey can't have a monopoly on faulty developments. The first development is the confusion that has set in between *teaching* and *learning*. Teaching is what educators do when they stand in front of a class and present their material. Teaching is what educators do when they provide readings and handouts and assignments for their classes. Teaching is what educators do when they serve as resource people and as experts in particular subject matters. Teaching is what educators do when they answer their students and when they try to get their students to formulate questions. Teaching is what educators do when they try to motivate students to pick up the textbook and engage in the chore of reading. This takes us to learning.

Learning is what students do when they read the textbook and make notes on what they are reading. Learning is what students do when they attend class, pay attention, and complete assignments on time. Learning is what students do when they *memorize* information—memorization is a practice that has fallen out of favor. Learning is what students do when they think about and ponder the topics they hear in class and read in the textbooks. Learning is what students do when they are by themselves and elaborating the subject matter in the privacy of their minds.

The distinction between teaching and learning has become blurred. The onus to study and memorize the information has fallen off students and landed on educators. The burdens of teaching have groan heavier. The burdens of learning have lightened. The assumption is that if teachers improve, students will improve. The assumption is that if teachers become better song-and-dance performers on a blackboard-ringed stage, students will join in the routine. And the assumption is that if teachers become better classroom managers, students will better manage their study habits.

There is an element of truth in this. Teaching is a skill and a profession. As in any occupation, there are levels of proficiency. There are competent teachers and there are incompetent teachers. There are brilliant teachers who put in long hours and there are dullards interested only in working short hours and taking the summer off with pay. But there is another side to this, the side that ignores the distinction between teaching and learning. No amount of teaching brilliance could have motivated Martin S—. If Robert E. Lee had taught the General Psychology section and given Martin a *third chance* to pass the course, Martin would not have availed himself of the opportunity. Teachers are only as good as the material they have to work with. If the material contains motivated grains of sterling, the teacher shines. The scores on state tests achieved by students of this quality make slackers look good. But sometimes the material teachers have to work with contains listless splinters of the dullest wood. Nothing can be shaped out of these inert logs. The scores on state tests achieved by students of this quality deflate the efforts of the most earnest and dedicated teachers.

I suppose I'm exaggerating. As in everything involving people, the outcome depends on the interaction of the parties involved. There are four possibilities. The happiest interaction is when superior teachers do their song and dance in front of superior students. Oddly, another happy interaction is when dullards of teachers do their act in front of classes of clods. Nothing gets accomplished in this situation and no one minds—as Daquan, a General Kearney High School student, once told me, "Mr. Ford, you pretend to teach us and we'll pretend to learn." The most aggravating interaction occurs when a prepared and competent teacher performs to an audience of clods—this has happened to me on occasion. The saddest and most troubling interaction is when a class of bright students gets instructed by a half-wit—I like to think this has never happened in any of my sections.

The second faulty development in education has been the idea that the solution to every problem is money. Pay teachers more and they will perform better. This notion is, of course, misguided. Dullards are not going to magically shine—paying dullards more darkens the dull. And teachers of quality are not going to get better. They're already performing at a high level. They would likely perform at this high level if their pay was cut.

There's a move, actually practiced in some schools, to pay students to study. (Parents have tried this for generations.) The logic is straightforward Behaviorism. Many students to not value an education and do not appreciate learning. These students likely value money. So, pay them to come to class. Give them a bonus when they get better grades. Dock them when they slack off. The idea that attending school is a job for hire is as misguided as the idea that skill in teaching depends on a fatted paycheck. Students who value education and appreciate learning are already receiving their rewards. They don't need money to motivate them. The dullards are not going to trouble themselves to make the effort to learn even if they get paid to. No amount of money could have motivated Martin to take the time and study for the second or third make-up test.

There is a literature on intrinsic and extrinsic motivation that suggests that paying people to do what they formerly loved to do destroys motivation. The same literature suggests that paying people to do what they do not want to do is a poor motivator. People persist in the behavior and perform it only as long as they are paid. Take away the pay, the behavior promptly disappears.

We can see these faulty developments in which money is thrown after students who don't want to advance academically in a recent *Press of Atlantic City* story (22 August 2010). Few low-income students in New Jersey bother to avail themselves of the *free* after-school remedial tutoring programs offered as part of the No Child Left Behind initiative. About 17% of eligible students enroll—this is approximately 21,000 of 124,500 students who qualify. Of the 17% who enroll, less than half attend every session. The program is free to the students, but not to the taxpayers. The program costs $1,318 per student to the tune of 28 million dollars a year. Tutors earn $35 - $65.00 per hour. Until 2010 there was no attempt to correlate the tutoring programs with overall academic success. Students appear to progress—classroom attendance improves—but it is not easy to determine whether progress was due to the tutoring or to some other factor.

Tutors have tried a number of techniques to get the 103,500 nonparticipating students to join the program. Simply-worded notices are mailed to parents who may be less literate than their children. Computer tutoring is offered. At-home tutoring is offered. So far, success is giving everyone the slip. "Motivation is the key," one tutor said, adding, "If the student isn't motivated, the tutor has to provide that motivation." If ever there was a clear statement of the blurring of teaching and learning, this is it. Tutors—teachers—can't do the learning for the students. Sick people don't get healed if the doctor takes the medicine. Out-of-shape people don't get in shape if their trainers do the exercise. Bald people don't grow hair if their stylists get a weave. Uneducated students don't get smart if the tutors do the learning.

"The tutor has to provide that motivation." Maybe we ought to make things simple and relieve students altogether and have the tutors take the tests.

119.   Robert E. Lee is one of the most beloved and respected figures in American history. He's up there in the first tier with Washington, Lincoln, the Roosevelts, and John Fitzgerald Kennedy. Generations of schoolchildren studied his life and accomplishments. Many edifying tales are told about his career in and out of military service. Generations of historians studied his tactics and strategies. Many excuses are submitted to preserve his reputation. He never lost a battle—it was always someone else who cost him victory.

His pedagogical talents aside, I've never understood this admiration for Lee, a man called "saintly" and "god-like". He fought for the Confederacy, after all, and was a traitor to the United States. He did take the oath of allegiance after the Civil War, setting a fine example for the Secesh ranks, but I have the feeling he wouldn't have minded passing his twilight years in a different country. As the leading Confederate general he was responsible for the deaths of thousands of Federal soldiers. He was also responsible for the deaths of thousands of Confederate soldiers. He pursued an aggressive policy that took war to the enemy. He was characterized as "audacious"—"reckless" might be a better term, considering the limited manpower resources of the South. (Manpower reserves got so low by the end of the war he considered conscripting African Americans.) The fact that the South was crushed and the Army of Northern Virginia destroyed suggests this overly aggressive policy was not the way to conduct the war.

Lee was as bloodthirsty a general as ever commanded in battle. He was as much a "butcher" as his nemesis, Grant. After sending thousands of Union men to their Particular Judgments in Fredericksburg, Virginia, in December of 1862 Lee famously proclaimed that "It is well that war is so terrible, otherwise we would grow fond of it." This is a misstatement, of course. What Lee really meant was "It is well that war is so terrible, which makes us grow fond of it." Some people dote on every word Lee uttered—there are military histories where his words are published in red ink, just like the Lord's in the New Testament—but he wasn't memorizing his own apothegms. Seven months later he showed he learned nothing from Burnside's blunders and sent a greater number of Confederate men to their Particular Judgments across the Emmitsburg Road in Gettysburg. He must have grown more fond of war in the interim.

Adulators of "Marse Robert" engage in sophistries when they consider that Lee exercised his martial genius defending a slave-owning society. Lee personally owned less than ten slaves. In 1857 he came into possession of 63 slaves when his father-in-law George Washington Parke Custis died. As executor of Custis's will Lee had the task of managing the slaves. The will specified that the slaves were to be manumitted within five years. In fact, it took Lee five full years to free the slaves. In those years he hired the slaves to pay off Custis's debts. Three of the slaves tried to flee to the North but were captured and returned. Under Lee's supervision they were whipped. Salt was scraped into their wounds. They were then sent to the Deep South where escape was unlikely.

Lee wrote to Mrs. Lee in 1856 that slavery "as an institution is a moral and political evil" (cited on Wikipedia web page). However, there is no doubt that he supported the institution. He made no effort to free Custis's slaves earlier than stipulated. To defend slavery he became a traitor to the country his father fought to create. To preserve slavery he commanded in battles that sent thousands to their deaths.

In the same letter Lee wrote that the "blacks are immeasurably better off here than in Africa." He viewed the "painful discipline they are undergoing" as "necessary for their instructions as a race." The length of this discipline depended on "a wise Merciful Providence." In the Lord's good time the black race would become like the white race and everyone would live in perfect harmony. Lee didn't condemn slavery in the letter. Rather, he condemned abolitionists who were trying to "change the domestic institutions of the South." He claimed that "emancipation will sooner result from the mild and melting influence of Christianity than from the storm and tempest" of the war he presciently saw coming.

We must, of course, see Lee as a man of his time and place—he may have been a man for the ages, but he was not a man of the twenty-first century. He was a middle-aged aristocrat and career militarist of a highly conservative and religious nature. He was not a revolutionary—

he fought to keep things the way they were. He would not tolerate uprooting any institution, whether by abolitionism or by war, since institutions were convened by God. Slave owners and a slave-owning society played the role of God's agents and ministers. Slave owners weren't really "masters". They were more like *school masters* whose motivation was to enforce God's curriculum and instruct the Negro race.

We can understand Lee in a social-cultural context, but we can't excuse him or pretend that he was "saintly" or "god-like". He was enmeshed in a ruthless economic system. He was a luminary in a society in which one class lorded over others and broke up families and sold human beings and whipped men and rubbed salt in their wounds when they ran away in pursuit of that most Caucasian virtue—freedom. Lee's religious slant on slavery—that slaves were being taught lessons and that these lessons were for their own edification—sounds blatantly self-serving. Lee was not above putting 63 human beings to work for five years for strictly economic purposes.

It is all so *disgusting*. The fact that one person can *own* another person and order that person about and have that person whipped for seeking freedom is pretty disgusting. There is no other way to describe what slavery was. The disgust doesn't recede if the slave owner is an icon of American history. Rather, it deepens and grows more turbid as we admire and study and worship a man who did disgusting things in his life.

120. Recruiting African Americans into the Confederate Army has got to be one of the zaniest ideas in history. Even if they went into the quartermaster corps and not into the infantry, this was a peculiar plan. It's like recruiting African-Americans into the Klan to boost up the dwindling numbers in white sheets. I suppose the logic was that black men would be as devoted to the ways of the Antebellum South as the men who whipped them and packed salt in the dermal fissures. The Confederate officers who suggested this must have thought that black men would be as nostalgic for the Old South as they were and that black men would rally to the cause of preventing the Union army from ending the institution of slavery.

"Please, Gineral Sherman, don't hurt our masters. We wants to stay slaves." "Please, Gineral Grant, go home and leave our masters be. We likes to get whipped." "Please, Father Abraham, take back that awful Proclamation. Things are fine jist the way they is."

An added incentive to recruitment was that the black recruits would become free men once the Confederacy won. This incentive makes little sense, considering they would become free men once the Union won. We know how the former Confederate States treated African Americans after the war. Anyone who believes the planter class would treat former slaves differently and with largess after the Confederacy won should stop by my office after-hours. I happen to own the rights to a nearby cotton field. I'll make you a generous offer. If you're smart about these things, you can make a bundle sewing boxer shorts.

121. The United States Postal Service should take a page from the end chapter of the Confederate States of America.

The Postal Service is losing billions annually. The prospects are not good that they can make up this deficit or reverse the stampede that would put them out of business if they were an ordinary corporation and not protected by law. The culprit is, of course, the Internet. No one writes letters anymore—if it wasn't for catalogs and charity organizations the mailboxes would be filled with dust. The Internet has killed a once intimate and literary art form, which is rather sad. There will never be compilations of American e-mails in the way there were compilations of American letters.

The Postal Service should surrender to the inevitable and join the wireless avalanche. The handwriting is on the keyboard. In the same way that desperate Confederate officers recommended recruiting African Americans into the military, the Postal Service should convert their offices to cozy Internet cafes. The former post offices can include coffee salons and pastry shops, as well as magazine stands and displays of imported chocolates. A small counter in the rear away from the hipsters lounging with their mocha lattes and scones can be reserved for the rapidly diminishing number of people who prefer to do things the old-fashioned way and write return addresses in flowery script.

122. This was overheard on the ferry to the Great Beyond. "If I told those kids once, I told them a hundred times, don't leave roller skates at the head of the stairs."

123. A recent scandal erupted at a South Jersey Wal-Mart when a racist prankster got on the loudspeaker and instructed all black people to leave the store. This is bad enough. Stephen Hawking, the renowned scientist, has gone one step further. He instructed all people of every color and complexion to leave Planet Earth. He believes that conditions have deteriorated to the point of anarchy and lawlessness on Earth and that, if the human race has one, the future lies in outer space. There is no future on Terror Firma. Doomsday is not avertable—this thought fills scientists and religious folk with glee. On the way off Earth we will leave our weapons behind. No weapons will be allowed on the big spaceship. Having learned the lessons of violence on our besmirched planet, we will live in perfect peace and harmony once we arrive at the solar system of the star Beta Canum Venaticorum in the constellation Canes Venatici.

Beta Canum Venaticorum is believed to be one of the best candidates to support rocky planets in its system. The star is 26 light years from earth. Traveling at the speed of the space shuttle—18,000 mph—it takes 96,720 human years to get there. Bon Voyage!

124. I stopped in town for a haircut at a place called the Senior Barber Shop. It's an old-fashioned barber shop run by an old guy. He gives discounts to senior citizens. Normally he charges seniors $8.00. He charged me $11.00.

It was one of the happiest days of my life.

125. This entry can be called "*In the Kitchen with Jesus.*"

Dr. Don Colbert has authored two books suggesting that in the same way we pattern our spiritual lives we should also pattern our gustatory lives after Jesus if we want to stay alive and healthy. As we sit down to dinner or as we shop the aisles of the local supermarket we should ask, "What would Jesus eat?"

This is an odd question to ask walking into McDonald's. I can't imagine Jesus ordering a Big Mac with a chocolate shake and a side order of fries. Dr. Colbert believes Jesus would order a salad and go light with the dressing. The assumption is that Jesus ate healthy foods like broiled fish and hummus and avoided what would have passed as "junk food" in Ancient Galilee. We like to think the Savior was svelte and in shape and that his arteries were unclogged, but that is an assumption. The Shroud of Turin aside, we don't know what Jesus looked like and we really don't know his eating habits. The Bible mentions Jesus eating a few times, notably at the Last Supper and after the Resurrection. The Bible also includes charges that Jesus was a wine drinker and a glutton (Matthew 11:19; Luke 7:34). These were charges hurled at Jesus by his enemies, so they need to be taken with a grain of salt (unless Jesus was watching his salt intake), but they indicate that Jesus was not averse to wining and dining. The Bible mentions Jesus going into people's houses and visiting, so he must have been the recipient of hospitality on a grand scale. I can't imagine that people would skimp when the Savior of the World visited. I know if the Second Person of the Trinity visited my home I'd spare no expense.

There are also a number of references in the Bible to Jesus fasting. We believe Jesus was dueling Satan in these fasts, but he might also have been watching his weight and maybe he needed to withdraw from the circuit to get back into shape.

Asking what Jesus ate opens up a few related questions. Who catered the Wedding Feast at Cana? What kind of entertainment did they provide? Was there a band? A stand-up comedian? A juggler and trapeze act? Did the guests dance at the wedding? Did they do the hootchie-coochie and put their left feet out? We know they drank a lot. It sounds like they were lushes—unless the host was a miser who went light with the wine. After all, Jesus had to change water into wine to keep the guests in their cups.

And who catered the Last Supper? It was the Passover meal, so we know the ingredients, but who prepared it? Did one of the Apostles prepare the meal? Or did one of their wives or one of the holy women who accompanied Jesus? Maybe it was a potluck production with each guest bringing a dish. This makes sense, considering the Apostles were poor folk. They would have had enough to eat if everyone chipped in and brought something.

126. If a person drowns while being baptized, does the person go directly to heaven? This can be asked about John Blue of Boston—the part about drowning. We don't know the part about going directly to heaven.

Mr. Blue was standing in Lake Cochituate in Natick, Massachusetts. Pastor Arliss Branch of the Church of Jesus of Nazareth intended to baptize Mr. Blue in a full immersion ceremony. They should have gone with the church font and forehead ceremony—it's drier. And safer. As Mr. Blue leaned to immerse himself he stepped into an eight-foot sinkhole. Since he couldn't swim a stroke, he promptly floated home to Jesus.

This is the kind of accident that really shouldn't happen. They were playing with fire performing this kind of baptism—I should say they were playing with water. They were standing in the black water of a lake. Mr. Blue couldn't swim. Neither could Pastor Branch. The pastor was fortunate he didn't follow Mr. Blue into the sinkhole or he would have provided the second demonstration in one day that while Jesus assuredly *saves* our lives he does not *guard* them.

127. We know we can *knock on heaven's door*. Can we also *ring heaven's doorbell*?

128. General David Petraeus, commander of the Central Command in Afghanistan and a prominent military strategist in the administrations of George W. Bush and Lyndon Baines Obama, suffered a weak spell during a Senate hearing. He leaned over the table and turned ashen. He had to be helped out of the room. All went well in the corridor. The general returned after a few minutes and the hearing continued without further incident. A military spokesman claimed the cause of the weak spell was dehydration. The general has been traveling back and forth from Baghdad to Washington, DC, to Kabul and back around again and he has been doing a lot of talking, explaining how our troop buildup in Afghanistan is going to secure victory just like it did in Vietnam.

I have a different conjecture about the source of the general's weak spell. I think what happened was that General Petraeus leaned over the table to get a glass of water or to retrieve a note and couldn't right himself because of all the medals and medallions he wears. There are so many rows of brag rags on his uniform they have started to curl up and over his shoulder. He may be the first general to wear brag rags on his shoulder blades as well as on the pectorals. He may even be the first general to require a subaltern—a major or colonel in rank—to stand behind him with a placard showing the smorgasbord of medals.

I'm sure General Petraeus is a superior officer who has been in many firefights in his career. And I'm sure he is an expert in tactics and strategy and has made many important contributions to the army. But the excess of medals looks a little odd given the scope of his command. My mother has a photograph of Field Marshal Montgomery and General Eisenhower when they visited Fort Myer, VA, after the war. As befits his place in the narcissist hall of fame the Field Marshal's chest holds a billboard of ribbons. But General Eisenhower has a single row of medals on his uniform and he commanded troops in a world war.

General Petraeus must be very proud of his military career and he must want to show off his accomplishments. It can be inspiring to lowly privates and corporals to see all the medals that can be garnered by diligent service. The general must also want to impress people in the civilian world—we don't get medals in civilian life. But General Petraeus's gaudy display may demonstrate the old and often forgotten psychological principle called "compensation" or "overcompensation". To say it bluntly—the general shows off too much. I hate to use this word when it comes to a military officer, but so excessively flashy a presentation looks like *overkill*.

129. It's the middle of the workday and time for lunch. An optimist thinks, "The day's half over." A pessimist thinks, "Four more hours to go."

130. We often claim "The devil is in the details." Consider this eventuality. When our lives are done and we descend through the charcoal turnstile into the pit of woe Old Coaley will greet us and read the particulars of our mortal misdeeds. Is this case "The details are in the devil."

131. The kids of today use cell phones that dial long-distance numbers at the touch of a finger, take pictures, download books, and access the Internet. My nieces thought I was joking when I told them about the phones I used in my youth. Black rotary phones as large as shoeboxes. Party lines. Operators. They could scarcely believe what they were hearing.

One of them blurted, "You must be a lot older than you look." Another commented, "Next, you'll be reminiscing about hitching posts." This niece will likely grow up to be a sociopath.

I realized I dated myself telling them about the phones we used in the old days. But *dated myself*? That's a tricky phrase—and a tricky relationship. Can dating myself lead to courtship and marriage? If we fall out of sorts, can I break up with myself and go our separate ways? And if we break up, who gets custody of myself?

132. Ophthalmologists have no sense of humor.

I realized this on a recent visit to Dr. Maury Bund, my retinal specialist. I was being examined for the floaters I've been experiencing. It seems the vitreous fluid in my left eye has been trying to bolt the socket and make a squirt for it. If the vitreous fluid goes, the retina can't be far behind. Dr. Bund is a slim man with thick black hair, glasses, and a noticeable slouch to starboard. During my visit he wore an odd headpiece made of wire that had an intense light bulb in the center like a miner's lamp. I was on a cot that reclined. I had on a yellow shirt, tan trousers, and loafers. My glasses were in my pocket. The conversation went like this.

"Well, Mr."—he looked at the chart—"Ford, do you have floaters in your left eye?"

"You mean the thumbprints swirling about whenever my eye moves?"

"And what about flashes? Do you have flashes?"

"Only of inspiration."

Dr. Bund stared at me—I had to squint to shield my eyes from the beam in his headpiece. He turned and stared at the computer screen with the most abject and dumbfounded look. He stirred and adjusted his posture and ran his hand over the chart. He would have run his hand through his hair except he was wearing the wire cap. After about a minute he made soft sounds that passed for chuckles, "He, he, he, he." He placed the clipboard on the counter, slid back into a slouch, and commented, "That was a joke."

"No, it wasn't," I replied.

133. Jainism is the ancient non-Hindi religion that originated in India before the sixth century B.C. The objective of Jainism is to free the soul from the karmic cords of negative acts, words, and thoughts. Liberation is achieved by adherence to the Jain principles of nonviolence, truthfulness, celibacy, and detachment from material possessions.

Nonviolence is the fundamental Jain precept. Jains believe that every living being has a soul and that every soul is potentially divine. In the Jain religion there is no creator god or deity analogous to God the Father or to Yahweh. Rather there are enlightened beings who have escaped the tethers of karma and become divine. Nonviolence extends from the ethical principles of compassion, mutual respect and assistance, to pacifism and anti-militarism. Jains believe it is wrong to waste life for trivial reasons.

Nonviolence involves not killing other beings. It also involves a psychological or interpersonal component that we should not insult others, that we should not talk harshly about others, and that we should not think of harming others in our fantasy lives.

The Jain precept of nonviolence extends to non-mammals. Jain monks are careful not to step on insects and will sweep the ground ahead of them in order to avoid inadvertently squashing ants and beetles. Jain farmers limit plowing at certain times of the year in order not to harm worms. Jains are strict vegetarians who will not eat plants or tubers that have to die to be consumed. They will eat only plants and vegetables that are not killed when harvested.

Jainism has a rich and scholarly tradition dating back twenty six centuries and longer. Historically, it has been influential beyond the numbers of adherents. Jain nonviolence and detachment from material possessions were important influences on the Buddha. There are approximately eleven million Jains worldwide—the number would be greater if they left out the precept about celibacy.

Jainism was introduced in America early in the twentieth century, but grew in number only in the 1960s when there was a wave of immigrants from India and when Vietnam War protestors found Jain precepts compatible with the peace movement. The number of American Jains is currently about 100,000. American Jains differ from Jains in India in that they tend to be nonsectarian, holding to no particular creed. And the laity play a greater role in America than they do in India, as there are far fewer monks.

American Jains combine the new with the old. Jain temples are built on the traditional plan, but they include modern amenities such as air conditioning, toilets with hot and cold running water, and pest control. American Jains have forsworn exterminating mice, rats, squirrels, and the pigeons that roost on the window ledges of the temples, but their magnanimity does not extend to the *Insecta* class. The long thin traps that use a blue ultraviolet light to summon flying insects to their electrocution can be found hanging from the roof beams of American temples.

In the middle of their prayer services sincere expressions of "I'm sorry" can be heard from American Jains as insects go sizzling into their next incarnation.

134. In spite of myself I've become something of a Jain.

This summer a spider the size of a quarter made its home in a panel adjacent to the doorbell outside my front door—it's a very public place to weave a web, but I suppose spiders have no choice when instinct impels them to take up residence rent-free in the siding of a townhouse. I was going to get the bug spray and send the spider packing on a one-way trip to the arachnid afterworld, but I thought to the contrary and restrained myself. "Why kill the spider?" I thought. "It's not causing any harm. It's not going to bite me. It's not a termite. It's not going to bite my house. It may even do some good and keep other insects, like flies and mosquitoes, from ringing the doorbell."

I didn't make it into a pet—I don't think you can do that with a spider—but I did have some fun with it. I made it a habit to sneak up on the spider on my way home from work. I noticed it was poised in the web trying to look inconspicuous. I walked slowly and bent over the web. Spiders may be the apex predator in the bug world, but they can't hold a candle to humans. I watched and waited for the spider to flee. When it didn't I lowered my hands and clapped and said "Boo!"

The spider performed what passed for an eight-legged double-take and dashed into a crevice in the siding. This went on for several weeks. I walked quietly up and waved my hands as if to clutch the web and the spider startled and scurried back inside the crevice. On a few occasions it knocked itself against the siding on the way inside. If the web wasn't in place and properly woven, the spider would have fallen to the pavement below.

I elaborated on the game. After I spooked the spider I opened and closed the door and pretended to step inside. I waited with my back against the panels for a second chance to scare it, but the spider never came out. Maybe the spider stayed in for the night—one fright a night was enough. Maybe it wasn't fooled and knew I waited patiently. It had eight eyes, after all. I wondered what it thought of my appearance and how it saw me in its eyes. Was I sharp and detailed in focus or blurry and indistinct? Did it know I was a solitary individual or did it think I was a squad of handsome clones?

At the outset of summer the spider waited immobile and defenseless as I loomed over it. If I were a different kind of person I could easily have swatted it into pieces and taken the web with it. The spider slowly improved—we expect no less of the species. It scrambled into the crevice as soon as I stood over it. I didn't need to raise my hands or holler "Boo!" to get it to flee—it nipped my laughter in the larynx. As the summer wore on it scrambled as soon as I started walking up the steps. It got even better and scrambled into the crevice as soon as the headlight illuminated the front door. I could see its marble shape start and swirl and somersault into the crevice—if you know what to look for, you can see a lot of things in the headlights of a car.

My spider vanished in October. I hoped it got so good at the game it hid as soon as the car pulled into the space and before the beams splashed the door, but sadly I didn't think that was the case. The web slowly scattered and blew apart—no self-respecting spider would allow that to happen. I hoped the spider went into hibernation. I hated to think it died of natural causes or that it got eaten by a peer.

If it didn't die or get eaten I hope the spider can survive the cold. It's a goner if it comes inside the house. Despite my Jainist inclination I'll whack it into nonexistence with the sports section of the *Press of Atlantic City* if I see it gliding across the living room floor.

135. Attracta Figueroa has left the firm. This is a tragedy of profound visual proportions. I may as well go blind. What's the point of having the sense of vision if not to look at Attracta? Over millions of years the process of evolution shaped vision precisely for that purpose. Evolution shaped intelligence for males to think up reasons to visit the Human Resources office. Evolution shaped long-term memory for us to be able to retrieve the images glommed on our visits.

Attracta was a specialist in Human Resources. No one knew what she was a specialist in, but that didn't matter. The operative word was *special*. No, it was *specialest*. If you look up the word "gorgeous" you won't find Attracta listed as an example. She's in a place beyond gorgeous, a place that leaves gorgeous panting in the dust and choking with envy. Attracta's eyes were brown and buttery. They always looked on the verge of melting—I was the one dissolving. Her lips were full and pouty and her complexion was a shade lighter than her eyes. Her hair was the color of amber. Everyone knew her hair was dyed, but that didn't matter. Males got stuck in her hair like gnats in prehistoric pine sap—we were encapsulated and could never break free. And Attracta's feminine endowments front and rear—well, *perfect* just doesn't match up as a word.

Attracta's finest moment came during the great fire in the old warehouse—I should say during the great smoke condition in the old warehouse. The rice that drops into cartons and serves as filler for the books somehow caught on fire. At first Segundo was suspected, but management remembered that he had been let go some time before. The culprit turned out to be a spark of friction that leaped from the conveyor into the rice dispenser. In no time the warehouse was filled with wisps of black smoke that wafted along the racks and into the picking lines.

The crew left the building in orderly fashion and waited in the truck yard. Everyone was worried that we wouldn't have a warehouse to return to in the morning. Some were filled with fear that the stacks of books would be ruined—they were rapidly becoming smoke stacks of books. Attracta appeared particularly upset. She kept her fingers raised in a feminine startle and walked excitedly from one trailer to another. It was fine by me that she was agitated. I could see the enticing curvature her long legs led up to.

Suddenly, Attracta ran toward the warehouse as fast as her four-inch heels allowed. She turned and waved us forward. "*Hombres, sigueme!*" she called, entering the building and disappearing into the smoke.

No one stirred, neither man nor woman bookseller. Oh, that I could *sigueme* her, but I couldn't at that moment. I love my company and my company loves me, but I didn't want to give up my one and only life for the bargain book business.

Attracta courageously ran from bay door to bay door. The smoke was thicker in the direction she headed. "*Hombres, ven aqui i ayudar a apagar el fuego,*" she appealed, but there wasn't a single *hombre* among us. Attracta looked so fragile standing on the loading dock with fingers of smoke stroking her shapely shoulders. I was beginning to lose control of my cowardice. I was surprised at what she attempted. I never took her for a company woman.

"*Hombres, por favor!*" she cried desperately, disappearing into the smoke. I waited, but she didn't emerge at the next bay door. I retraced her steps mentally. Maybe she was circling back and withdrawing. But there was no sign of her at any of the bay doors.

I couldn't suffer the thought that Attracta had been injured or that she succumbed to the smoke. It was one of the moments I knew I'd regret, but I couldn't help myself. She wanted us to put out the fire in the buckets of packing rice. She started a fire in my heart—I couldn't let her battle the blaze by herself.

"Attracta, I'm coming!" I shouted, racing into the building.

It was like running into black gauze. I knew what it looked like, but I couldn't see the back of my hand in front of my face, the smoke was so thick. And it wasn't only the darkness, it was the suffocating burnt popcorn odor of the roasted rice.

"Attracta, where are you?" I called, trying to shout with my mouth closed. Breathing the foul aroma was bad enough than to have to swallow it. "Attracta, are you here?"

I had a cognitive map of the layout of the warehouse and a general sense of how far I could go before I bumped into a conveyor. I didn't have a map of the location of the pallets strewn against regulation on the receiving dock. I felt a sharp nudge at my ankle and then I felt myself falling. I couldn't see the direction, but I was pretty confident it was down.

I woke up twenty minutes later stretched out in the truck yard on a corrugated stretcher. My clothes were torn and oily. I smelled badly. A quiver of smoke washed in front of my face as I raised my hand to cover the cough. Attracta was leaning over me. I had never seen her from that angle before—the view was worth the welt on my forehead. "You're so brave," she said. Her amber hair was blowing in the breeze. Her brown eyes were tearing. Her face was darker from the soot the smoke had streaked on it. She looked worried, but she was smiling. "You're the bravest *hombre* I've ever seen."

It took a week for the grime to rinse out of my hair and a month for the welt to change back to the color of skin. It took a little longer to get the taste of burnt popcorn out of my mouth. I could never forget Attracta's compliment. I could tell she was sincere and I appreciated what she said. Everyone within earshot heard. From that day forward I was treated with respect in the warehouse and with more than respect. I raced into the smoke-filled warehouse when no one else dared, not even the assistant managers. My fellow booksellers could never think of me in the same way. Attracta could never think of me in the same way—I alone of every *hombre* in the company ran to her defense. We laughed about it when we passed in the corridors. We told jokes about our adventure, but they were the kinds of jokes that relieve the fear of what could have been a grim situation.

Now that Attracta's no longer with the company I often repeat what she said. I know it's not true, but I like to hear her say it. It gets me over the rough patches and the times when cowardice starts to creep up. I may not be the bravest *hombre*, but for a few minutes Attracta thought I was and that meant everything in the world.

136. There's a slang expression "*to off* a person", meaning to kill a person and to end a life. For example, "Lee Harvey Oswald *offed* President Kennedy and was shortly thereafter *offed* by Jack Ruby."

It follows that "*to on* a person" means—or should mean—to give birth or, better still, to conceive a person and to start a life. For example, "The man and woman had relations and *oned* a baby nine months later."

137. One of the simplest security devices for travelers is the neck wallet. This is a zippered pouch that hangs on a string and is worn under the

shirt or blouse. Rather than keep money and important documents like passports or credit cards in pockets or in pocketbooks travelers keep these items close to the body and under the clothing where they will, presumably, be more secure. In theory the neck wallet is an excellent idea. Pickpockets can't reach between the buttons without being noticed and thieves have no easy access to items that are otherwise vulnerable in back pockets or purses.

In practice the neck wallet is less than an excellent idea. Pickpockets and thieves have limited access to the contents. So does the wearer. When it comes time to pay for dinner or for merchandise the wearer has to unbutton, reach inside the clothing, unzip the wallet, and count money without seeing the denominations of the bills. This is not a large problem for men, who are allowed to show chest hair in public, but it can be a problem for women, who are not allowed to show their chest hair. Women have to make apologies and turn and face the wall to get at the bills. Sometimes they have to crouch beneath a table or duck behind a display case. Talk about calling attention to oneself. Every thief in the room notices what's going on as the lady indignantly positions herself to get at the wallet.

Neck wallets call attention to themselves even when the wearer does not engage in metacarpal contortions. We have photographs of ourselves posing on a bridge over the Neris River in Vilnius in 2007. We're trim people with enviable body masses—in Lithuania we could pass for Balts with no questions asked. But each of us has a noticeable bulge under our shirts at the level of the solar plexus. The unsightly mounds beneath our blouses are not round. They're the flat square outlines of wallets crammed with money and important papers. It looks as if we tucked first base beneath the polyester.

It's as if we carried a billboard instead of a partially concealed billfold. The message couldn't be more clear if we wore arrows and a bull's eye painted on our garments. *Here is where we keep our stash. Come and get it!*

138. As readers get near the denouncement of a thriller they can rightfully say there's an incoming outcome.

139. It's rare that a town long in existence changes its name, but this has happened to Wildwood Crest.

Located on a barrier island at the southern tip of New Jersey "The Crest" is one of the premiere family resorts in the Northeast. People come from near and far to enjoy the Jersey Shore at its most sedate and seductive. The ocean at The Crest is unusually serene. There's scarcely any surf. Sandbars allow bathers to venture a good ways from the beach. Even at fifty yards the water doesn't reach above the knees. The beach is legendary—I believe it is the greatest beach in the world. Five miles long, it's more than a fourth of a mile wide. And the beach is growing.

The bay on the interior side of the island is as tranquil as the ocean and more amenable to water sports. People sail and jet ski on the bay. Piers allow fishermen and crabbers to haul supper home. Excursion boats sail to watch whales and sightsee along the coast.

The architecture of the motels has a bright and cheerful look. The style is dubbed "doo-wop" and dates to the 1950s. The buildings come with shiny statues of dolphins and mermaids over the rental offices and with chrome facades in the shapes of convertibles and musical instruments.

The Crest is famously family oriented. There are few bars in town. The liquor stores are in Wildwood proper along Rio Grande Ave. The restaurants serve meals American style and are of the "bring your own" variety when it comes to alcohol. There are no fast food restaurants and no strip malls. There's one convenience store and it's located at the southern edge of town.

The Crest is a most pleasant and idyllic setting. We spent many happy weeks there in the 1990s and we still make frequent day trips. If there is an afterlife and if I have any say about it, mine is going to look a lot like The Crest. The only difference will be the number of liquor stores.

Of course, this is all too good to be true. Wildwood Crest was a special place, but it was part of the United States. Like the nation at large, the citizens of The Crest became afflicted with the mortal sin of greed in the early 2000s. A considerable number of motels—especially those along the beach—were replaced by garish new townhouses offering street level garages and rooftop swimming pools. The motels that weren't razed got converted to condominiums. The doo-wop decor came down and got replaced by "For Sale" signs. People who formerly rented were given the option to buy and then, after turning a quick profit, to sell to the highest bidder who could make his or her profit in turn. Each revolution of the real estate carousel was sure to boost the selling price. If there were no bidders, owners could meet the mortgage obligations by renting to vacationers from Philadelphia and Quebec.

In their haste to get rich people forgot that the ghosts of pirates stalked the calm waters in the long ago and that a few miles to the north Boardwalk scams proceeded in delirious progress. The real estate market collapsed, the national economy tanked, and people who expected to reside half the year in luxury oceanfront apartments belly flopped into the poorhouse instead.

The city of Wildwood Crest went under ahead of the rest of them. The city lost a fair number of motels. The city lost a fair number of motel rooms. Raising the tax on the saps who rented the rooms that were left couldn't make up the difference. People weren't coming in the same numbers. Vacationers found other places to spend their paychecks. Day trippers found closer places to unfold their beach chairs and blankets. The tax base dried up like the shallow pools caught between sand dunes—much of it had been given away as abatements. There were vacant lots where prosperous motels once stood. There were carpets of sand where cars once packed parking lots.

Wildwood Crest in now known by the name of Wildwood *Crestfallen.*

140. On the steamship of life I travel steerage class.

141. The horror movies I watched when I was a child can't compare with the blood splatter in today's movies or with the computer-generated gory effects, but they were scary nevertheless. The violence was off-camera and in the world of imagination, so when we saw something untoward on the screen it was truly frightening. The world back then was in black-and-white and bloodless. Today's viewers are exposed to the most outlandish spectacles brought to them in living color and in 3-D. When they see the tame old movies, they yawn and scratch themselves and reach for the remote control.

One of the most frightening scenes I remember from my youth occurred in *Son of Frankenstein*. This was the third entry in the Universal Pictures series and the last to feature classic sets and scenes—the Monster was on his way to meeting Abbott & Costello. The movie had a great cast including Basil Rathbone, Bela Lugosi, Lionel Atwill, and Boris Karloff in his final appearance as the Monster. In the movie Baron Wolf von Frankenstein, son of the Monster's creator, returns to the ancestral castle. He has no intention to recreate the mayhem his father unleashed, but the Monster is found alive and severely injured—he didn't die at the end of *Bride of Frankenstein*. The crazed and deformed Ygor, who wants a new body built like Hercules, blackmails Wolf to restore and heal the Monster so he can engage in the usual off-camera carnage. The movie ends happily when the Baron saves the village by drop kicking the Monster into a vat of acid that just happens to be bubbling outside his laboratory window.

The scene that has stayed in memory all these years occurs immediately before the Monster is dispatched. Inspector Krogh, the stern but good-natured constable played by Lionel Atwill, has an artificial arm. The flesh original was previously mangled by the Monster. In the fight scene at the end of the movie the Monster grabs Krogh by the arm—it immediately comes off, allowing the Inspector to elude certain death. I found the scene disturbing and I still do. Viewers know the arm is a fake, but forget that fact even at the moment the Monster rips the arm off at the shoulder and clear through the sleeve. We don't want the Inspector to die and we are relieved that the prosthetic device saved the day. We are somewhat put off, though, and shocked by the violent manner of his escape. Getting an arm torn off, even if it is an artificial arm, must be painful. It must be like getting false teeth punched out of the mouth.

There are creatures like salamanders and starfish that escape death by sloughing body parts. Some creatures regenerate their appendages. Others don't and put in for disability. Evolution has not equipped the human species to re-grow body parts. If we lose appendages, it's for keeps. If we get lost body parts back, it's in the form of wood, stainless steel, and glue.

Fashion designers have succeeded where Mother Nature has failed, if she ever tried. Our clothing is detachable, unlike the flesh underneath.

You can strip my jacket and I have shirt and pants on. If you tear my shirt or pants off, I have underwear on. If you yank my shoes off, I run away in my socks. We shed our clothing in lieu of ourselves. It once happened that a detachable article of clothing kept my good looks from taking a mangling.

I'm not sure I'm ashamed to say I never learned to knot a tie. I was never good at it when I was young and I've worked for years in a "business casual" environment when knotted ties infrequently appear. The executives in the Distribution Center rarely wear ties—they rarely wear suits—and the professors at Manhattan Community College dress in a nerdy fashion of dress slacks and sweaters. When I need to dress formally, I wear a clip-on tie. There's no bother with a clip-on tie. No carpal hassle. No vexation of skeletal contortions. No need to stand in front of a mirror and watch fingers turn into toes.

A clip-on arm comes in handy when a monster attacks. So does a clip-on tie.

After Junior's wedding a bunch of us went for late-night drinks at a local tavern near the reception hall. I think the name of the joint was *Club Zanzibar.* It may have been *Club Gibraltar.* I know it was *Club* something or other. Whatever the name, the tavern catered to a cutthroat crowd of truck drivers and blue-collar workers—I suppose every bar caters to a cutthroat crowd at two in the morning. We didn't know that when we went in. We must have thought it was a yuppie establishment where people in sweaters drink white wine and discuss haute cuisine. As soon as we walked in we realized we made a mistake. We couldn't pivot and walk out. That wouldn't be political. And we couldn't settle in till closing. The unspoken consensus was that we would order one round and leave.

We ordered the round and hunkered down in the corner. We tried to remain innocuous, but that was impossible. We were strangers and newcomers in an hour when intoxication breeds familiarity among bar regulars and we looked different. None of us had beer bellies or five o'clock shadows. Our hair was properly combed. A few had plastered hair gel on. We were in suits and button-down shirts that weren't flannel and didn't have American flags pinned on the lapels. We reeked of cologne. I could feel the bloodshot gazes of the regulars burning the back of my neck. They must have thought we were insulting them by walking in at a private hour. If it wasn't an insult, it was certainly an intrusion.

We weren't helped by Junior's Uncle Felix, who was loudly pondering the sexual orientation of Lance, one of the groom's men. Uncle Felix had consumed too many martinis at the wedding and he quite forgot where he was. His comments about the mess President Obama inherited from George W. Bush didn't lessen the provocation.

By the furthest bad luck one of the bar regulars was named Lance— either he was Lance or his drinking buddy was. When he heard Uncle Felix rant on about lisps and limp wrists he grabbed hold of the bar and hoisted himself to a standing position—for a moment I thought he was going to bring the bar with him. He walked toward us at a deliberate pace. Probably, he was waiting for sobriety to catch up. He stood about six foot six and weighed well into the 200s. He had a grizzled and hairy face and the twenty or so beers he consumed pasted a hepatic sheen to his angry look. His eyes were slits, smallish and screwed up. The fact that he was seeing double didn't change the odds that a massacre was about to take place.

Everyone in our group shrank, Uncle Felix furthest of all. The collective brawn of all the people in our party didn't equate to the brawn of this single patron. Since I sat at the outskirts of our group it became my lot to negotiate or to be the first to fall. To maintain the peace I thought I would offer a round of drinks. I intended to imitate Duke Wayne in posture and in voice. I hoped I didn't sound like Barney Fife. I trusted he had so much hair in his ears he couldn't possibly hear my knees knocking.

"Listen, he doesn't mean any harm," I said, appeasingly coating my voice with a soft Texan slur. I stood and turned to face him. I'm pretty tall, but I came up to his shoulders. "He's had too much to drink."

This guy wasn't hearing any excuses. He wasn't amenable to negotiation. He wasn't interested in another beer. He wanted only to come through me and slaughter Uncle Felix. That was not especially difficult to do.

He raised his fist—it was the length, width, and depth of a tree trunk. He grabbed me by the collar and yanked. He intended to hold his fist in position and pull me into it. The ignominy was all mine—I was going to knock myself cold. I felt myself scrapping on tippy toes along the floor, but only for a second. I came to an abrupt heel-dropping halt a half inch from his thumb, which resembled a nose inserted between the middle and ring finger.

The joke was on him. He grabbed my clip-on tie and nothing else. The collar tore open and the top button of my shirt popped off, but I remained intact from the neck up. As I ran out the door I could see the word "What!" puff his brows in a ponderous startle. He must have thought he tore my head off. I added the "Huh?" and a second "Huh!" a block later. I was saved by a clip-on tie, just like Inspector Krogh had been saved by a clip-on arm. Sometimes it pays to come apart at the seams.

I walked till I found the motel and passed out in fright in my room. I never found out what happened to the other members of the wedding party. We never met again. I checked the headlines the next day, but there was nothing about multiple murders or about the riot squad being called to a dive in the wee hours. I read the obituaries for a week to be sure that nothing happened. I wasn't close to that side of the family and I wasn't sure of their names, so I looked for a decedent named Felix. I didn't find anyone listed by that name, which was a good thing. I like to think they made it out of the bar intact. Maybe they were wearing clip-on articles of clothing just like I was.

142. Now *sledge*. This word sounds like something best handled by a *shovel* than by a *hammer*.

143. This was overheard on the ferry to the Great Beyond, "This is what I get for being too cheap to take swimming lessons at the YMCA."

144. *Riverworld* is a sprawling and plot-heavy fantasy mini-series that once aired on the Science Fiction cable channel and is now available on DVD at a bargain price. *Riverworld* answers the question whether or not they use dope in Hollywood.

War correspondent Matt Ellman, his fiancé Jessica, and two gay friends are blown up by a suicide bomber in a Singapore café. Jessica disappears, but Matt and his friends revive in a river. They swim ashore to a scenic place called Riverworld. This is a strange afterlife run by blue-faced beings who may or may not be aliens—they don't look like angels. Glowing orbs keep the peace. A huge machine dispenses box lunches like an outdoor automat. Beards never grow. Faces never get dirty. Clothing never gets soiled. People stay immaculately clean despite living in the great outdoors.

People from all periods of history emerge unpredictably from the river. They tumble ashore like driftwood after a storm. The Conquistador Francisco Pizarro and his henchmen have a nonaggression pack with the explorer Francis Burton and his Russian mob associates. Together, Pizarro and Burton rule Riverworld and brutalize the peace-loving arrivals.

Matt no sooner arrives in the Great Beyond than he sets out to find the missing Jessica. He soon learns his mission also involves saving Riverworld from a fraction of evil blue beings who, in league with Burton, seek to pulverize it in some kind of atomic blast. Along the way he learns that he also needs to save Planet Earth. We are told by an arrival on the riverbank that the world blew up in his absence. He's joined on this quest by no less a personage than Mark Twain, who commands a paddleboat, wields six-shooters with unerring accuracy, and has an Italian countess and poisoner for a mistress. One member of Twain's crew is a female physicist with an inferiority complex that causes her to hate men.

Matt and Mark are soon joined on their quest by Tomoe Gozen, a most honorable twelfth century Samurai who promptly slays Pizarro's army as they charge at her one foot-soldier at a time. This is pretty much the plot—the commencement of the plot, anyway, which grows more complicated with every station break. By the end of the movie Matt has exchanged Twain's paddleboat for a ride in the zeppelin *Hindenburg*. An alien spacecraft flies into view and hovers outside a Medieval castle where an ominous atomic device is set to blow Riverworld into a sequel.

The setting of the movie is gorgeous. It looks as if it was filmed on location in the Great Northwest. Despite the setting and the unusual amalgam of characters from different time periods, the move is standard fare involving good guys and bad guys, their bosom buddies, and their bosom molls. The story is interchangeable with any other fantasy extravaganza.

In three hours of movie making there is one surprising scene worth the price of the DVD. The bad-tempered Pizarro stabs one of Matt's friends to death. This unexpected development immediately leads to the theologically thick question, "Can you die in the afterlife?"

I don't know the position of Holy Mother Church on this question, but you cannot die in the afterlife that is Riverworld. Matt's friend soon reappears in the guise of one of Pizarro's soldiers—he is dispatched a second time later in the move, but only for a while. Bad guys die and come back. Good guys die and come back. Matt and Tomoe die and are promptly revived as themselves. We expect no less of the hero and heroine.

Riverworld is a place that takes the poet's insight to heart, *Dead, once dead, there's no more dying then.*

145.   Beethoven adapted Schiller's epic poem *Ode to Joy* for the magnificent choral finale to the *Ninth Symphony*. In German it's *Ode an die Freude*—it sounds better in English, but everything sounds better in English. The theme of the poem concerns universal solidarity among people. Selections of the poem usually have uplifting and inspiring titles such as "Brotherhood", "Fraternity", "Harmony", so the listener knows what the theme is. After all, the *Ode to Joy* sounds slightly salacious. Just what kind of joy are they singing about? If we didn't know better we might have off-the-scale thoughts of scantily clad sopranos scampering about in drunken debaucheries.

Andre Rieu, the noted conductor of the Strauss Symphony Orchestra, calls his version *All Men Are Brothers*. This describes Schiller's theme to perfection, but it is sexist in the extreme. *All Women Are Sisters* is equally true, but you won't find that on the CD box. A better and nonsexist title to Rieu's version might be *All People Are Relatives*. This is true in a philosophical sense and, broadly speaking, in a biological sense. Unfortunately, it's an awfully bland title for the rousing fourth movement of a thunderous masterpiece.

146.   All my life I've been surrounded by intelligent people. I went to a university run by the Jesuit order. They're so intelligent they contributed a word to the language—Jesuitical. I worked in a bookstore for a while and booksellers are known to be of a scholarly inclination. Some of the people I've known might be called "intellectuals". You might even call

me an "intellectual"—you better call me that behind my back because if I hear you I'll have to drill you full of bullet holes.

After dealing with these people for years and with the authors of the books that made them intelligent, here's the conclusion I've come to—*smart people aren't.*

147. Election time is on us again and the professional class of sleazebags called "politicians" is stuffing my mailbox with campaign literature. "If elected, I will lower property taxes," the Democrat candidate insists. "If elected, I will lower every tax," the Republican candidate counters. "If elected, I will create jobs." "If elected, I will create a business-friendly environment." "If elected, I will make government more efficient." "If elected, I will draw back the drapery and open government to the people." "If elected, I will repair the highways and infrastructure." "If elected, I will restore the transportation trust fund to solvency." "If elected, I will promote family values." "If elected, I will terminate the corruption that squeezes the life blood out of the State."

Right. Like the late Glenn Edwards of Manhattan Community College used to say, "If you're going to the cafeteria, bring me back a cup of world peace."

I don't know why politicians tell fibs when they could tell true lies and whoppers. No one believes a word they say about lowering taxes or creating jobs or making the environment more business friendly or making government efficient and transparent or repairing the infrastructure or restoring the transportation trust fund or promoting family values or terminating corruption. If they're going to lie and if we know they're going to lie, they may as well amuse us.

"If elected, I will cure the common cold." "If elected, I will cure cancer." "If elected, I will build a luxury hotel in the Sea of Tranquility." "If elected, I will send a man to Mars and return him safely home by the end of the decade." "If elected, I will bring every dead zone in Barnegat Bay back to teeming life." "If elected, I will reverse global warming and return the earth to a permanent springtime." "If elected, I guarantee no one will have to grow old in my administration." "If elected, I will see to it that no one dies on my watch." "If elected, I shall go to the cafeteria and bring back a cup—no, a gallon bottle—of world peace."

Those are the kinds of lies a citizen could cotton to. They're almost enough to get a fellow to actually go and vote.

148.   I was sitting on the deck poolside in our housing complex pretending to read my copy of Sartre's *Being and Nothingness*. I was eavesdropping instead on the two ladies at the next table. They looked to be in their fifties. The one closest to me was dressed in a white terry-cloth beach robe. She was full-faced with dyed blond hair that was as frizzy as the robe. She was on the plump side, which didn't stop her from shedding the robe periodically for a dip in the pool. The second woman was dressed in a white button-down shirt and blue shorts that hugged her hips about as tightly as store-bought fabric can pack flesh in. She wore sunglasses and had thick hair the color of coal, some nuggets of which looked jet black, others of which looked as if they had been sitting in the grill throughout mealtime. She twirled a half-empty water bottle as she spoke. She was older than the first woman and on the plumper side. Their conversation went like this.

"It was just yesterday when my niece graduated kindergarten," the woman in the terry-cloth robe said. "She graduates high school in June."

"Children grow so rapidly," the older woman advised. "One minute, they're babies, the next minute, they're grown up and gone."

"I can't believe how the years have flown."

"Mine are out of the house. They have careers and families of their own."

"One day, you're young."

"Mine don't even live in the state anymore."

"The next day, and before you know it, you're old."

"Wait till your niece gets married. You'll find out how fast time really flies."

I was growing depressed by their conversation and thought I should get back to Sartre's upbeat masterpiece when I hit on a solution to what sounded like a threat of aging. If we do away with the institution of marriage, then we don't have to find out how fast time flies. Without marriage we can stay permanently youthful and never have to age.

This insight solved the problem of aging for me, but not for the ladies. I was going to share my insight with them, but stayed silent and turned page 109 instead. They didn't look like the types who'd take kindly to an intrusion, even if it was neighborly, and I wanted to survive long enough to put my theory to the test.

149. Everyone has a dark side, an unseemly smelly side consisting of small and petty deeds, spiteful and spiritually mean thoughts, and a plentitude of sins of omission and commission. We keep this side well hidden and tucked in beneath the hem of consciousness. It behooves us not to notice these deeds when we commit them—they're the kinds of deeds we wouldn't overlook if we saw other people commit them. Sometimes these unsavory deeds slip out and then we're stuck. It's too late. The damage has been done. We can't take back what we did. We can only feel the regrets.

Sometimes we acknowledge these deeds publicly. Maybe we want to live an honest life. Maybe we want to repair wrongs and make restitution to the people we've harmed. Maybe we want to confess and pump out the sulfurous slurry that wipes the shine off our souls. Whatever the motivation, when we confess we say that we *come clean* about who we are and what we did. Given the iniquities of these unwashed and unwashable deeds, a better term for this kind of confession is *come dirty*.

150. The *wazoo* is an imaginary body orifice. The word is in common parlance, but there is no consensus where the wazoo is located on the body, whether in the ventral or dorsal or cephalic or caudal zones. *Wazoo* sounds like something that belongs in the dorsal and caudal zones, but this is purely speculative. Presumably, it is an orifice common to both sexes.

And no one knows whether objects *come out of* or *go into* the wazoo. Possibly, objects can do either, but the language is not clear on this. The fact that this is not known with certainty can cause grief if a person fiddles with the wazoo in the wrong direction.

151. There is nothing sadder, or more commonplace, than when my ballpoint pens run out of ink. I carry these pens in my shirt pocket seven days a week. I hold them in my hand nearly every waking hour of the day. They become a kind of extension of my being. And every now and then I have to deposit them in the trash bin. It's an undeserved fate—I always feel like I'm throwing a finger away. There's a *Twilight Zone*

episode in which a magical flask never runs dry of whiskey. I wish my ballpoint pens were like that flask and never ran out of ink.

I never forget to say good-by when I place a pen—I never throw it— in the bin. And I never forget to thank the pen for the many productive thoughts it gave me.

Ballpoint pens deserve better. Maybe I should set aside a space in a drawer of my desk where I can inter pens that have run out of ink. The drawer can become a kind of mausoleum to pens of the past.

152. It's also sad when writers run out of ink and expire.

This happened to Robert B. Parker who passed away at the age of 77 in January 2010. Parker wrote more than 50 books, including 39 featuring the redoubtable private eye Spenser. I followed the Spenser series since the middle 1980s, when I read *Crimson Joy*, one of the best in the series. I subsequently went back and obtained the earlier novels— the series debuted in 1973. And I dutifully bought each Spenser novel that followed. The rumor is Parker has a few Spenser books that will be published posthumously. I'll buy those as well. I have to be candid and say that the books in the first half of the series were superior to the books in the second half of the series. Spenser never changes. Nor do the plots. Regardless, I consider Parker an outstanding writer. I learned a lot reading him.

Parker went out in what seems ideal fashion. He was at his writing desk and at work when he unexpectedly breathed his last. We like to think he finished the chapter he was working on when the plug was pulled. If not the chapter, then at least the paragraph. Let's hope he ended the sentence with a period.

This seems like the ideal death for a writer, but it is trickier than it sounds. Parker's wife Joan left him at work to go for her morning jog and returned to find that he had expired. This is tragic enough, but it can be worse if they parted on bad terms. A lot of times people go out of the house in angry and regretful moods. It not infrequently happens that people make their partings full of bad thoughts and ill-chosen words. And it sometimes happens that people leave the house without saying good-by.

Even if Parker went out on good terms with his wife, he might have placed a last-minute phone call. He might have called a relative and complained about some irksome family matter. He might have called his agent and berated him over royalties. He might have called an editor and argued over the choice of words or plot machinations. ("You ****, how dare you change a word! I'm going to punch you in the ****ing nose the next time I'm in your office!") Or he might have called a critic and used swearwords and vows to God Almighty and his Divine Son in protest over the observation that the books in the first half of the series were superior to the books in the second half of the series.

This kind of sudden death, when the consciousness is shut off with the flick of a cosmic finger, sounds like the way to go, but it can lead to trouble in *the other place* depending on what was said and done when the light was extinguished. It may be preferable to have a little time to get our affairs in order. If a person knows he is leaving *this place* for good, he is usually careful in his choice of words—we like to make a favorable final impression. But if a person doesn't know he's going and not coming back, he's often not careful in what he says at what is the last moment and that can get him in big trouble.

It's not proper form to pass through the pearly expurgates uttering swearwords.

153. Every car in the state of New Jersey will eventually display a gold State Police decal above the inspection sticker on the lower left corner of the windshield. These decals entitle drivers to break traffic law with impunity. Drivers can't be pulled over if they display such decals. If by some chance drivers get pulled over by troopers with diminishing eyesight, they earn lesser tickets for failing to wear seatbelts than tickets for running stop signs or red lights or for driving at twice the posted speed. Drivers who display a gold State Police shield in the lower left windshield can disregard any traffic law they wish. Regardless of the offense, these drivers receive no tickets when pulled over. Instead of a ticket they receive an apology. The word "brother" frequently occurs in the apology.

Every driver in the state of New Jersey will eventually possess a Medical Permit that can be used to park in handicapped spaces near the entrances to stores and public buildings. Since there are a minimum number of handicapped spaces, this is going to cause considerable mayhem and considerable flashing of State Police decals and shields.

("My shield trumps your decal, brother, so pull out of the spot before I phone headquarters.") The solution to the mayhem is to make every parking space in every lot a handicapped space. Police decals and shields have no right-of-way in ordinary parking spots. It will be business as usual finding a place to park. No one will be sued, cursed, spat at, or run over.

154. Some people have character and charisma. When they enter a room they are said to show *presence*.

I'm not like those people. When I enter a room I show *absence*.

155. In the old days the term *Jersey Fresh* referred to things like cranberries, blueberries, and tomatoes. In our time *Jersey Fresh* refers to a surly and half-civilized standard of misbehavior demonstrated by Mafioso types and illiterate twenty-somethings. When people thought of New Jersey in former years pictures of beaches and bogs came into mind. People thought of factories where middle-class laborers worked themselves frail to make a better life for their children. When people now think of New Jersey they picture smoke-filled strip joints inhabited by thugs and beach houses rented by foul-mouthed floozies. People in New Jersey are no longer perceived as making an honest day's living. Instead they are seen as crooked and corrupt characters looking to score outside the law.

As if it were something to be proud of, the reputation that New Jersey people are arrogant rejects and incompletely socialized has spread throughout the land. Some people in New Jersey revel in the perception that we're considered goons and loons—they're overjoyed that residents in other states think we're tough and give us wide latitude. Some people believe this reputation brings in tourist dollars. Tourists visit the Garfield bar where the Don whacked his Number Two. Other tourists visit the Seaside Heights bar where the frats passed out when they couldn't match the floozies in vodka shots.

When I was in the used book world I got a call from Dusty, a bookseller in Iowa. After we conducted business he asked whether New Jersey is like what he sees on television, a place that is mean, miserable, and situated between oil refineries and garbage dumps that are mountain high. I don't think Dusty was planning a visit—I suppose he was curious about life on the other side of the Appalachians. I told him, "In all honesty, Dusty, New Jersey is not like what you see on television. It's worse." I don't doubt he believed me.

There's a sign at the border of Plumstead, a town along County Road 539. The sign claims, "Expect to be charmed", which seems unlikely since alcohol is banned there. A wag suggested that billboards be raised at the borders of New Jersey. The signs would read, "Welcome to New Jersey—Expect to be conned." But that can't be true. In fact, the opposite is true. The con is—there is no con. If anything, the sign should read, "Welcome to New Jersey—go ahead and con us." Because that's what happens all the time and everywhere.

I don't believe there's a state in the Union where the citizens are more often ripped off and conned. We have the highest tax rate or nearly the highest. The return from the Federal government is the lowest in the country. Our roads are among the worst in America and the costliest to repair—everything in New Jersey is the costliest to repair. New Jersey ranks near the bottom in making college accessible to its residents. College students in New Jersey pay a larger percentage of out-of-pocket expenses than students in nearly every other state. We have the most corrupt political system in America—maybe Illinois is worse, but second place in corruption does not bestow bragging rights. We pay a state tax, a county tax, a sales tax, and a property tax. Taxpayers not only pay for the education system in their communities, they also pay for the failed education systems in the inner cities of Trenton, Jersey City, Camden, Newark, and elsewhere. Fees in the state have multiplied like the cogon grass in the Old Confederacy. There are fees for hunting, fees for fishing, fees for using the beaches, fees for using the sidewalks, fees for driving the streets, fees for crossing the streets. There are fees for electricity, fees for gas, fees for water. Soon, there will be fees for using the air and for breathing.

No wonder we swagger and act tough. No wonder we pimple our vocabulary with a rash of swearwords. No wonder we pass out from drinking shots of vodka. While we're busy pretending to be wise guys and picking our teeth play-acting the roles of lowlives we're being suffused with radioactivity from the contaminated soil.

Our money. Our pride. Our self-respect. Our reputation. These are great things and they are taken from us. But nothing is too small to take. I picked up four pictures I had developed at the pharmacy. It was 15 cents a picture. The bill came to 64 cents. The state asked for its cut of this purchase—four lousy cents. I wasn't angry that the state wanted four cents so I could get my pictures developed. I wasn't amused at having to add another coin to the purchase. Rather, I experienced the most terrible sadness. This is what life in New Jersey has come to—paying a tax of four cents. And they say we con people.

Four lousy cents—something this pitiful can tip a fellow into major depression.

156.   The inquiring mind would like to know—when does a *wag* graduate into a *wit*?

157.   Social scientists claim that laughter does not result from hearing jokes or funny lines but from the necessity of short-circuiting aggression in social situations. Laughter is a way of defusing potentially harmful encounters. Laughter indicates to the other person that you are not a danger and that you are not making a threatening pronouncement or a provocative gesture. Laughter indicates that you are not going to assault the other person verbally or bodily.

I have doubts about many topics in the social sciences, but I believe this claim about laughter. I've noticed that people rarely laugh at my jokes, so laughter can't be primarily related to humor. And I've heard enough arguments in which strong and offensive statements are followed by laughter. The laughter serves to signal that, however aggressive, the statements should not be taken seriously. Laughter informs the other party, "I just called you a name or said something derogatory about you or about your beliefs, but don't be offended. I'm not out to hurt you. No response on your part is required."

I witnessed a particularly crass demonstration of how laughter defuses aggression in the Subway sandwich shop at Hudson and Beach Sts. in Lower Manhattan. Visiting a Subway sandwich shop is one of life's most aversive situations. On a scale of vexation it is exceeded only by a visit to the Post Office. (Please don't laugh. This is not a joke.) I just want to order a sandwich. I do not want to be interrogated. The last thing I can do is make up my mind. How do I know what condiments

I want on my sandwich? How do I know what kind of bread I want? Or what kind of cheese? I hate being put on the spot.

Anyway, after waiting 45 minutes to order my five-dollar foot-long hero I was next in line. The counter girl was a young Latina woman on the height-deprived side. My guess is she was Puerto Rican. Probably, she was a senior in high school or a freshman in college. Maybe I'll see her in one of my psychology classes. She didn't look like she enjoyed the job. I can't say I blame her. The clerks in the Post Office ask only a question or two—"Are the contents of your parcel liquid, fragile, or perishable? And is there a bomb in the bubble envelope?" The counter girl in Subway has to ask a litany of questions as she laboriously builds sandwich-after-sandwich, cold-cut-by-cold cut, condiment-by condiment.

The customer ahead of me was a middle-aged African-American lady. She was professional in appearance, with a carefully combed coiffure, a white sweater and blouse, and a black skirt. Her high heels made her look taller than she was. She must have been watching her figure, which was a little on the chunky side. She ordered a foot-long vegetable hero.

"What kind of bread?" the counter girl asked.

"Oh, dear me," the customer responded, running her hand over the notice pasted on the inside of the display case. She had, let me see, 45 minutes to think about the kind of bread she wanted. "Herb and cheese," she decided after a few moments.

"Cheese?"

"Herb and cheese, I said." The customer chuckled.

"No, cheese in the sandwich?"

"Yes."

"What kind of cheese?" I thought I'd hear a laugh at the tail of the question, but the counter girl remained silent. She had been through the paces before.

"Swiss—wait, provolone. No, Swiss is fine."

"Lettuce?'

"Yes."

"Tomato?"

"Yes."

"Olives?"

"Are they whole or diced?"

"Diced."

"Olives are fine."

"Pickles?"

"Yes." I realized at this point that the entire ordering process could have been shortened if the word "everything" was spoken.

"Onions?"

"Just a little."

"Peppers?"

"They're not hot, are they?"

"Hot or sweet."

"I'll take sweet."

"Pepper?"

"I just said sweet."

"Pepper and salt?"

"Oh, yes."

"Oregano?"

"Yes."

"Oil and vinegar?"

"Extra oil and extra vinegar, if you don't mind."

Here comes the part about laughter—the counter girl took the oil cruet in one hand, the vinegar cruet in the other, turned them upside down, and vigorously shook them over the sandwich. The customer suddenly leaned forward and grabbed the rim of the display case. "Not that much!" she yelled. If the glass were a little lower, she was poised to leap over it.

The counter girl looked startled and then she made a face, an obviously angry face of drawn-in lips and lowered brow. The look was enough. She didn't need words to say, "You asked for *extra* oil and *extra* vinegar." She quickly returned the cruets to the counter. Mentally, she reached for a carving knife.

The customer immediately backed down and blathered something about not making the sandwich too wet as she had a long trip home and she didn't want the bread to get soaked. And then she started laughing. Chest laughter, loud and breathy laughter, serrated laughter filled with kinks in the frayed cords of breath. If I didn't know better, I'd have thought she just heard one of my jokes. "Yes, yes, we don't want too much now," she said in a conciliatory tone of voice that grew progressively softer as she spoke. "We have to go—go easy."

The counter girl was not amused. She hastily wrapped the sandwich and rang the sale. She didn't look at the customer as she returned the change. She was looking at the meat slicer instead. I hate to think what would have happened if the customer didn't laugh after yelling, "Not that much!" The counter girl was thin, probably not more than a hundred pounds when she was soggy, but she looked as if she had a temper and all the metal objects with sawed-off edges were on her side of the glass. I don't think it would have taken much provocation for the counter girl to go the Subway version of Postal.

My turn had come. I stepped to the counter and gulped. "Can I have a foot-long roast beef hero?" I had the type of bread prepared, "Italian." I added the word "Please" and then, to be on the safe side, I started laughing. I didn't stop laughing until I answered every question and told her to skip the oil and vinegar.

158. *The Andy Griffith Show* was one of the most beloved programs in television history. It ran for eight years on the CBS network and featured Andy Griffith as the wise and kindly sheriff of Mayberry, North Carolina. Sheriff Taylor handled local crime in a relaxed folksy manner. He intended law enforcement to be a learning experience for the culprits rather than a punishing experience. But "culprits" is too strong a word. "Well-meaning but misguided souls" is a better description. There was little crime to address in Mayberry. The Sheriff's workday mostly consisted of sitting in the stationhouse and reminiscing about past incidents in an edifying manner.

Sheriff Taylor was disably assisted by Barney Fife, a classic character in television history played by Don Knotts. High-strung and inept, Deputy Fife served as comic relief and as a foil for the earnest sheriff. Deputy Fife could always be counted on to make the wrong decisions and come to the wrong interpretations. Fortunately for the well-meaning and the misguided, he carried a single bullet that he was not allowed to place in the chamber unless Sheriff Taylor instructed him. This may have happened once or twice in the history of the show—there was little need for loaded firearms in Sheriff Taylor's jurisdiction.

Mayberry was a tranquil place, maybe the most tranquil place on television. They actually featured shows in which big-city slickers suffered anxiety attacks owing to the immobility of the townsfolk. There was Opie, Andy's son. He always strolled to the fishing hole after school. On the way he was distracted by wounded birds he brought home and mended till they could fly again—one of the birds might have been a *night hawk*. There was the fusspot Aunt Bee. She ran the house for the widowed sheriff. Helen Crump was Sheriff Taylor's lady-friend—love-interest is too strong a description. Helen was a dedicated schoolteacher who managed to teach the hopeless hillbilly Emmett T. Bass a few grade school lessons. Dim-bulbed Gomer ran the gas station until he joined the Marine Corps. His sharper cousin Goober took over the business when Gomer left town. Gomer and Goober patched tires and pumped gas once they roused themselves from loafing. Otis Campbell was the town drunk. Otis obligingly locked himself in the slammer to sleep a bender off. And, of course, Floyd was the barber. Floyd moved so slowly and talked so deliberately visitors mistook him for an inanimate object.

Mayberry is beautifully rustic and rural. It's inhabited by good people who care for one another. In the early years of the show Sheriff Taylor pronounced it, "Gu-uuoood people." But there's something missing in Mayberry. There's something wrong there. It becomes obvious once you notice the absence of dark complexions. There are no people of color in Mayberry. There are no Hispanics. There are no Mid-Easterners. No East Europeans. No people from the Black Sea region. No Asians. No Hawaiians. No Polynesians or Malaysians. No Eskimos. No Pygmies. There are no people in Mayberry except those whose ancestors sailed from Anglo-Saxon Europe.

The fact that there are only white people in Mayberry needs explanation. There are possibilities. Located in the mountains, Mayberry may be so far off the beaten path non-whites find it only by accident. There may be a sign at the entrance of town that reads, "White people only—expect to be charmed." *The Andy Griffith Show* aired after Jim Crow laws were stricken from the books, but the place was in the sticks and the star of the show was the sheriff, so there may have been suspicious goings on in the back woods. Non-white people who arrived by accident may have got railroaded out of town by the local chapter of the Klan. We hate to think of this possibility, but Mayberry was in the former Confederacy and, sad to relate, that sort of thing happened.

If there was a local chapter of the Klan, there had to be a Grand Wizard. This invites conjecture over the identity of the head man. We can rule Opie out. Aunt Bee would have to be in the ladies auxiliary. Deputy Fife was too nervous—he'd set his robes on fire instead of a cross. Gomer and Emmett T. Bass are too dimwitted and they leave a lot to be desired in the leadership department. Goober has managerial potential, but by the time he arrived on the scene all the non-whites were gone, so he couldn't be the one. Otis could set a cross on fire with his breath, but he was too wobbly to conduct business. This leaves two candidates. Sheriff Taylor has the gravitas and leadership skills, but it's disrespectful and even a little sacrilegious to think he wouldn't extend his wisdom and compassion to all peoples and races. By the process of elimination this leaves Floyd the barber. At first glance it's preposterous that Floyd the immobile and slow-speaking barber was the Grand Wizard of Mayberry or that he could conduct a Klonvocation. But on closer consideration it makes sense. It's the ones we least expect who turn out to be the criminal types. It's the soft-spoken quiet people we have to worry about. No one could be so hypnotically calm without concealing a sinister side. By day Floyd trimmed sideburns and mustaches; by night he peppered the humid air with gunshot in pursuit of ethnic cleansing. By day Floyd was a kindly barber who patted customers' shoulders and massaged their cramped neck muscles; by night he poured kerosene on crossbeams and chased non-whites into the trackless forest.

When Floyd put on the white barber smock he was the personification of Small Town America. When he put on the anonymity of the white sheets he became as ferocious and as furious as any Klansman.

159. A recent study asked a group of women to rate the manliness and, presumably, the attractiveness of the male voice. The participants in the research heard snippets of men clearly enunciating prose passages. These snippets were interspersed with snippets of the same voices mumbling passages. Overall, the women rated the mumbling voices as more masculine than the precisely enunciated voices.

Go —gure. Buff, clean-cut, and dry enunciation was heard as less attractive than flabby declarations slippery with drool. Mumbling must go with sweaty t-shirts, Brut aftershave, and ellipses filled with lust-choked thoughts.

The result of this study must be a fluke. It can't be correct. There must be something the matter with the procedure or with the sample. They mustn't have controlled for experimenter bias. The sample must have consisted of lumpish working women. If mumbling was the defining quality of mascu—nity, I'd be the head-of-household of a harem. The fact that I'm not the Sultan of Ocean County —dicates we need to take the —sults with cau—.

160. The result of the study mentioned in the previous entry suggests this advice—when in doubt, mumble. You can never go wrong mumbling, especially in mixed company.

161. I'll have to find an Australian and ask, "If you have to, can you back out of the Outback?"

162. It was the eve of the summer solstice. To be in fashion I put my wicker wear on—straw derby on top and moccasins on bottom—and went into the forest looking for a four-leaf clover. I read that if you find a four-leaf clover on this night you get dominion over the plant and animal world, not to mention the plant and animal world on the other side of the astral drapes. I rarely have dominion over any species on any plane. Usually I'm the butt of dominion of other species from mosquitoes on up the evolutionary scale. So it seemed like a good idea to stroll around the forest in search of magical power. Nothing ventured, nothing gained.

I walked for hours. Some of the time I reverted to the pongid status of my ancestors and walked bent in two with my knuckles scraping the grass. Some of the time I proceeded on my hands and knees. I burned out two flashlights. I pulled up an acre of sod—quite a number of earthworms saw the moonlight for the first time. I accidentally pulled up a patch of a rare plant that grows only in the Pine Barrens—I didn't see the warning sign "Don't uproot this plant!" until it was too late and the yellow petals of the Lace-lipped Ladies orchid (*Spiranthes laciniata*) lay crinkled in my palms. I wiped my fingerprints off the petals and tossed the stalks of the orchids behind a shrub where the forest rangers would never find them. Really, if they want the rare Pine Barrens plants to be preserved they ought to make taller signs that glow in the dark.

I crossed dry grassland and wet moor, piercing thorn briars and sandy plains leached of moisture by the pine sap. I was in the deep woods, but in places the soil was like beach sand. I didn't bother to go around them—that required too much labor—but proceeded directly over rocks deposited by some ancient fist of a glacier. By the end of the night I was exhausted. Every muscle in my body ached. Every bone hurt. It was back-braking labor and I'm not use to labor of any type. If I didn't think I'd get attacked by Mrs. Leeds' Devil or by a beer-guzzling variant of the Devil in overalls and a Philadelphia *Eagles* football jersey, I'd have laid on the sod and taken a nap before heading home.

At the last moment I saw a clover on the rolled-up patch below me. I looked closely. It had three leafs and a tiny stem or bud that didn't officially count as a leaf but was noticeable enough to count for something. I bent and plucked it, carefully peeling the roots out of the soil. I raised it toward the sliver of dawn that emerged in the East. Yes, it was a three-and-a-half leaf clover. An edge of the fourth leaf must have got torn off. Maybe an insect munched on it. Maybe there was a genetic defect that caused it to grow shrunken and misshapen—the same thing happens to human beings on occasion. Maybe it never opened up and never reached maturity—this happens to humans too. Regardless of what happened, it was the rudiment of a fourth leaf and that was all that mattered.

I don't know how much dominion three-and-a-half leafs give me, but I was definitely in the clover. A three-and-a-half leaf clover was better than no clover. It must give me dominion over something. Maybe it gives me dominion over three-and-a half plant and animal species. I hate to think that clover-picking was all-or-none and that the night could have been better spent tossing and turning under the covers.

163. *Blood Diamond* was an acclaimed 2006 movie directed by Edward Zwick and starring Leonardo DiCaprio as a Rhodesian mercenary and diamond smuggler. The movie is set during the ferocious Sierra Leone Civil War that lasted from 1991 – 2002.

The conflict involved the attempt of the Revolutionary United Front (RUF) to topple the Sierra Leone government. The RUF was aided by forces belonging to Iberia and by arms supplied by the late dictator Moammar Gadhafi. The government countered with a private South African army. The course of the war led to two coup d'etats against what was left of the government. The second coup—a re-coup d'etat—involved an alliance between the RUF and renegade Sierra Leone military officers. After a decade of bloodshed the United Nations intervened to defeat the RUF and restore order.

The war was financed by the diamond trade, hence the title "blood diamond". The conflict was horrendously brutal. More than 50,000 civilians were killed. Atrocities were commonplace, including rape, mutilation, and the massacre of unarmed villagers.

The movie is spectacular, with brilliantly photographed crowd and battle scenes. The movie spares no element of the conflict. The scenes are brutal and realistic. There's no attempt to stylize or prettify the violence. At the outset of the movie a unit of the RUF rides into a village and massacres the people with machine guns and machetes. The old men who survive are lined up and their hands are systematically chopped off. The logic of this is to prevent anyone from raising a hand in defense of the government. Young men in good condition are transported to work camps where they stand in streams and fish for diamonds. Anyone caught stealing is shot on the spot. In what may be the movie's most horrific scene a ten-year-old villager is taught to kill. He machine guns a man to death. Later, the boy is shown firing a gun in combat.

The camera never blinks. I did. I stopped the DVD after a half hour. The carnage was unwatchable. For one half hour there was no end to the violence. I guessed there would be no end to the violence in the next hour and a half. Filmed in gore-geous color, the incessant violence made me wonder—these events happened, but why would anyone make a movie showing them? And why would anyone watch the brutality? Nothing can be learned. Nothing edifying can be concluded. The movie has nothing to do with conscience. We already know the horrible things that people do to one another. We don't need to see the blood splash walls and limbs get chopped off to know what people are capable of.

Why would anyone spend tens of millions of dollars to make a movie that amounts to watching people get killed? It's obvious. People make this kind of movie for the same reasons diamonds were bought and sold and smuggled in and out of Sierra Leone—to make hundreds of millions of dollars in profits. Why would anyone watch a movie like *Blood Diamond*? There's no financial gain—I was out the six dollars the DVD cost. There's no political gain. The political dimensions of the conflict are complex, involving a number of changeable factions. Viewers have to summon Google to decipher all the players. There's no psychological gain. Nothing new is learned about human nature—the movie confirms our worst suspicions. There's no spiritual gain. We're not cleansed or pacified for watching the movie, a half hour of it, anyway. We're not inspired to become more kind or more compassionate. We're not made into better people for having watched the movie. If anything, we are worse off. We've taken another half step into savagery. We watch this kind of movie for a transparent motive—it satisfies our bloodthirsty cravings and fulfills the monstrous nature of our species. I can't think of any other reason why we would sit and calmly watch our fellow beings get shot and stabbed and hacked to death.

The fact that *Blood Diamond* is all fakery and special effects doesn't excuse anyone. They're just actors, we tell ourselves. No one actually got killed. They just represent people who got killed in the real conflict. I can imagine writers in their conferences competing among themselves to come up with ways to enhance the blood splatter. "Let's show the guy's head get blown off." And I can imagine the excitement and visceral delight of the audience. "Did you see it? The guy's head got blown off!"

In *Frankenstein*, released in 1931, the Universal studio could not show the Monster unintentionally killing a child and throwing her into a lake. It barely got away with showing the girl's body floating. *Blood Diamond* shows how far we have degenerated. The makers of *Blood Diamond* showed a ten-year-old machine gunning an adult hauled into view to serve as a target. We don't know who the stranger is or what he did to deserve execution and it doesn't much matter. The camera doesn't bat an eye when the blood splatters the walls and the stranger tumbles into death. Nor does the audience.

164. This is a sermon I heard Pastor Chad D. Strong preach in the Second Reformed Authentic Church on Route Nine in Little Egg Harbor. The church advertises that they preach only Jesus and "Heem crucified" and I believe they do.

"Brothers and sisters, open your Bibles to Genesis 18. This chapter tells the familiar story of God destroying those citadels of sin, Sodom and Gomorrah. The chapter commences with Abraham lounging outside his tent 'in the heat of the day' (v.1). It must have been a summer day like unto our own in Little Egg Harbor. Brothers and sisters, you know how warm and muggy these kinds of days get. Let's hope the humidity wasn't as bad in Mamre as it is in Little Egg Harbor.

"Suddenly 'The Lord appeared' to Abraham and 'three men stood over him' (v.1-2). The three are soon identified as angels. Immediately Abraham extends hospitality to his guests, offering them water and bread and then a meal of butter and milk and a 'calf tender and good' (v. 7). The strangers inquire where Sarah, Abraham's wife, is. Abraham informs them that she is in the tent. They go on to say that Sarah will have a son.

"When she hears this Sarah laughs—she must have been eavesdropping on what the men were talking about. She and Abraham were 'well stricken with age' (v. 11) and Sarah was past the time when a woman can conceive and bring forth issue. The Lord hears her laugh and chastises her in verse 14—'Is anything too hard for the Lord?' he asks. Brethren, that is not a rhetorical question.

"After dinner the three men proceed toward Sodom. Abraham accompanies them a part of the way. In verse 20 God says, 'The cry of Sodom and Gomorrah is great' and 'Their sin is very grievous.' Abraham knows what their fate will be and he dares to act. Brethren, here's what I'm coming to. In verses 22-23 Abraham boldly asks whether God will 'consume the righteous with the wicked' and whether God will spare the cities if 'fifty righteous be found there.' God replies in verse 26 that he will spare the cities if fifty righteous can be found.

"In many sermons emphasis is placed on Abraham's exceeding boldness—he is a mortal daring to ask Almighty God for a favor. I would like to stress a slightly different theme—it is the same theme found in the gift of a son to an elderly couple. God answers Abraham's appeal in a way that signifies *ask for more*. We don't know how God communicated this to Abraham. Maybe it was in his tone of voice or in a look. Maybe it was an empathic feeling or a subtle expression compatible with the moment. However God communicated it, the message was clear. *Abraham, you don't have to stop. You can ask for more*. Of course, it had to be God who made this initiative. A man cannot dare to pester God and Abraham must have known he asked for something that was impossible.

"In verse 28 Abraham ambitiously asks if God will spare the cities if forty five righteous people be found inside the walls of Sodom and Gomorrah. God immediately agrees. And Abraham asks for more. In verse 29 he asks if God will spare the cities if forty righteous people be found. God agrees. Abraham immediately asks for more. In verse 30 he asks if God will spare the cities if thirty righteous people be found. At this point Abraham must have realized he was asking for a lot, as he begs the Lord not to be angry at him.

"The Lord isn't angry. He wants Abraham to ask for more. In verse 31 Abraham asks if God will spare the cities if twenty righteous people be found there. The Lord still isn't mad. 'I will not destroy it for the twenty's sake,' he answers and Abraham asks for more. In verse 32 Abraham asks if God will spare the cities if ten righteous people can be found. And God agrees—he will spare the cities if ten righteous people can be found inside the walls. I believe that God would have agreed to spare the cities if one righteous person could be found, but Abraham stops at ten. Probably he realized ten was the best deal he could get.

"As it does for the wicked, the story of Sodom and Gomorrah ends badly. We find terror and consternation in the judgment God renders on those places and we are right to worry about our own city and state. Brothers and sisters, we may not be very much better than the people of Sodom and Gomorrah and we may be a great deal worse. That's for God to decide. But the message I read in Genesis 18 is one of mercy and divine munificence. God works miracles in our lives, as he did in Sarah's life. And God invites us to ask for more in our prayers and in our yearning. Abraham must have been terrified asking God for more, but in every case—in *every* case, brethren—God agreed. He spared the cities for the sake of fifty and then for forty five and then for forty and then for thirty and then for twenty and then for ten righteous people.

"Genesis 18 shows God's intentions towards us. He is ready to answer our wishes if we ask, like Abraham did, in righteous regard for the lives and souls of our brethren. He is ready to answer our appeals even if they are, like Abraham's, impossible. If we ask God for small and insignificant things, that's what we will receive. If we ask God for great and significant things that's what God will grant to us. Abraham knew God's generosity and he systematically went from fifty to ten righteous people. He knew what he was asking. He knew the unlikelihood that his appeals would lead to success. But he asked and in every case the Lord agreed. In every case the Lord indicated that Abraham should ask for more. I believe Genesis 18 elucidates the mysterious saying of Jesus in Luke 8:11, 'For to him who has shall be given and from him who does not have, even the little he has will be taken.' If we challenge God and ask for great things, God will give us what we ask and more. But if we ask God for small things, the pittance that we have will be taken and we will be left with nothing.

"The final chapters of the Book of Job remind us of the might and majesty of Almighty God. 'Where were you when I created the earth (38:4)?' Indeed, where were we? The glory and the greatness of the Lord frighten us. How dare we ask the Creator of the universe for anything? How dare we ask for more? Brothers and sisters, do not be intimidated. Our Creator is not stingy. There is no smallness in our God. The power and wonder of the universe are not incompatible with our prayer requests. Indeed, the gifts given in answers to our appeals lie in the power and the wonder of the universe. Do not hesitate, brethren. Ask God, ask God for more. In not a single case did the Lord turn Abraham down. If we live righteously, I have every confidence that the Lord will not turn us down.

"Brethren, please open up your hymnal to page 164. Let us glorify God with the precious words of *Amazing Grace*."

165. In the first *Star Wars* movie—this was the fourth in the series, but the first released—the illustrious Knight Jedi, Obi-wan Kenobi uses the Force to avoid paying a toll. He waves his hand as he rides by and the toll taker is convinced the fare was paid. The scene is amusing, but if you ask me it is a rather petty demonstration of the Force. It makes me wonder whether Obi-wan used the power of the Force to defraud lowly servers of their tips and vending machines of their coinage.

What worked for Obi-wan may work for me. It was worth a try.

I stopped in the New Delhi Deli on my way home to buy my usual bingo cards issued as scratch offs by the state. Hashan is the proprietor of the inconvenience store and the sole employee. (He used to be named "Saddam", but changed his name when things went bad for the Baghdad strong man.) I ordered four $2.00 bingo games. Unless they changed the math, this was $8.00. Hashan peeled the cards from the roll and handed them to me. I handed him $4.00. "The Force, the Force," I started to think with the most intense concentration. "I gave you $8.00, the Force, the Force." I held the games in my left hand and made circular waving motions over the counter with my right hand.

Hashan counted the bills with George Washington face up and then to be sure he was short-changed he counted the bills a second time with George Washington face down.

"Four tickets, $8.00," Hashan insisted.

"The Force, the Force, I gave you $8.00." I thought so strenuously my mind compressed into a psychical frown.

"Four tickets, $8.00," Hashan repeated.

"No, Hashan, I gave you $8.00, the Force, the Force." The idea crossed my mind, but I rejected the thought that Hashan should give me change of $20.00.

"You give me $4.00," Hashan said, glancing at the display case. The case was stocked with buckets of salads, balls of cheeses, and bats of cold cuts. Black flies rounded the bases in haphazard fashion.

"The Force, the Force." I switched waving motions from the horizontal to the vertical dimension. I looked like the Pope blessing the faithful from the balcony in the Vatican.

Hashan didn't know what to do—until that moment I was a reliable customer. Making the universal sign for *dinero*, he rubbed his thumb and index finger over the counter. He flapped the four bills in front of me. He didn't scare me. He did, however, scatter the flies that hovered over the pastry trays.

"The Force, Hashan, the Force."

Hashan looked dazed. He stared at the door and then at the frozen food case. He clicked his lips and started to work his mouth in soundless desperation.

"$8.00, Hashan, I gave you $8.00. The Force, the Force, the Force—."

"Four dollar more!" Hashan cried, regaining the power of audible speech. He lunged over the counter and grabbed the bingo games out of my hand. He tossed the four bills at me and fell back, knocking over the circular container that held strips of beef jerky.

The Force—so much for that idea.

166. The Distribution Center published its dress code. Item fourteen advises that *doo rags* are forbidden on company property. What's a *doo rag* and did I ever wear one?

And *doo rag*? Isn't that the same as toilet paper?

167. I think I got off a pretty good line in learning theories class, but first I have a little explaining to do. I have to set up the context in order for you to appreciate the line.

Donald Hebb, a prominent learning psychologist of the mid-twentieth century, had an interesting view of the origin of fear. This view arose out of his physiological orientation. Hebb believed that learning theories had to be based on neuroscience. This view was not shared by all learning theorists. B.F. Skinner, for a prominent one, believed that it was possible to develop a theory of learning without any physiological concepts.

That aside, Hebb suggested that with practice and experience new pathways are established in the brain and new connections are formed among neurons. With repetition circuits develop in the brain that become active in unison, such that when one neuron in the circuit *fires* all neurons in the circuit fire. He called simple neural connections *cell assemblies*. Complex collections of cell assemblies were called *phase sequences*. A simple example of a cell assembly is "lightning—thunder". A phase sequence involves "lightning—thunder—raincoat—umbrella—shelter." Another example of a cell assembly is "turn on faucet—water follows". A phase sequence is "turn on faucet—water follows—soap—shaving cream—razor blade—bandages." This view of learning and of neuronal activity is pretty much taken for granted today, and it is pretty much correct, but when Hebb postulated it in the 1940s it was quite novel within psychology, which plodded on at that time with minimal regard for the brain's involvement with behavior.

Hebb believed that expectation and foresight derived from the cell assembly—phase sequence model. When I see lightning I expect thunder to follow. When I turn on the faucet I expect water to flow.

These events are linked or associated in reality. They are also linked cognitively. When we think about lightning thunder always rumbles in our thoughts. And the water always flows in our imagination when we turn the faucet on in our minds.

When lightning occurs without thunder or a faucet turns on and no water flows, we experience *surprise*. Hebb used the stronger word *fear*. Hebb conjectured that we do not experience fear (or surprise) when we come across something *completely familiar*, because the event corresponds with the phase sequences. We are not the least bit surprised when thunder follows lightning or when water pours from the faucet. We expect such events to follow. There is no clash between reality and the phase sequence. Hebb further conjectured that we do not experience fear (or surprise) when we come on something *completely unfamiliar*. No phase sequences have been built in the nervous system. There is nothing to expect and there is no clash between reality and a phase sequence—we don't have one.

Hebb suggested that we feel fear (or surprise) when a *familiar object or event is experienced in an unfamiliar way*. We have phase sequences that have been established based on our experiences. But something other than thunder follows lightning and something other than water flows from the faucet. Real events do not correspond with our expectations. Something else occurs, something different than what we expect. Lightning is flashing and thunder is sounding in our minds. Neurons are firing, but they're not running for cover. We turn on a faucet and water starts to pour in our minds. Neurons are firing, but they're not getting wet. There is a clash between the event, which doesn't happen or happens in a different way than we expect, and our phase sequences. Reality does not match our expectations.

This brings me to the line. After the lecture I have students break up into small groups in which they talk among themselves. Their assignment is to come up with original examples of fear based on Hebb's conjecture about the clash of events and expectations. Here's the example one group came up with.

"Two sisters live together," Eileen, the group's spokesperson, told the class. "There's a long foyer in their apartment. The kitchen is at the end of the foyer. One sister has the habit of sitting in the kitchen doing her psychology homework. Her loads of psychology homework."

"Can't be from this class," I commented.

"The sister is sitting there," Eileen continued, "and hears footsteps in the foyer. She's built a phase sequence where the footsteps get closer and her sister eventually appears in the doorway. But this time her sister doesn't appear as expected. Instead her sister's fiancé appears. That's when she experiences fear."

"What's so frightening about her sister's fiancé?" I asked naively. I didn't think it was a joke, but it must have sounded like one, since the class laughed.

Eileen bent over the desk and thought for a few moments. "I don't know," she said, but she didn't give up thinking. She sat up suddenly. "Her sister's fiancé is naked. That's why she's frightened."

"And the wedding is off and she proposes to her sister's fiancé," I said to everyone's amusement. The line was so good I would have earned a round of applause except that the students—the ones who wanted A's—were too busy holding their sides as they convulsed in laughter.

I must admit this was a lot of buildup for one clever line. And the buildup was quite esoteric, involving a difficult theory of learning. But that's how we are in psychology. Our clever lines are decidedly humorous and pointedly heady.

168. This afternoon four people told me to "Have a good one." A cashier at the pharmacy. A stock boy in the frozen foods aisle of the supermarket. A teller at the bank. A gas jockey at the pump. They all the said the same thing when we parted and told me to "Have a good one." This got me thinking. What exactly was the "good one" they wished on me?

Presumably it was a day, as in "Have a good day." But it could have been a good night. For that matter it could have been an extended interval of time, like a month or a year. If they never saw me again, it could have been "Have a good forever."

Maybe the "good one" was an object, like a shiny new car or a high-definition television set or a lottery ticket with six winning numbers. Or the "good one" may have been a good meal or a good dessert or a good after-dinner cocktail. Or the "good one" may have referred to an emotional state, like "Have a good laugh" or "Have a good cry."

I appreciate their intentions, but if they don't tell me, how I am supposed to know what the "good one" is when I encounter it? I may not recognize it when I come across it. And how am I supposed to know they're wishing me the same "good one"? For all I know they may be wishing four different "good ones" on me.

169. Manhattan Community College has sixty five clubs on campus. One of them is named the *Beauty Club*. The objective of the club, as advertised on the flyer, is "to empower women in the 21st century." The advertisement features images of women who are as thin as pencils and presumably as beautiful as movie stars. The message is unspoken, but loud and clear. Chunky women in the shape of appearance-challenged magic markers need not apply.

Inspired by the *Beauty Club* I'm going to found a *Handsome Club* on campus. Modesty forbids me from mentioning the name of the first president.

170. San Antonio remains the friendliest city in the United States. I found out on a recent trip just how dangerous friendly can get.

I had just paid my respects to the John F. Kennedy Memorial, which is something I religiously do on every visit. I was driving on the beam bridge across the San Antonio River when my rental went the way of the fallen president. The radio was the first to go—the country singer was silenced in mid-wail. The headlights flickered and went out. The air conditioning swished off. The electrical system was last to go. It stopped as if an extension cord had been ripped from the exhaust pipe. I had all to do maneuvering the car to the shoulder of the road. It took all my strength to turn the steering wheel. Fortunately, traffic was light or I might have gone the way of the car.

I got out, popped the hood open, and stepped to the passenger side. I reached inside, opened the glove compartment, and pulled out the always reliable cell phone. I started to dial for road service and the light on the screen flickered and went blank. I took a few steps to the east. The screen stayed blank. I took a few steps to the west. Still blank. I hustled across the street. Nothing. I returned to the side of the car. There was no dial tone. This is nice, I thought. I have to go to the motel, pick up my bags, and get to the airport for a night flight to New Jersey, and I break down on the only stretch of wireless dead zone in the state of Texas. I assumed that least enviable occupation—I became a stranded motorist.

At least it was a picturesque place to break down. I walked to the railing and peeked over. The river was about thirty feet below. The surface was a peculiar green gray color that jealously reflected neither sky nor riverbank. The current was barely existent—the river looked like a serpent that was in no hurry to arrive in the tangled woods that grew on the banks to the water's edge. The gable of a single great house was concealed in the woods to the left. To the right I traced the upper floors of a block of townhouses. The vegetation was so thick, I couldn't see below the tree line.

Somewhere in the woods to the south was a pet cemetery. There was also a people cemetery in the vicinity. I became uneasy and stepped back from the railing. I noted the guardrail wasn't very high—it was lower than my waist. I wasn't in New Jersey where the government keeps its citizens from toppling over railings and into riverbeds, where we take the first few snores in the *Big Sleep*. I was in the great state of Texas. The government in Texas doesn't put guardrails on bridges that are taller than a man's height and impossible to climb over like the government in New Jersey does. In Texas every man is on his own and at risk of tumbling over a low railing if he isn't careful.

I remembered—true enough, I was in Texas, but I was also in San Antonio, where no man is without a friend. I was a motorist, but I wouldn't be stranded for long. I stepped to the trunk of the car and leaned against the taillight. I was confident someone would stop and help. I waited fifteen seconds when a white pickup truck coated in the yellow sheath of Texas soil pulled up. When the driver cut the engine, the decibel level dropped by eighty ear-blistering points.

A huge man, well over six feet and two hundred pounds, dropped out of the truck. He was what I expected of the driver of a pickup in the state of Texas. He wore overalls over a red flannel shirt. His hair was thick and wavy and he had a scratchy furze that covered his face like the soil did his truck. His eyes were barely visible in the cellulite pads of swollen cheeks. He belonged to that category of person called "Tiny"—it was an appellation no one other than track stars ever said in his hearing.

"Howdy," he said. It came out "Hardee."

I started to say "Hardee", but corrected myself and said "Howdy" instead. The last thing I wanted was to imitate a Texan drawl while in Texas.

"What's the problem, friend?"

It seemed obvious, but I told him anyway. "My car died. So did my cell phone."

"We'll fix that," he said. He walked back to his truck and retrieved a cell phone from the cabin. He dialed as he returned to my side. He waited a few seconds and then jiggled the phone. He held it upside down and then right side up. "Dern these dang-blasted gadgets. They never work when they're supposed to." He hurled the phone over the river and into the next county. I watched till the speck in my eye surpassed the mote of my vision. If Tiny started for the Texas *Rangers*, he was in deepest centerfield and had just pegged a runner out at home plate.

"Let's have a look-see." He walked to the front of the rental and bent over the engine.

As he did another car pulled up behind his pickup. It was a spotless white sedan that looked as if it just sailed through a car wash. A middle-aged gent in a bright blue suit and frilly white shirt that puffed out in front emerged from the car. I should say his shiny leather boots emerged first. The rest of him followed. When he was erect he removed a handkerchief from a jacket pocket and wiped his bald head. He bent, reached in the car, and pulled out a beige cowboy hat. The hat was so large it wasn't a ten-gallon hat, it was a twenty-gallon hat. He revolved the hat for a few seconds and placed it on his head with a downward tug of the arms. Immediately a shadow fell across his face.

"Howdy," he said, strolling over. It sounded like "Hardee." "What seems to be the trouble?"

"Well, my car died. I don't know what happened. It just went dead—I was lucky to make it to the shoulder of the road."

He walked to the engine. Tiny moved over a half step. "A car going suddenly usually means the alternator."

"Battery," Tiny said.

"Alternators can go like a snap of the finger." He raised his hand and snapped his finger. The snap sounded unusually loud. I think it came with an echo. "Alternators don't give any warnings."

"Battery," Tiny repeated.

A red sports car pulled up while the two men assessed what went wrong with the rental. A young couple got out. They looked like Lone Star versions of Manhattan metrosexuals. They wore color-coordinated white blouses and trousers. The man wore loafers without socks. The woman wore flip flops. They were on the slim side and in obviously superior shape. They were both highly tanned and had black hair. His hair was thick and shoulder long. Her hair was cut short not far off the scalp. He wore tiny reflective sunglasses that barely covered his eyes. She wore large pink-framed sunglasses that covered the upper half of her face.

"Hardee," I said. They didn't seem to mind the accent.

"Car trouble?" he asked tossing his hair back.

"It died just as I got on the bridge. I barely made it to the shoulder."

"Lucky for you," the woman said, walking to the side of the engine. The cowboy tipped his hat. Her partner stood by her side and looked at his image in the window on the driver's side. She must have been the mechanic in their relationship.

"When cars go without warning, it usually means computer trouble," she said.

"Battery," Tiny said.

"Alternator," the cowboy corrected.

In no time a row of parked cars stretched off the bridge into the woodsy distance. A stream of people, all intending to be helpful, hurried to look under the hood. Pedestrians started to arrive. Like the drivers, they offered suggestions why my rental gave up the ghost. One pedestrian was a jogger in blue spandex—he looked like a deep sea diver more than a jogger. Another pedestrian walked a horse-sized Doberman Pincher on a long leash. Another was an elderly man with American flags pinned in each lapel of a shabby suit. A blue naval cap with gold lettering sat crookedly atop what was left of his hair. At one time the cap revealed the name of the ship the man served on. So many threads had come unraveled in the interim it was impossible to tell other than he was a "Vet—ran" of the *U.S.S. Something or other.*

Two elderly ladies approached. One wore a cucumber-colored blouse and white pants. The other wore a blue blouse with lime-colored pants. Both ladies carried black purses the size of shopping bags. Both wore white tennis shoes. Their hair was a color somewhere between gray and blue.

"We don't know anything about cars, but we'd like to help," the lady with the blue blouse said. The other lady smiled in kindly fashion.

A crowd had formed around the rental. I was technically responsible for the car, but I was shoved to the side and I could no longer see the red exterior. Each person in front of me excitedly pointed at the engine and stated what the problem was. I thought it strange that everyone attempted to offer mechanical advice, but no two people agreed. I thought everyone in Texas fixed cars as a hobby.

"I'll get a battery," Tiny said. "That'll solve the problem."

"Where are you going to get a battery?" the cowboy asked.

"Why bother with a battery?" The young woman in white asked. "It's a computer problem."

"Alternator," the cowboy corrected. He tipped his hat again. "With all due respect, Ma'am."

"I'll give him the battery out of my engine." Tiny pushed his way to his pickup and got a screwdriver out of the toolbox on the flatbed. Then he walked to the front and opened the hood—it made an ugly cracking sound as it rose a story in the air. He started to unscrew the battery.

"Why give him a used battery?" the cowboy asked. "I'll buy him a new battery."

"I know just the place," the jogger said, going from zero to fifteen miles an hour in a few steps. "I'll be back with—." He ran so fast we couldn't hear what he was coming back with, but the chances were good it was going to be a battery.

"Never mind the battery," someone in the crowd yelled, "I'll get him a loaner rental."

"Rental, nothing," a woman yelled. "He can have my car."

"That piece of junk," another person yelled. "I'll buy him a car."

"Dear me," the lady with the cucumber-colored blouse commented, "someone should take the nice young man to dinner for the inconvenience of breaking down."

"Helen," the other lady asked, "where are your manners? The nice young man can come home with us. We can cook him one of our famous steak and potatoes dinner." As she spoke she looked at me and smiled cozily. "He can have apple pie for dessert."

At this point I thought I had better retreat. I had learned on my previous visit where the famed San Antonio friendliness can lead. I had no intention going to dinner with the kindly old ladies—they would soon start brawling over which house I visited. And I had no intention taking a swan dive into a river, even if I were propelled into orbit by a friendly person committing a friendly deed. I started to slip away and hike off the bridge.

It wasn't a moment too soon. Those kind-hearted and well-meaning folk started to jostle and to push one another. I heard barking and growling and cursing and the shouting of the names of auto parts. "Battery!" "Alternator!" "Computer!" Hearing that commotion I started to worry about body parts—my own.

Tiny gently placed the battery he unscrewed from his engine on the pavement and barreled a passage into the crowd. He flipped the cowboy's hat off and then flipped the cowboy up and over the railing. I heard a scream and, a full five seconds later, a splash. Tiny was working himself up into a state that can be described as "berserk", but he wasn't long for the bridge. The metrosexual male slipped behind him and crouched on all fours. His girlfriend charged Tiny and sent him over the railing with a perfectly pointed savate kick to the jaw. She was obviously the warrior in their relationship. The elderly gentleman with the indecipherable naval cap held a handgun at the ready and, cursing like a sailor on shore leave, challenged anyone to make a move on him. The man with the Doberman Pincher strained to keep the dog on the leash—it took so much strength to hold the dog in check, he stood at the oblique. The two elderly ladies opened their purses and removed tubes of pepper spray from inside. They aimed the tubes in the faces of anyone within walking distance.

I reached the end of the row of parked cars. I had no intention of going back. It was suicide to return. The rental company can pick the car up later—if it isn't tossed into the river. The scene on the bridge looked like the pandemonium that breaks out in the final reels of silent film comedies. Everyone was chaotically lunging and grabbing one another. There was little coherence to the mayhem. Occasionally, the crowd surged in the same direction, creating a human wave one way and then another. Mostly, they went in every direction with pockets of violence breaking out at different points of the compass. A red rectangular object went flying over the edge of the bridge. I took that for the hood of the engine. A second red rectangular object bounced across the double yellow and skipped onto the west-bound lanes. I took that for the hood of the trunk. People on the verge of the crowd rubbed their eyes vigorously. They stood stooped over the pavement and looked to be crying. Deeper in the crowd people got knocked over the edge of the bridge and into the river. A few people climbed the railing and threw themselves off the bridge under their own volition—I suppose they intended to save a step and avoid the knocking part of departure. A lithesome woman in white acrobatically leaped through the crowd. She spent more time off than on the pavement. The footsteps she took were on the jaws of defenseless people. The elderly veteran twirled his cap in one hand and, making high-pitched whooping sounds, shot at cumulus clouds with the pistol he held in the other hand. Other armed people unlimbered their weapons and commenced to pollute the air with lead. If they weren't preoccupied with being so friendly, they could have organized themselves for a run at Santa Anna and the Alamo.

I walked to the curb. I wet my thumb and unrolled my pants to the knees to show some beefcake—they like beefcake in The Lone Star state. I must have waited all of thirty seconds for a hitch. The first car that passed stopped. I entered a spacious SUV with three aisles of seats, adjustable air conditioning over every seat and drop down screens for viewing DVDs. A cheery thirty-something couple in bright apparel sat in the front bucket seats. They were on the way to pick up their son Rusty at elementary school. When they heard what happened and how I had no car to get to the airport, they insisted on driving me—all the way to New Jersey. I tried to talk them out of it, but they wouldn't hear a word to the contrary. They said that no visitor to San Antonio was going to suffer the insult of missing the return flight home. And they had heard about the indignities visited on people who travel on planes. No way a visitor to their lovely city was going to stand in front of a screen that shows him in boxer shorts for all the security agents to see. Besides, it was the friendly thing to do to drive a stranger home.

I argued, but it was to no avail. Once they got Rusty, we would set out. We wouldn't stop until we reached my doorstep. It was no great bother my doorstep was 1,739 miles away. Distance counts for nothing among friends. And, no, it wasn't an inconvenience to stop at the motel so I could my pick up my bags.

171. This was overheard on the ferry to the Great Beyond. "The next time I use a wood chipper I'm going to read the directions."

172. I attended college in the early 1970s, which were the cusp years between profound intellectual changes in orientation. Previous to that time an environmental paradigm predominated in society. The previous decades had seen a progressive agenda focused on education and on social progress. This agenda matched the orientation in the social sciences. Indeed, the social sciences provided the intellectual skeleton for the political meat. In psychology the psychodynamic orientation stepped out of the consulting rooms and advanced into the public domain. It was the heyday of family dynamics and group therapy. The Palo Alto group conjectured that mental disorder lay in conflicted messages between verbal and nonverbal communication—this took clinical psychology into the experimental chambers. In the field of learning operant conditioning dominated. Behavior modification and behavior therapy were the fast tracks to mental health. B.F. Skinner became a household name. People took Skinner's utopian schemes seriously. Behavior analysts were going to advise presidents. Better yet, behavior analysts were going to become presidents and rule the nation—I was promised Rhode Island for a fiefdom. Alas, that part of the plan never came to fruition.

By the century's end everything had changed. Social programs were turned into carcasses. The psychodynamic approach was viewed as a futile practice engaged in by dilettantes with East European accents. Family therapy and group dynamics were considered palliative and not curative. The study of nonverbal communication could improve one's social standing, but it couldn't make a person mentally ordered. Even operant conditioning, which once strove to rule the world, was seen as a small and insignificant twig on the tree of knowledge. Genetic explanations came to dominate. Previously, criminals and mental patients and geniuses were seen as the products of socioeconomic class struggles and of schizogenic mothers and of elite training programs.

Criminals and mental patients and geniuses were now seen as the products of genomic processes beyond anyone's control.

David Shenk's new book, *The Genius in All of Us* (Doubleday, 2011) challenges this genetic determinism in a number of ways. Shenk points out that the relation between genetics and personality is bidirectional. Genes turn on proteins. Experiences turn on genes—they also turn off genes. The older view was that experiences influenced the finished products of bodies and brains built by genes. The new view Shenk develops is that experiences affect genes before—and as—they build bodies and brains. In the new, and not widely known, view the relationship between nature and nurture mimics the dynamic and ever-altering brain "plasticity" that baffled Edwin in entry # 18. Genes—and what they do—can be altered by experience.

The thrust of Shenk's attack—of his attempt to correct the current tilt in favor of genetic determinism—is on the "fallacy of giftedness" (p. 94). As with criminality and with psychological disorder, the general view held by civilians and many scientists is that people—geniuses—create works of art because of some inborn talent or gift. These gifts are special and unique to the creator. These gifts are beyond the capabilities of the "average person". In some as yet unknown way these gifts relate to the structure of the genius's brain and to his or her genome.

Shenk's theme is that genius is not only the *cause* of creative works, it is also the *result* of something. That something is not a mysterious essence strung together by genetic glue. That something is *incredibly hard work*. Shenk points to people like Mozart and Ted Williams, both of whom were considered as "naturals" and as geniuses in their respective fields. In fact, both worked incessantly at their crafts and were immersed from a young age in the skills it took to write a symphony and to hit a baseball. Virtually every day of their lives they practiced some element of their craft.

Shenk's presentation is an example of B.F. Skinner's concept of the "incomplete causal analysis." In this analysis creative works of art are construed as dependent variables (effects). They are usually traced back to an internal or intervening variable called "talent" or "gift". In today's paradigm this intervening variable is held to be genetic. The assumption is that the analysis—or explanation—is now complete. We can stop explaining things once we climb the helical stairway. Like

Skinner, Shenk suggests we need to extend the analysis an additional step to the true independent variables (causes). As with the intervening variable, with which it is confused, these independent variables are held to be genetic. We are still busily climbing one gooey strand at a time. Shenk suggests, to the contrary, that the true independent variables are experiential and the result of incredibly hard and repetitive work. He optimistically suggests that they are acquirable by everyone willing to make the effort.

Shenk offers a number of practices that lead to the development of talents and gifts and to creative productions. He notes that people called "talented" and "gifted" work at their craft every day. They exhibit an intense repetition of skills and a passionate persistence in pursuing these skills. Their craft becomes a preoccupation. He notes that, as part of the repetition and persistence component, talented people constantly revisit and revise their works of art.

Shenk includes a few additional factors besides the sheer work factor. People called "talented" receive support and encouragement from their family, peers, and teachers. They are fortunate to have a life style, or to be allowed to have a life style, that allows for this strenuous repetition. They have the time to practice their skills and they allocate whatever time they have to the performance of the skills that go into creativity. They manage time better than their peers. While they ride a bus or wait in an airport or work out on a tread master, they are preoccupied with their projects to the exclusion of anything else.

Shenk's book is an important corrective to the "genomization" of our personalities and accomplishments. And it is a cautionary tale warning against the current craze of multi-tasking. Trying to do and to be everything results in hyperactivity and in divided attention. Rushing dizzily from task to task results in nothing getting done and to a glum state where we are gifted only in haste and in disorder. Shenk suggests we can become productive if we work hard and repetitively at the skills needed to create works of art and science and if we allocate time in ways that deviate from frivolity and from frenzy. Shenk offers the helpful and hopeful message that there is a genius in all of us—in most of us, anyway.

173.   There's a Lithuanian folktale in which a jealous mother-in-lore magically turns her daughter-in-lore into a tree. She then induces her son to chop the tree down for firewood. The tree bleeds human blood when he strikes it. Until recently the notion that people could turn into trees was far-fetched and in the realm of folktales. But this has changed, like so many other things in the modern age. A British firm called Biopresence announced plans to graft strands of human DNA into apple trees. The DNA would be inserted into an apple stem cell that would be nurtured into a tree. The DNA would be in every cell of the adult tree. The process would take several months and cost hundreds of pounds sterling. The plan has not been approved by British authorities, who want guarantees that only "junk" DNA will be used rather than the biologically active portions of DNA that turn proteins into bodies and brains. The last thing British authorities want is for trees to grow limbs in place of branches or to have recognizable faces on the fruit.

The original idea was for trees to replace marble headstones. The body would be interred at the foot of the tree, which would serve as a living memorial rather than the usual cold stone chiseled with names and dates. This is a version of a "green" burial that would do justice to a Native American chieftain. At harvest time apples could be gathered and the departed relatives eaten in a weird and somewhat distasteful ceremony—their junk DNA eaten, anyway. The departed could be digested raw or baked in pies. They could even be squeezed and drunk as juice. When the tree got old and started to rot, the departed could be cut up and used as firewood, as in the folktale. Or artisans could sculpt the branches into death masks. The trunks could be carved into statues.

The departed don't have to stay that way forever, which is good news for them. The original idea of a green burial has expanded to include the concept of an arboreal cryogenic. Safely preserved in an apple tree, a person's DNA could be retrieved after a period of time and then returned to human form. Or the seed from the apple could be planted in nutrients and grown into a new human being. These possibilities set up an interesting philosophical conundrum whether or not the revived person is a clone or the original McCoy, since the person is not only the "chip", but the "block" as well.

Cryogenics of the human dead frequently involved preserving only the head. When the technology became available at some future point in time the head would be thawed and attached to a new body or to a robot. Arboreal preservation circumvents the rather icy problem of attaching heads to new necks or to robotic necks, since the person is preserved in his or her genetic entirety.

Thawing has always been the problem for cryogenics. Absolute zero leads to things like chipping, fracturing, and freezer burn. Arboreal cryogenics avoids these devastating effects—everything is done at room temperature—but opens up problematical issues of its own. Issues like pest control. And worms. And bird nests. And spiders' webs. And splinters.

174. The problem with television game shows is that they are stiflingly insipid. "What's behind door number two?" "I'll take the square in the middle." "Will the real Cary Grant stand up?" Television game shows are not even up to the action at the bally stands in amusement parks. In those places people risk losing their pay checks to keep the big wheels spinning, not to mention their retirement funds. In television game shows there are no consequences for losing.

That's the problem. Contestants can win bundles, but there's nothing for them to lose. There aren't even trivial consequences for losing. In some game shows contestants get to keep the prizes they won up to the point of losing. They don't have to give anything back. In other game shows contestants who come up empty are given consolation prizes to carry home and cherish. Since no one loses anything, certainly nothing of value, there is no reason to watch. The situation would be different if contestants stood to lose their pay checks or their retirement funds. Losing a few hundred out of one's pocket for picking door number two makes the show interesting. Losing a few thousand for taking the square in the middle makes the show a *game* rather than a slobbering demonstration of greed punctuated by station breaks. And losing one's car or one's home for choosing a Cary Grant imposter keeps the hyperactive fingers of viewers from pressing the change buttons on their remotes.

Other than the television cameras and the station breaks, losing money in games of chance is not especially unique. We can witness these financial losses any night in any casino or amusement park on the New Jersey Shore. Television game shows become viscerally interesting

if contestants wagered something of greater value than money—
something like bits and pieces of their bodies. Win—or lose a part of
yourself. We're not talking internal organs like kidneys or lungs. We're
not even talking about unnecessary organs like tonsils and appendices,
however medically troublesome they can become. Contestants can keep
those. We're talking small and inconsequential body bits like finger tips
and little toes. Many people live without the end pieces of their fingers.
And there's no evolutionary reason why people need their little toes,
especially when they can win astronomical prizes in their place.

These shows might include a sliding scale of prizes for bits of the
body. Risk a fingernail on the pinkie for a $1,000 prize. What is behind
door number two and who needs a fingernail? Risk the top phalange on
the pinkie and win a $10,000 prize. The square in the middle is?—we
can live without the tip of our pinkie. In fact, we can live without a
pinkie. Risk the whole pinkie for $25,000 and bet who's the real Cary
Grant. We can wear mittens in winter rather than gloves. The sky's the
limit when it comes to the thumbs and other fingers of the hand. Of
course, limits would have to be set. There are always foolhardy people
who would risk their hands from the wrists forward and their legs from
the knees down for the chance to hit the mega-prizes in the millions.
We have to be sure to keep that from happening. We don't want people
to get maimed in pursuit of the almighty dollar. We just want television
game shows to become watchable.

175. "So how was your day?" Darlene asked when I sat down to dinner
two hours late.

"So how was my day?" I replied. "This is how my day was. I awoke
at the ungodly hour of 5:00 AM to find that it snowed three inches. The
snow was not in the forecast when I went to bed. I had to shave an inch
of ice off the windshield and shovel the car out of the parking space.
The roads were icy and wet. An accident at the intersection of Routes
539 and 537 stopped traffic dead in its tire tracks. I arrived at work an
hour-and-a-half late. The e-mails had built up so badly in the interim
the computer crashed—the messages turned out to be e-mauls. Once
the computer was up and running I was called into the warehouse. An
import vendor had placed pallets so snugly into the container they had
to be unloaded by hand. My hand. After 59 cartons at 35 pounds apiece

I went to lunch. The tuna and tomato salad must have gone germy. My stomach turned inside out. It was like being seasick, only worse. When I recovered sufficiently to return to the desk I discovered that the data in the spreadsheet I've been culling for the past ten days was corrupted and unreliable. It's back to the drawing board on this project. On the way home a slow-moving dump truck kept traffic to a crawl. So did the snow that started falling—this snow was also not predicted. I had to swerve to avoid a deer that strolled onto the road. A branch cracked and fell onto the shoulder of the road. If the branch was a foot longer it would have crossed the white line and bounced on the roof of the car. I found a parking space three blocks from the house. I slipped and nearly fell on the ice on the steps of the house. I took the garbage to the dumpster. The bag ripped on the way over. I spent fifteen minutes kneeling in the snow picking up yesterday's linguini. I couldn't help myself—at this point I started drifting into major depression. Other than that, my day was just fine."

"It could have been worse," Darlene noted. "You could have experienced spontaneous human combustion."

"You're right." I realized that would not be a good thing. "What would I be if I spontaneously combusted?"

"Embers?"

"I was thinking more of the order of wings and a halo."

"Don't kid yourself."

Darlene's comment got me thinking. Spontaneous human combustion is one of those weird and inexplicable phenomena that float in the misty cusp of science and para-science. There are reports going back centuries of people burning to crisps for no apparent reason. There are photographs that show the charred corpses and gory photographs they are. The body is incinerated except for the hands and the feet. The clothing is singed but not consumed. Furniture in the vicinity of the corpse is not burnt. There are no scorch marks on the floor. There is no obvious source of the combustion.

There are a number of explanations, each residing in the land of the ridiculous. The preferred explanation is the "wick theory". This theory posits that, before passing out, the person may have suffered a wound somewhere on the body. The wound surreptitiously secrets subcutaneous fat that drips from inside the body and somehow sets on fire. In the same way wax keeps a candle burning the fat keeps the "wick" of the body burning. There are other explanations. They are equally dotty. Ball lightning is conjectured to penetrate the building and engulf the person in some manner. Alternately, gamma rays or other bolts from the deep blue zap the person. A visceral explosion is conjectured. In this scenario explosive mitochondria are the usual suspects. In another explanation the kundalini dragon slithers up the chakras and out of the body, leaving in its departure an overcooked shell. In another explanation Satan or one of his pointy nose deputies prod a person with a pitchfork still warm from the dismal inferno. Or the event is beaterrific—an angel inadvertently brushes the victim with a wing.

Sometimes simpler explanations are advanced. The person may have fallen asleep or died while smoking. The person may have been intoxicated and unable to comprehend that he or she was getting lit from a nonalcoholic source. The person may have scuffed his feet on a rug. The scuffing may ignite a spark that travels up the pants leg. By the time the person realizes what's happening he or she is ablaze. In this scenario the traveling spark is misinterpreted as an itch. The person does himself in by scratching.

Darlene's concern was misplaced. These explanations are irrelevant for me. I like to think I would be cognizant if subcutaneous fat were dripping from a hole somewhere on my person. And I like to think I could bat ball lightning into the next room. I'm not sure if gamma rays give advance notice of their approach. Maybe they make a whistling sound like incoming artillery that would give me a chance to run down the stairs and into the vintage Cold War air-raid shelter in the basement. I think I would feel it if my mitochondria started playing with matches. I'm confident I have the kundalini dragon corked and docile in its velvety chambers. There's not much I can do if Satan climbed in through the basement window or if the wing of an angel whisked my easy chair. I don't smoke so the chance of a lit cigarette kindling my pajamas is nil.

About the only way I could spontaneously combust is by scuffing the floor. I walk with a heavy and plodding pace that scrapes the hard wood. I shuffle along and rarely lift my feet off the surface. I don't so much glide as trip along with bent knees and raised heels. This kind of walk seems problematic only to the shoe salesman, but it could lead to major trouble as Darlene pointed out. It would be an ignominious way to end life, shuffling along and suddenly scuffling with sparks shooting up the inseams.

From this day forward I'm going to walk with a brisk pace and with my heels solidly planted on the floor.

176. We know Nowhere has a middle. That's been well established on many occasions. Travelers might find it useful to know whether Nowhere has a beginning and an end. That way, they'd know whether they are lost or not.

177. On the drives home from school I sometimes listen to a National Public Radio show called *To the Point*. It should be called *To the Pointless* for all the good it does me. I lose the signal below mile-marker 105 on the Parkway and miss the feature stories.

The show has a maddening habit of announcing an intriguing lead story and then playing it last, long after the signal beams into the ether. I understand it's a standard practice in radio journalism to entice listeners with important stories that are put off to the end of the broadcast, but this is National Public Radio. We expect better than cheap gimmicks.

So the headline screams, "Aliens land on the Capitol Mall! But first this story. Seniors grouse about rising costs in podiatric care." This is what's called a "tease".

And "The existence of the Afterlife proven! But first this story. Gone from American rivers—paddleboats." Another tease.

And "World peace established! But first this story. Skyrocketing insurance costs threaten neighborhood block parties." Another tease.

And "Jesus Christ seen in the sky over Jerusalem. But first this story. Fluoridation—a Cold War plot resurfaces or the antidote to tooth decay?" We're up to a tangle of teases—enough to get me to cancel my membership in the next pledge month.

I understand the producers want us to listen to the entire program and not just to the lead story, but there are no commercials on National Public Radio and nothing to sell other than high-brow broadcasting. We like to think the audience of *To the Point* is going to stay with the program after the lead story evaporates, even if the segments involve the gimpy legs of seniors or disappearing paddleboats or threatened block parties or fluoride in the drinking water. This is National Public Radio, after all. No story is so obscure the audience won't hear it out to the conclusion.

178. A stranger came to my cube at work and asked if I were *the one*. I answered, "I am not the one who is the one." This makes me *the other*.

179. What a difference a word makes.

Goodnight, Irene is a popular song and folk standard made famous by The Weavers. The origins of the song are unknown and may date as far back as the late nineteenth century. The song, as we mostly know it, was written or rewritten by the singer/songwriter/murderer Huddie "Lead Belly" Ledbetter (c. 1888 – 1949). Lead Belly first recorded *Goodnight, Irene* in 1932, but sang it for decades previously.

Lead Belly's version was not commercially successful. In 1950 the left-leaning folk quartet The Weavers scored a number-one hit with their version. The Weavers consisted of Pete Seeger, Ronnie Gilbert, Fred Hellerman, and Lee Hays. (I checked into this—there is no truth to the rumor that Lee Hays was the originator of Socialism.)

The Weavers' version of *Goodnight, Irene* included violins and a sweetened orchestra background to their folksy banjo sound. Their version—it's the version now commonly played—is cheery and airily upbeat, despite the song's restless themes of marital separation, faithlessness, and thoughts of suicide. There is a one-word difference between The Weavers' version and Lead Belly's that makes *Goodnight, Irene* into two separate songs.

The Weavers sing of Irene, "I'll *see* you in my dreams." Lead Belly sings of Irene, "I'll *get* you in my dreams." That one-word change—*see* for *get*—makes a dramatic difference in content and context. To paraphrase someone, that one-word change is the difference between a flashlight and a lightning bolt.

We *see* the cop lady and the cashier girl in the supermarket and the girl who pumps gas at the Getty station. We *see* the girls in the class and on the train and on the sidewalks and on the television set. But we *get*, or want to get, the girl we want sex with. Singing that we want to *see* Irene rather than to *get* Irene deflates the meaning of the song and erases the intimacy and sexual tension inherent in the original version.

Changing *get* to *see* alters the nuance of the song as well. In The Weavers' version Irene is taken for the wife of the singer. She is the person he deserts. In Lead Belly's version Irene may be the wife or she may be a loose woman the singer wants to cohabit with on his "stroll downtown". We don't know of course, but given his scandalous character it may be possible the singer wants to *get* someone other than his wife.

Yes, one teeny word of three letters makes all the difference.

180. Speaking of words, the other day I heard two words that surprised me—I hadn't heard them in a long time. And I used a word I say only one day a year.

I heard the first word in Ralph's Barbershop on my way to class. (Ralph calls it a *tonsorial palace*, but that's overstating what he does.) I was in the chair nearest the door when a teenager walked in. The teen looked to be fourteen or fifteen. He was on the tall side with stringy brown hair that hung over his forehead and collar. He immediately occupied the second seat near the television set. Giuseppe, the assistant barber, promptly sprang to work, pinning a tissue around the teen's neck and wrapping a black smock around the rest of him. Giuseppe reached for the scissors and comb and asked, "What-er?" Giuseppe didn't complete the sentence, but the teen knew what he asked. Giuseppe never completed sentences, but somehow or other all the customers knew what he meant.

"Give me a six on the sides," the teen answered. "Give me a three on the top and take two inches off my *bangs*."

His use of the word *bangs* surprised me. I shifted in the chair, but not too far, since Ralph was busily snipping away at earlobe level. I hadn't heard the word *bangs* in years. I didn't think I ever heard a male say it, certainly not in the period I was growing up. I considered his use of the term inappropriate, but I've been told by people who claim to know that I was wrong. I had reserved the use of *bangs* for what hangs on the foreheads of teeny-boppers, but I've been told the word can refer to the forehead frill on both sexes and that its use is not uncommon among today's male adolescents. I suppose I'm not in the cradle of the current culture and I'm not often in barbershops. Giuseppe wasn't surprised. He understood what the word meant. He got out a ruler and started cutting.

I heard the second word when I entered class. The students were chatting rather loudly. I placed my case on the table, took off my jacket, and waited. After a few minutes a student noticed I was in the room. "Prof.'s here," she announced. Another student noticed I got a haircut. "Prof. Ford got a haircut," the student whispered, giggling for some reason. A young lady in the back of the room commented with a voice that quavered, "Prof. Ford's here. I'm in a *swoon*." Fortunately, she was seated.

Swoon is another word I hadn't heard in years. People don't often *swoon* nowadays—or people don't often admit that they *swoon*. The student's use of the word was entirely appropriate. She used *swoon* correctly. In former years *swooning* is what ladies did when a handsome gentleman entered a room and caused the heart to flutter and the legs to melt to jelly. If the ladies were lucky, there was a couch nearby. If they were not lucky, they would be found supine and panting.

In the old days a *swoon* was sometimes brought on by a mysterious substance called *the vapors*. No one knew what *the vapors* were or what ethereal chemical filled the air, but when *the vapors* blew into a room ladies started dropping. Some people claimed *the vapors* smelled like roses. Other people claimed they smelled like witch hazel. Whatever the odor, *the vapors* carried potent effects. Couches filled up and gentlemen had to be careful where they stepped. Handkerchiefs became in short supply.

I used the third word in the lecture. Actually, it was a phrase. I described the theory of learning of Clark Hull (1884 – 1951), a Yale psychologist who was inordinately influential in psychology in the 1940s and '50s. Hull organized his theory in a series of postulates, which were summaries of learning experiments stated in a precise manner with multi-syllabic words coined by long-dead Greeks and Romans. In one of the postulates Hull wrote about *"stimuli that impinge on the sensorium"*—now, that's a sterling scientific phrase if one were ever heard in a psychology lecture. I say it—*stimuli that impinge on the sensorium*—in a slow and deliberate manner. When I say it I raise my voice and stress the *"pinge"* in *"impinge"*. Students are impressed. They look at me with stares less vacant than usual. They don't know what to write. They rarely hear the word *impinge*. They never heard the word *sensorium*. They don't know how to spell it. Sometimes I help them by writing the word on the board.

I leave *sensorium* alone and stress the word *impinge*, repeating it several times for fun. I tell the students that it means "to strike an object in a collision and to press against something." I give them an example—"The deer *impinged* on the hood of the car." I give them another example—"The football linemen *impinged* on the tackling dummy." I give them a third example—"Thrown from the upper story window, the television set *impinged* on the pedestrian on the sidewalk below." I tell them *impinge* is a solid word, a good and useful word, and a word that, like *swoon*, should achieve wider circulation outside classrooms. I don't know what students will do with *impinge*, whether they will use it or not, but after the lecture on Hull I gently lay the word to rest in my notebook where it will stay comfy and curled up with the other postulates until its next utterance in a year's time.

181. There was an unexpected flap on the radio during the morning rush-hour commute. Drivers noticed that an American flag was flying upside down outside a civic organization on Route 33. For some reason the drivers were motivated to call the station as if the program host, ensconced far away in the studio, could do anything about it.

Conjectures multiplied as callers tried to discern the reason the flag flew upside down. Was it an intentional act of desecration? If it was, what was the motivation behind the desecration? Was it a deliberate affront to the American flag? Was it a deliberate insult to the American people perpetrated by a radical organization? Just what was going on behind the closed doors of that unnamed civic organization? Was it a prank pulled by adolescent malcontents or by some barely socialized gang of unpatriotic punks? Was it a fraternity initiation rite of passage performed in the middle of the night by drunken collegians? Or was it an oversight, a mistake pure and simple with no anti-patriotic overtones? There are a lot of immigrants in residence along Route 33. Many of them do not know in which direction the *Stars and Stripes* is supposed to fly. Maybe the caretaker of the building was an undocumented foreigner. Maybe he didn't recognize the American flag. Talk on the airwaves grew hot—the possibilities were many.

After a half hour of agitation over whether the upside down flag was an act of desecration or dimwittedness, John from Pennsauken called to berate the audience. John proved to be a Yankee flapdoodle dandy and somewhat of a literary type. "What's wrong with the people who saw the flag?" he yelled. "Why didn't one of the drivers pull over and right the flag?" he asked, sensibly enough. "I'll tell you why," he continued without giving the host a chance to interject. "People are scared to do anything, even the right thing. They see the American flag flying upside down. Instead of stopping and flying it right side up, they drive past and reach for their phones and complain." John concluded abruptly, "This demonstrates yet again that New Jersey people are *feckless*."

This is absolutely true. We like to think we're tough and belligerent, but John was right. We are *feckless*. The word means "inept", "cowardly", "spineless". The word should be used a lot more frequently in reference to the citizens of New Jersey.

Feckless exists, but we need an antonym to describe people who are assertive, competent, and courageous. We need a word to describe the kind of people who, like John from Pennsauken, take matters into their own hands. *Feck* would do nicely to fill the gap in the language. The adjective is *feckful* as in "full of *feck*." The verb is, of course, *feck*. The past tense is *fecked*, which is also absolutely true of the people of New Jersey, but not in the sense I'm using the word.

182. Here's a scoop from the Raleigh News wire:

"Stop the presses … call back the flagships at sea … Borderlands Book Co. announces with regret that it is closing its superstore in Croatoan, North Carolina, owing to a lack of readership."

183. Behaviorism was one of the most important developments in American psychology—and one of the oddest. In its less radical forms, as in the theories of Tolman, Mowrer, and Bandura, Behaviorism involved the tortured application of operationalism and operational definitions to capture cognitive concepts without forsaking the then-current standards of scientific methodology. In its radical forms, as in the highly influential theories of Watson and Skinner, behaviorism

rejected the study of the mind and of cognitive concepts as fit topics for scientific research.

In a 1929 paper *The Unconscious of the Behaviorist* Watson explicitly claims, "There is no mind." Watson made this outrageous statement because he saw no difference between mind and brain. For him, the mind was the brain and vice versa. Watson also saw the mind as a collection of "verbalized responses" and as "subvocal speech". Mind means talking to oneself. If we can say a word, we can have a thought. If we can't say a word, we can't have the thought.

Skinner pretty much concurred with Watson's view. In the 1950s Skinner devised a selectionist scheme that was an important conceptual tool for behaviorists. In this scheme behavior is selected across the life of a species through natural selection, across the life of an organism through operant selection, and across the life of a human individual through cultural selection. For Skinner, personality and conscious awareness of personality arose only with language. One's identity—selfhood itself—depended on verbalizing what we know of ourselves. This depends on what the culture teaches and allows us to put into words.

I tend to think the origins of the tortured and radical forms of Behaviorism derived from the choice of laboratory experiments—mazes and bar-pressing—and the choice of subjects—rats, pigeons, cats, and dogs. The assumption was that the nature of learning found in experiments on lower organisms could in some manner explain the free-wheeling activities of higher organisms. The assumption about learning was analogous to the performance of combustion engine vehicles. Every car on the road, despite differences in make, model, and design, runs on the same principles of internal combustion. Similarly, every response of every organism, however simple or complex, runs on the basis of classical and operant conditioning.

I've taught these ideas in the Theories of Learning course for more than twenty years. I believe these ideas in part, but not in whole. We would have seen a very different and far less confident and assertive Behaviorism if the choice of experiments and subjects were different from the outset. There is a vast difference between a rat learning to run a maze and a child learning to behave in a socialized manner. There is a vast difference between a pigeon learning to peck a key and a student learning a difficult topic in high school or college. There is a vast difference between an experimenter managing a cat in a puzzle box and a teacher trying to manage a classroom full of rowdy children. There's a vast difference between lower organisms and human beings. This may sound on the narcissistic side, but I tend to think—I like to think—there's a world of difference between Pavlov's dog and me.

A common criticism made of Behaviorism in its radical form is that it works by excluding the wonderfully unpredictable complexity of the human mind. (The tortured forms of Behaviorism tried to capture aspects of the mind through posturing the existence of intervening variables defined operationally. Their effort was historically interesting, but not particularly successful.) The elements excluded by radical behaviorists point to an essential contradiction. Watson and Skinner were thoughtful intelligent men. They came up with *ideas* about learning that they then applied in experiments. These ideas were creative—unpredictable—experiences that they later verbalized. They mulled these ideas over, contemplated them, and *thought about them.* They spent a vast amount of time in conscious deliberation of these ideas. Maybe they even dreamed about these ideas.

As they considered these ideas they were in their homes and gardens and offices. Maybe they were on vacation, hiking a blue mountain trail or splashing in the Atlantic surf. The ideas they entertained—thoughts about the laboratory and the design of experiments—had no relation to the environment they were in. The ideas were primary and of greater relevance than whatever was going on outside them. Maybe they were so preoccupied with the ideas they paid no attention to what was going on outside them. What I'm describing is not unusual. It is part and parcel of our ordinary human experience. It happens to any person who's thinking about something not physically present—not physically present but very much *present in the mind.* To overlook this commonplace experience is to state warped and limited theories that deny the thought processes behind the theories.

Watson and Skinner were gifted writers who captured large audiences and made bundles of money with best-selling books. Both men must have worked laboriously on their books, outlining presentations so their words would make sense to an audience that existed *in their minds.* Their presentations varied as they wrote for housewives or for credentialed peers. Both men would have taken great care in the choice of words, consciously choosing words that could not be misunderstood. Since both men were polemicists, they would have selected words they knew would have enflamed adherents of different schools of psychology. In this endeavor to be clear, critical, and controversial, they would have referred frequently to dictionaries and to thesauruses. They would have run their fingers across lists of words before *making up their minds* which felicitous phrase worked. Phrasing their theories, they did what any writer does, whether a student in high school or college or a writer of fiction—they addressed an audience that was not physically present but *very much present in the mind.* To overlook this creative and strictly mental process is to write—to verbalize—limited theories that are true at the least important fringe of our human existence and not at the cognitive core.

184.   By focusing exclusively on external stimuli and observable responses radical behaviorists miss things like personality, creativity, and a lot of interesting private experiences—private experiences like the truly weird dream I had last night.

I dreamed I was in what vaguely resembled the office in the great Distribution Center. I was with dream characters who vaguely resembled my co-workers. We were in an agitated state, holding wrapped newspapers and chasing an insect described as a "May fly". Into this dream walked Ed, last name unknown. He says something to the effect, "I'll take care of it." That's the dream in all its stark absurdity.

Ed was a sales clerk in Macy's Cellar at Herald Square where I worked in the late 1980s. I haven't seen Ed since the late 1980s. I haven't thought about Ed—not for a single moment—since the late 1980s. I didn't think much about him in the late 1980s. We weren't friends. We weren't close except to say, "Hey, how's your day going?" as we passed on our way to and from the break room. We just worked on the same sales floor. (I was in Éclair Bakery. Ed floated from department-to-department.) There wasn't any reason to dream about Ed. Nothing reminded me of him the day before the dream. No one I saw the day before I went to sleep resembled him. I didn't see a photograph in the newspaper or a character on a TV show who looked like him. I didn't meet anyone named Ed. He doesn't resemble any of my co-workers. His work standards weren't like theirs—he was obsessively diligent only at shirking work and goofing off. Yet more than two decades later—and for reasons unknown—this person who I haven't thought about in years floats into a dream about swatting a May fly. Strange, very strange.

And what's stranger is that I recognized Ed on the instant and thought while I was dreaming, "That's Ed from Macy's Cellar. I haven't seen him in years. What's he doing in the dream?" Ed's appearance was so unusual I noted it even while in the middle of the dream. Experts call this *lucid dreaming*—except that the term "lucid" really doesn't help clear things up.

I don't know what dreaming about chasing and swatting a May fly means. I don't know what Ed's unanticipated appearance in the dream means. I don't know if any of it means anything. But the experience was fun when it happened, fun while I was dreaming it and fun while I was thinking about it afterward. And it was the kind of fun behaviorists can never have by their refusal to poke about inside a dreamer's thoughts.

185. Here's a surefire way to make New Jersey financially solvent and to eliminate the state property tax, not to mention the state sales tax and the state income tax—enforce traffic laws.

Owing to the fact that it happens to be broke, the state of New Jersey has reduced funding or even stopped funding many municipal programs. The state tried to solve its enormous problems—it's on the precipice of defaulting and one holey boot is already over the edge—by fobbing financial responsibility onto the individual municipalities. This maneuver solved the problem for the state, but not for the individual communities. This was an unusual situation for 565 municipalities to be in. They were not used to being kicked off the state dole.

Some municipalities responded in the habitual way. They immediately raised taxes, thereby fobbing responsibility onto emaciated taxpayers. Other municipalities responded by cutting back programs and laying off city workers, including police and fire fighters. But other, more clever, municipalities took a different approach. They started to enforce traffic laws. The result of the enforcement was astonishing. The municipalities that enforced traffic laws recovered all the lost state revenue. In some cases they exceeded the revenue the state ordinarily bestowed on them.

The implication is as clear as a well-washed windshield—the enforcement of traffic laws can make municipalities a load of cash. Done properly, the enforcement of traffic laws can save taxpayers a load of cash. Taxpayers may even start to fatten up, since they will have extra money to spend on food rather than to pay in taxes.

Some municipalities enforced the traffic laws the old-fashioned way. They instructed police to leave the parking lots where they hang out and hit the roads in search of lawbreakers—they aren't hard to find. Some municipalities went high tech in pursuit of revenue. They installed cameras at intersections to catch drivers running yellow or red lights. And they installed speed cameras that catch people exceeding the limit. Other municipalities introduced decoys and sting operations to catch drivers in the act of breaking the law. One prominent decoy tested whether cars yielded to pedestrians at the crosswalks as required by law. As we might expect, drivers did not yield.

In the decoy effort at crosswalks police officers were trained how to cross the street. If a car didn't yield the right of way the officer radioed ahead and the car was pulled over and ticketed. The fine is no mere ticket but in the $200 price range. (For an additional $200 drivers can fix the fine with their insurance companies.) The total take in these decoy operations can run as high as $10,000 a day.

The potential dollar value of fines is nearly incalculable if we consider the amount of money that can be taken in from decoy operations and from cameras that catch drivers running red lights and refusing to yield the right of way and making illegal turns and exceeding the speed limit and failing to signal when changing lanes. The money taken in from handymen in pickup trucks alone will eliminate the sales tax—it has never happened since the time of Henry Ford that the drivers of pickup trucks obeyed a traffic law. The cost to municipalities is miniscule. They don't need to hire more police, they only need to rent the equipment from the companies that write the tickets. Police don't issue the tickets. The work is done by the United States Postal Service and by computer geeks in the Midwest who, for a portion of the take, watch the films and drop the tickets in the mailboxes.

The argument might be made that it is unfair to pick on traffic violators to generate revenue and not on violators of other crimes. This argument is valid to some extent, but there are not enough murderers and rapists and drug dealers and robbers to fill up the coffers. There are plenty of law-breaking drivers. The police need only cruise any road in any municipality in any county in the state to find drivers who are breaking the law. Place a camera at any intersection and the film will run out before the morning rush hour turns into the midday lull. We have to remember that drivers are breaking *laws*. If we don't want to catch and punish people who break laws, then the laws themselves should be rescinded. The current law enfarcement system in place is laughable. A few hundred police ticket a few hundred lawbreakers— there are tens of thousands of lawbreakers at every mile marker in the state. How many drivers can police pull over on their shift? How much are they being paid to ticket drivers? How much revenue are they pulling in for the municipality? Cameras are able to catch every lawbreaker and they operate at a fraction of the cost of flesh-and-blood police officers. Cameras catch lawbreakers and they allow the police to do the heavy work of tracking serial killers, solving cold cases, and preventing terrorism.

Another argument is that the enforcement will cease to work once drivers start to collect tickets in the mail. After a few tickets drivers will refrain from running lights at intersections and yield the right of way and stop making illegal turns and stay within the speed limit (or a few miles over it) and signal when changing lanes. Highway fatalities will plummet as everyone becomes a defensive driver. Insurance rates will drop. And revenue to the municipalities will dry up.

I don't believe fatalities will plummet or insurance rates drop. And I don't believe revenue to the municipalities will dry up. To the contrary. Drivers are constitutionally unable to obey any law once they get behind the wheel of a motor vehicle. And drivers are constitutionally unable to exercise a modicum of caution and defensive driving once they turn the key in the ignition. I say this with confidence because revenue from cameras at intersections has not dropped despite their presence being publicized in newspapers and in signs warning drivers about the cameras. Drivers don't exercise discretion and stay within the law even when there are street signs informing them about cameras at the next intersection. Drivers don't pay attention to the signs. It's a fair bet they don't even see the signs.

The use of hand-held cell phones, which is now a primary offense in New Jersey (meaning that drivers can be pulled over for this and for no other reason), has not reduced despite widespread publicity campaigns and public announcements. Since the law was enacted more than 225,000 citations have been given to motorists caught using cell phones. Despite an increase in the fines for the offense, surveys indicate that the use of cell phones has *increased* rather than decreased. The use of cell phones—and text-messaging while driving—has increased despite the finding that such practices are as dangerous as driving under the influence of alcohol.

New Jersey drivers will not be able to help themselves. No matter how many tickets they receive, they will not be able to obey the law. There are many reasons for this failure. Drivers become distracted, causing the foot to press heavier on the pedal. Drivers are fatigued and hung over. They are under the influence. They are stupid. They have a psychopathology of some sort. They have frontal lobe damage and cannot foresee the consequences of their actions. They are simply oblivious of road conditions, of the rules of the road, and of traffic laws. In the review of crosswalk decoys, for example, a fair number of drivers honestly state that they did not yield to the pedestrian because they did not see him. "What pedestrian?" they ask the officer as he writes a $200 ticket.

Drivers also refuse to accept responsibility. They are behind the wheels of their cars, they rule the road, and the rest of humanity can be run over the hoods of their speeding vehicles for all they care. In a radio program on crosswalk decoys driver-after-driver called in and complained that it was the responsibility of the pedestrian to watch where he or she is going. Never mind that the law clearly states that it is the driver and not the pedestrian who has the responsibility of yielding the right of way at crosswalks. The attitude of the drivers was, "It's not up to me to watch, it's up to the pedestrian."

There's a last reason why New Jersey motorists will not obey the law. This reason lies in the social psychological concept of *anonymity*. The rationale is this—"You can't see me in my car, you don't know who I am, and I can't see you in your car and I don't know who you are, so I am not obligated to obey the law in your presence. I can do whatever I want until I'm caught and the chance of that happening in this state is slim to none." When they enter their cars and electronically roll up tinted windows and turn on amplified CD players drivers put on war paint and hoods and masks. They feel snug and secure and safe from identification. This attitude, helped by the horsepower in their engines and by the size of their vehicles, produces the mindset that they can break the law with impunity. "I'm behind the wheel of a 2,000 pound machine going 75 mph, you can't see me and I can't see you—this gives me the right to run the yellow or red light and not yield the right of way and make any turn I damn well please and drive at whatever speed I feel comfortable at and to signal whenever I want to or not."

Drivers identify with their cars, with their custom-designed interiors and sleek exteriors and with their makes and models and horsepower and with all the amenities credit can buy. Fortunately for the taxpayers, drivers do not identify with the license plate the camera catches. You can't see me and I can't see you, but the camera sees both our license plates. So, thanks, New Jersey drivers. Keep up the good work and keep on breaking the laws. Break all the traffic laws, break every last one of them. I intend to use the money I'll save on taxes to buy a new and shiny foreign-made luxury sedan.

186. We frequently say that a *person has taken leave* of his senses. When a person goes blind or deaf or numb or when he loses the sense of taste or smell we can say that his *senses have taken leave* of him. Except that we don't.

187. Call forwarding—isn't this the same as an echo?

188. "The Little Gem on the Bay", as my adopted hometown of Little Egg Harbor calls itself, is a rural place with vast salt marshes that lead to the Atlantic to the south and with a remarkable forest of pygmy pines to the north. The township consists of a number of diverse habitations. There are modern housing developments alongside free-standing old-frame homes. A reticulation of houses line lagoons that slither to open water—these houses have piers for back porches and garages full of powerboats. It's probably safer to get around town by boat than by foot. Only the business district has sidewalks. Everywhere else citizens have to walk on lawns and on the scrawny shoulders of the roads. Half the

citizens are on the senior side of the calendar. Half are on the child-rearing side. Regardless of age there are few original "Piney" types left in Little Egg Harbor. The majority of residents are pilgrims from North Jersey seeking safe places to raise their children and to live out their retirement years rusting beside community pools.

The "Little Gem" is mostly a peaceful place. The usual crimes involve driving under the influence and blackened eyes in arguments over whether the *Yankees* are a better ball team than the *Phillies*. Occasionally, the police are called to quell domestic violence before it erupts into spousal abuse. Every now and again someone gets caught growing marijuana in the garden. Those kinds of crimes—rather a run-of-the mill sort—were the extent of it until the fall of 2010 when the peace was permanently broken. Little Egg Harbor became the murder capital of Ocean County. In that wicked season Little Egg Harbor became *Scrambled Egg Harbor*.

On October 4 Craig Muller, an unemployed electrician age 54, shot and killed his brother Bryan. Muller then killed Cara Ellis, newly married and all of 21 years of age, as she ran to Bryan's assistance. Getting murder – suicide in the wrong order, Muller then killed himself. A week later, Karen Murphy, also age 54, deliberately ran her husband over, killing him while he waited at a bus stop. Initial reports indicated that she used a baseball bat to dispatch her husband to his Particular Judgment, but the story changed to a car making a K-turn as the murder weapon. Five weeks later, Michael Cahill, 41, stabbed a roommate to death. Cahill also stabbed his mother, but she survived. No motives were stated for any of the murders. In the case of the bachelor Muller brothers it's unlikely any motive will ever come to light.

This spree of violence is inexplicable. It's one of those things that happen, no one can say why. The spree may reflect a cluster of random events that have no connection but are perceived as related. There is a tendency, well established in cognitive psychology, for people to perceive patterns where none exist and to decipher meanings in events that are random. In medicine clusters of rare and unusual diseases break out in a locality and have no apparent connection—no connection is ever found among the cases. And in gambling there are clusters of unrelated people living in a locality that hit big prizes in the same limited time period. There are also clusters of vehicular accidents. There are no wrecks on a particular stretch of road and then, for no apparent reason, a number of wrecks occur.

What happened in Scrambled Egg Harbor may reflect copy-cat violence. We like to think that middle-aged people can control their impulses, but that appears not to be the case. For whatever unknown reason Craig Muller goes berserk and kills people. Karen Murphy has been holding the berserk in. She reads about Muller's spree in the local paper and the tethers loosen that kept the rage in check. She reaches for the car keys and acts on the unbearable anger. Michael Cahill reads how Karen Murphy settled things with her husband and he reaches for the carving knife. Considering the build up of anger, resentment, and rage among the general population it's a wonder violence in the "Little Gem" stopped with Michael Cahill.

What happened may reflect something more elemental. In the same way that multiple acts of creativity and compassion sweep through a place, ennobling everyone, something vicious may have blown ashore across the salt marshes or slithered into town from holes in the nearby Pine Barrens, debasing everything it touched. Angels of mercy sometimes descend on places and inspire peace and compassion. Angels of hatred can also descend and instigate despicable crimes and outbursts before they depart.

What happened may reflect something simple and straightforward and without profound implications. The fall of 2010 may have been time for the "Little Gem" to catch up with and become part of the violence that besmirches our land. It may have been time for this sedate community to show that it is like everyplace else in the mental asylum the United States has become.

Whatever the explanation, the events in Little Egg Harbor are very sad, especially the killing of Cara Ellis. She rushed to a neighbor's defense—this is what people are supposed to do. She didn't die instantly, but survived for a few minutes. Neighbors heard her moaning. This set up an awful choice—a choice that will haunt people for the rest of their lives. No question the neighbors wanted to rush to Cara's side, but if they stepped outdoors they would have shared her fate. This is the grimmest situation possible, one the people involved can never win. The choice was the worst one possible—death or life encumbered with the bad memories of being powerless to act when a Good Samaritan lies dying on the sidewalk.

The sadness transcends what happened in *Scrambled Egg Harbor*. The horrific events that occurred in a mostly tranquil place happen in every city, small and large, across the United States. They happen in other countries and other continents as well. Of the hundreds of thousands of species that have appeared on this earth only humans have evolved consciousness. Only humans have evolved the awareness of who we are, what we do for right and for wrong, and what we might become. What do we do with this gift of consciousness? To what end do we sometimes use it? A man kills his brother. He kills a person who did him no harm and who tried to do a good thing. He kills the conscience of everyone within earshot of the bullets. Another man kills a friend and tries to kill his mother. A wife kills her husband. In comparison to what our species is, these ends are pathetic.

189. Danish researchers have discovered that all blue-eyed people now living are descended in part from a single ancestor who lived around 8,000 BC. Blue-eyed people who are no longer living are also descended from the same ancestor. He lived in what is now Scandinavia. His name was Karl.

The researchers discovered a mutation in a gene that results in turning off the chemical processes that lead to the development of brown eyes, which had been universal among humans till the time of Karl. A partial turning off of the gene produces green eyes. The mutation also results in a greater incidence of blond hair and fair skin. The fair skin provided Scandinavians like Karl an advantage in survival, as it enabled them to obtain sufficient vitamin D in the sun-deprived Northern latitudes.

The researchers claimed this mutation is neither favorable nor unfavorable and bestows no special survival benefit on the people who inherit it. This can't be true, as it's well-known that blond blue-eyed people "have more fun" and are preferred as mates. Or so they keep telling everyone.

What is scary is that this gene is adjacent to the genes for skin and hair color. If nature didn't prefer blonds, blue-eyed people might have been albinos. What is also scary is that Adolf Hitler shared this ancestor, so all living (and all dead) blue-eyed people are related to *Der Fuhrer*. I know if I were blue eyed and found out I was related to Adolf Hitler I'd put in brown contact lenses, even if that meant having a little less fun and fewer mates.

The question was raised about green-eyed people. Are they related to *Der Fuhrer*? They are, but only to Adolf.

190.   I just read an article about "leadership". The author suggested leadership was the defining quality of—a leader. He wrote about a recent visit to an aircraft carrier in which he viewed the leadership qualities of the American sailor. He saw that everyone was doing their job. From the admiral on the bridge to the cook in the galley, from the pilot in the situation room to the swabbie in the latrine—everyone knew his and her place and everyone performed their duties with skill, confidence, and competence.

I've been on an aircraft carrier and I saw precisely what the author noted. We have every reason to admire the sailors and to feel confident that our liberties are protected. But I'm not so sure the correct word is "leadership". I think the more accurate term is *followship*. Except for the officers, no one on board seemed to be doing much leading. The enlisted sailors were following the orders of the junior officers and the junior officers were following the orders of senior officers higher up the chain of command. Everyone was performing their job descriptions as they're written in the manuals. Every mate knew their assigned roles and performed them well. Every mate on board knew their station. Some knew their battle station.

Followship applies in the civilian world. It applies in the corporate world and in the public sector. And it applies in a religious organization. The laity know their place. The clergy know their place. Everyone mans their station—sometimes it's a Station of the Cross. The laypeople report to the parish priest. The parish priests report to the bishops. The bishops report to the cardinals. The cardinals report to the Pope. The Pope reports to God. All is well in the *followship* of the Holy Spirit.

191.   We say a plan *backfires* when it goes awry or produces unintended consequences. It follows that a plan *frontfires* when it works according to schedule and produces the results intended and no other.

192. In entry #69 in *Thinking About Everything* I pointed out that screenwriters and directors do not always think out the implications of the scenes they create. In that entry I used the example of the improbable wardrobe exchange. No matter how disparate in height, weight, or build, characters exchange clothes that fit perfectly as if they were tailored for identical twins. There are two other improbables that always capture my attention when I spot them in movies and television shows, which is frequently. The first is the awakening of perfectly composed and coiffed sleeping beauties. The second is the parking space that is immediately available.

When I wake up I resemble something out of a zombie movie. It takes a minute to figure out in which direction gravity works. It takes another minute to plug all my bones in their sockets. My hair looks like I spent the night cuddled up with an electrical outlet. I use a bowl of ice water to unwrinkle the corrugations and a spade dipped in boiling water to loosen the sand from my eyelids. While this is going on memory and personality regroup and let me know who I am and what I'm supposed to do.

This is not how it works in movies or television shows. Characters instantly spring into vivacity on awakening. They turn cartwheels and perform ballet the moment they glide out of bed. Their hair is perfectly combed, their skin is baby smooth, and their eyes are clear. Murphy never pours sand in their eyes like he does in mind. Characters don't have to look around the bedroom to recollect where they are or who they are. They awaken into the instantaneous bloom of full consciousness. It must be star power that makes them rise and shine without so much as a jaw-cracking yawn.

Another improbable occurrence is the amazingly available parking space that appears whenever characters need to park their cars. Whether it's in front of a bank or a restaurant or a supermarket or an apartment complex, characters find these spaces without so much as driving around the block. And it's not just a parking space for a car, it's a space long enough to glide a tractor trailer in—the thought occurs that in my fifty years of watching television I have never seen a character parallel park. Maybe they don't teach parallel parking in acting school.

This has not been my experience. Back in the day when I cavorted in taverns in Hoboken parking spaces were about the rarest things in materiality. I counted myself blessed if I found a parking space anywhere in the vicinity of my destination. Usually I gave up and took the first available space, even if that meant walking across town. If I found a space like television characters do, directly in front of the place I was visiting, I became instantly suspicious that I died and drove to heaven.

Awakening from sleep without so much as a yawn? Finding a parking space without using up the gas in the tank? Maybe things would work better for me if I were in pictures.

193.   I heard a radio program the other day that made me realize how strong the need to believe is—and how important criticism and refutation are. This program had a psychic on the air. Listeners called in and gave their first names. The psychic hemmed and hawed for a few moments and then disclosed bits of information gained through the extrasenses. He told one lady caller that a man named "Jim" would pursue her. He told another lady that she had best be on her guard, as someone was looking to take money from her. He told a gentleman caller that there was something the matter with his stomach. He told another caller that he feels full after eating a big meal.

This kind of thing went on for nearly an hour. The information that flowed from *the other place* was entirely pedantic. We might call it *the banality of ESP*. That to the side, what struck me were the responses of the callers. There was some hesitation on their parts—it was their turn to hem and haw—but I could hear through the process of empathy their attempts to find the truth in what the psychic told them. So the lady replied hesitantly that she didn't have a suitor named Jim. "Ah, but you will," the psychic claimed confidently. I could hear her thinking through the FM signal, "I wonder who it could be." She didn't doubt that somewhere in the world a man named Jim was donning his Sunday attire and placing a rose in his lapel.

The other lady listener paused and made gargling noises when she was told to be on her guard. She was thinking, "Who could it be? A relative? Someone at work? A clerk in the shopping mall? A server in the restaurant?" As she rank-ordered the possibilities the psychic repeated his warning in a serious voice, "If I were you, I'd be especially careful about my finances in the next few weeks." Coming from a psychic, that statement caught her attention, if anything on the radio did. I'm sure she tied her purse strings with a double knot.

The gentleman who had been told that there was something the matter with his stomach replied that, as far as he could tell, his digestive system was in working order. The psychic replied that his problem may be in the process of manifesting itself. That was precisely what the listener wanted to hear—undiagnosed stomach ailments. He intended to stock up on antacid and watch his diet in the coming weeks. He would take every nutritional precaution. He would schedule an appointment with a doctor earlier than planned. He wondered how much time he had left.

The caller who had been told that he feels full after eating big meals didn't need to think twice. "That's exactly right," he responded. "Oh man, after Sunday brunch I have all to do to stay awake. I always let my wife drive so I don't nod off behind the wheel." "And after a party you need to open your belt a notch or two," the psychic commented. "Make that three or four notches. I'm lucky my pants don't tear open."

Each of these callers immediately tried to figure out the truth of what the psychic told them. They reviewed their memories and interpreted events. They reinterpreted events. They tried to peer into the future to make sense of things. The lady who was told that she would be courted by an unknown Jim made a mental note to listen for the name as she went about her business. The lady who was told to watch her money reexamined just why her niece paid an unexpected visit and why the cashier in the supermarket was so nice. And the man who was told his stomach was on the blink reviewed certain odd feelings and unusual sounds he experienced during his last visit to the toilet. He didn't think anything of those feelings and sounds at the time, but in the light of what the psychic said—well, one never knows.

Not one of the four contradicted the psychic. Maybe they were being polite and didn't want to appear contrarian—who calls a radio program to argue with a psychic? Maybe they believed the psychic and just couldn't get a hit in memory at the moment. Not one of them asked how a man sitting in a studio hundreds of miles away, a man who didn't know them from the on-off switches on their radios, could produce pieces of information that were unknown to him before he heard their voices and predict things that were going to happen to them. A small dose of critical thinking—a smidgen of critical thinking—may have given them pause. But this small dose would have spoiled the act.

There was a selection process in play. These people called a program with a psychic guest, so they were prepared to accept whatever he said. They were happy to get on the air and find out what was going to happen. They were predisposed to believe whatever the psychic said. This kind of uncritical acceptance goes on all the time and in every field. Every guest on every radio program, whether endowed with psychic talent or not, is believed. "Yes, that makes sense," listeners say to every broadcast statement. "That's the truth, if ever I heard it," we say to every statement on the air. "By golly, this guest knows what he's talking about."

It happens to psychics on the call-in shows. And it happens to me in the classroom. When I'm in the swing and hammering away on the chalkboard I could say anything, however preposterous, and the students will believe it. Of course, they assume I base my statements on the granite edifice of psychology and not on the ethereal wisps gathered by a sixth sense. Believing that, they wouldn't be far from the truth.

194. *Tests & Measurements* is the huge, powerful, and lucrative subfield of psychology that studies the structure of normal and abnormal personality through projective instruments and objective self-report questionnaires. Tests & Measurements is a vital component of clinical psychology and of trait personality theories. It is involved in nearly every psychological study, given the excessive reliance on surveys. The subfield is the bane of undergraduate and graduate students with its emphasis on sampling procedures, statistical inference, and the assessment of internal and external validity. Students are taught to administer and evaluate surveys and to assess the results. Usually, this assessment means the comparison of *single-word diagnoses and personality descriptors* with established norms.

Tests & Measurements is found everywhere in psychology. It is an integral part of differential diagnosis in clinical psychology. School psychologists employ psychological tests to evaluate and place children in special education and in gifted programs. Personnel officers employ psychological tests to identify employee strengths and weaknesses.

Court officers use psychological tests to assign custody and determine competency.

The number of single-word diagnoses and personality descriptors derived from psychological tests is extraordinary. Going back to the origin of psychology the number must be in the thousands, if not in the tens of thousands. Some tests were created for a specific research project and survived for the life of the project. They were never seen again and reside in the unvisited stacks of journals in the crypts of libraries. Other tests—and the single-word descriptors derived from them—have become part of popular parlance and well-known to civilians. To name three, there are the Myers Briggs Type Indicator, the Big Five theory of traits, and the Minnesota Multiphasic Personality Inventory.

Derived from Carl Daddy-o Jung's masterpiece *Psychological Types*, the Myers Briggs Type Indicator reduces personality to extroverted or introverted thinking, feeling, intuiting, and sensing types. The Big Five trait theory reduces personality to scores on extroversion, agreeableness, conscientiousness, openness to experience, and emotional stability. In the clinical sphere the Minnesota Inventory outlines ten varieties of psychological disorder. These varieties are: hypochondriasis; depression; hysteria; psychopathic deviance; masculinity/femininity; paranoia; psychasthenia; schizophrenia; hypomania; and social introversion. As with the other instruments, individuals who take the Minnesota test receive a score on each of the ten subscales. The scores are compared with norms for age, gender, and ethnicity.

This desire to categorize personalities is understandable. Human beings are the most complex things on the planet. Knowing a person is an extroverted thinking type and that he is conscientious and that he scores high on the paranoia subscale of the Minnesota Inventory provides orientation. Presumably, these single-word descriptors say something important about personality and something accurate about the person. Prediction becomes possible. I expect the person to be scientifically oriented, thorough in his work habits, and not particularly trustworthy.

These single-word descriptors govern my behavior toward the person. I feel free to discuss the latest scientific research with him. I am confident the person will finish whatever projects are assigned.

And I won't try to become friends with him—this will only make him suspicious.

But there are problems with this drive to categorize people on the basis of single word descriptions.

Trait psychology and much of clinical diagnosis relies on surveys as the main source of data. This is problematical at best. People are *asked* about their behavior and they are *asked* to rate themselves. This is not something everyone can do—many people are not particularly reflective. On many surveys people are asked to evaluate their behavior on a scale from "one" (never) to "five" (always). They are asked to make carefully drawn distinctions and to be consistent in changing a self-rating of "two" to "three" or "three" to "four". Sometimes words like "never", "seldom", "occasionally" and "often" are used in place of numbers. The problem is the same. Individuals have to make judgments when "seldom" becomes "occasionally' and "occasionally" becomes "often" and to do this consistently. The interpretation of numbers and words grows immeasurably when the sample size starts to proliferate.

Psychologists claim responses on surveys reflect the category being studied (Jung's types; the Big Five; and the particulars of psychological disorder), but it's trickier than that. The self-ratings on surveys may also reflect what the respondents want to reveal about themselves and the presentations they want to make. The self-ratings may reflect what the respondents think the test administrators want to hear. The self-ratings may also reflect the understanding, competence, and motivation of the respondents. Over the years I've given a number of surveys in the psychology classes at Manhattan Community College. Despite my lucid explanations, many students do not have a clue about what they are answering. Other students complete the surveys so thoughtlessly rapidly I can't believe they take the questions seriously. The responses of these students reflect the trait of haste and nothing else.

At the simplest level the answers to survey questions may reflect the working vocabularies of the respondents. Many years ago I distributed the Extroversion Subscale of the Minnesota Inventory to an undergraduate General Psychology class. This survey is roughly forty questions of the true – false format. One of the questions was "I am a good mixer." A student walked to the front of the room and asked if the word "mixer" meant the tool bartenders use to stir drinks. I had to explain that the term "mixer" meant a person who likes to socialize at parties and who fits into groups easily. If the student didn't ask what the word meant I may have scored a "false" response rather than a "true" response.

Reliance on Tests & Measurements of traits and clinical diagnoses invites us to look for essences inside people. He is *deep down* an extroverted thinking type. He is *really and truly* conscientious. He is *through and through* a paranoid. This focus on stable and pervasive essences can easily overlook a situational and contextual analysis. We examine the person in isolation from the environment and from culture. As far back as the 1930s knowledgeable social scientists suggested this was misguided and harmful to a full and accurate analysis. The exclusion of environmental factors in assessing personality is ironic given the cultural biases in surveys—the word "mixer", for example. The meanings of words change and words date. Some of the category names (psychasthenia) on the Minnesota Inventory are no longer in general use. They are still retained in the manuals but are always accompanied by modern synonyms (anxiety-proneness).

Finally, this reliance on Tests & Measurements conflates partial knowledge with a more complete or thorough knowledge. Too often, a trait name or diagnosis is mistaken for the individual in all his or her complexity. We say, "He is extroverted" and think we capture everything the person is. We say, "He is conscientious" and think he will always act in a conscientious manner. We say "He is paranoid" and think he will never trust us. Human personality cannot be captured by single-word descriptors or by any combination of descriptors—human personality can't be captured by the entire alphabet or by the entire number line. The person we characterized is more than extroversion, more than conscientiousness, and more than suspicion and distrust. The person is more than all the descriptors in all the psychological literature since its inception in Wilhelm Wundt's Leipzig laboratory. It is not possible to say anything final or complete about a human being. Humans are too complex, too changeable, too creative, and too unpredictable to be sorted and parsed into however many catalogs of trait names and clinical diagnoses.

To describe a person using single-word descriptors is like scooping a cup of Bay water and saying, "This is the Chesapeake." Yes, it is Bay water, but there's a lot more Chesapeake out there and it's not in the cup.

195. Physics, chemistry, and biology are commonly referred to as the *hard sciences*. This has to do with the belief that topics such as supernovae, molecules, and mitochondria are inherently difficult to study. It may also have to do with the ruthless and unforgiving dispositions of the hard asses who teach these subjects.

If the natural sciences are *hard* it follows that the social sciences of psychology, sociology, and anthropology are the *soft sciences*. But this can't be right. Human beings are the most complex beings in the universe. (I suppose I should clarify this and say that humans are the most complex beings thus far discovered in the universe. There may be more complex beings lurking in outer space, but we probably don't want to know about them.) Supernovae can't think or use language. Molecules can't write books or come up unpredictably with witticisms. Mitochondria don't have relationships—they don't mess relationships up. It's a safe guess that mitochondria don't know who they are or what they do for a living.

Physics, chemistry, and biology may be the *hard sciences*, but when it comes to the subject matter the social sciences are the *harder sciences*.

The perception that the social sciences are not hard likely derives from the soft asses who teach the disciplines. I can't speak to sociology or anthropology, but the bleeding hearts who teach psychology aren't mean and merciless like their peers in the natural sciences. I know psychology teachers agonize over grades. Psychology teachers are tormented when they have to give a student a low grade. They hate it even when the student deserves the low grade. When they fail a student psychology teachers can't sleep at night. They break out in eczema. Their immune system falters. They experience heart palpitations. They suffer crying jags. They can hardly live with themselves. They drift into major depression. They have all to do resisting the urge to open the window and hurl themselves to the campus green.

196. There's a 2008 comedy called *Ghost Town* that is remarkably un-funny. It is so not funny it could air on Comedy Central. The plot concerns a nerd of a guy who's revived after being clinically dead. He returns to life with the ability to see ghosts. Manhattan is full of ghosts—we might expect this in a city of eight million. Being dead

does not inspire wisdom or grace. Being dead involves no rewards or punishments, such as the clergy state. Being dead does not involve extinction, as scientists claim. Ghosts pretty much carry on and do what they did when they were alive. They retain the same basic personalities as when they were among the living. The locale being Manhattan, they retain the same basic neurotic personalities as when they were alive. On paper the movie must have sounded hilarious. On the screen it's un-hilarious. I sat and watched it headstone-faced.

There is one joke that is effective. The movie explains the origin of unexpected sneezes—when a person sneezes a ghost has passed through his or her body. Being incorporeal, ghosts can do that. When a troop of ghosts file through, the person sneezes a number of times in rapid succession. I'm not sure what this phenomenon of multiple ghosts walking through a person can be called. We have a pod of whales, a pack of wolves, a gaggle of geese, and a smack of jellyfish—probably, this should be renamed a *sting* of jellyfish. I suppose we can call a procession of ghosts a *shroud*.

The movie leaves unanswered a number of questions. Maybe it answered them, but I wasn't paying attention once I realized the movie wasn't funny. We know what happens when a ghost walks through flesh and blood. What happens when a human walks through a ghost? What happens when two ghosts walk through one another? Do they sneeze? Cough? Hiccup? Pass gas? If they did, we can call ghost gas *ectoplism*. And finally, what happens when a ghost stops dead inside a person?

197. Once January 1 is over and people recover from their hangovers and go back to the noxious grind of work they complain that it's 364 days to go and that they will have to laboriously trod their way uphill the rest of the year till the next New Year's Eve celebration. The next January 1 is something to look forward to from the blurriness of January 2. The intervening months of days are not.

I have a solution that could stop the griping. Let's do something different next year. Let's replace January 1 with a second December 31 and count the days backwards. That way, we wouldn't have to summon motivation from its hiding place and drudge uphill from 1 to 365. Instead we can slide downhill from 365 to 1. The year will scoot by much faster if the days go in the reverse direction and downward. And having two days marked December 31 on the calendar won't confuse anyone, not even the people in Ocean County. After all, each December 31 will be in different years.

Of course, we may not want time to scoot by rapidly. Time is the most precious commodity we possess and it's the one we squander most readily.

198.   Yea, though I walk in the valley of microbes thy antibiotics refresheth me and thy alcohol swab comforteth me.

Against my better judgment I went ahead and did it. I took a chance and got a flu shot at the local supermarket and nothing happened. Absolutely nothing. I watched and waited as the pharmacist wiped my upper arm with cotton dipped in rubbing alcohol. I sat still as a stone as she taped a band aid over the needle mark. It was like I entered a meditative state. I was aware of the inspirations and exhalations of my breaths. I was aware of the nooks and crannies of consciousness. I was aware of every motive and every conative impulse. There was no urge to drop to the floor and push a can of franks-and-beans across the aisle with my nose. There was no urge to rush to the pet food section and rip open a bag of birdseed. There was no urge to run to the parking lot and roll on the pavement and dust bathe. There was no urge to climb a tree and flap my arms and chirp. Consciousness was clear and devoid of animalistic impulses. I was certain—evolution was not going in reverse. I got a flu shot and I remained a human being.

My friends, I strongly urge you to go to your local supermarket and get a flu shot. It doesn't hurt, not in the slightest. It costs $25.00—this may hurt a little. You won't change species. You'll stay a human being. You'll be doing your family and friends a favor. You'll be doing everyone in the world a favor. If everyone got a flu shot our enemies, the microbes, would disappear and no one would have to suffer fevers and chills and stomachs pumping in the upward direction.

It's none of my business if you choose to act irresponsibly and refuse to get a flu shot. As for me and mine—our bloodstreams are awash with inert bubbles of H1N1. Your germs can't get to us no matter how hard they try.

If it turns out to be that we are the only people to get flu shots, I'll do the right thing for humanity. The rest of the world may be collapsing in puddles of pus and poo, but I'll stand tall in Little Egg Harbor. I'll step up and walk upright, except for the slight slouch I have from all the years I spent bent over keyboards. The rest of the citizens may turn septic green, but I'll carry the tradition of learning into the unpopulated future. I'll keep the history of our culture alive till the race recovers and the nation rises from the river of phlegm. I'll keep music, art, and literature alive. And I'll keep the lights of science burning—not all the lights. I don't know much biology, chemistry, or physics. I suppose those lights will grow dim and extinguish. But the lights of the social sciences will not go out. I know a lot of the social sciences. Those lights will burn the brighter for the disappearance of the natural sciences.

199.   In Carl Daddy-o Jung's theoretical universe the collective unconscious that everyone is born with is inhabited by a number of archetypes. (If this is any help, the archetypes are the inherited structures that underpin our thought processes.) The archetypes include the anima, the animus, the persona, the shadow, the self, the *senex* or wise old man, and the *puer aeternus* or eternal boy.

In mythology the *puer aeternus* was linked to the natural cycle of planting and harvesting and to such dying and reviving gods as Dionysus and Adonis. Psychologically the *puer aeternus* refers to an adult male who has never grown beyond adolescence. Such an individual exhibits a combination of playfulness and rebelliousness, along with a fear of independence and an excessive attachment to the mother. Daddy-o didn't see the *puer aeternus* as particularly negative, since the archetype represents the opportunity for creativity. Popular psychology tends to view the *puer aeternus* in a more negative light as a man-child who refuses to grow up and as a "mama's boy" dominated by a mother figure.

I don't know if any of this is true—it's vague enough to be true— and I don't know if my psychological state reflects the *puer aeternus* or not. I tend to think I reflect another, equally potent, citizen of the collective unconscious, the *poor aeternus* or, better still, the *poorer aeternus*.

I realized my identification with the *poorer aeternus* archetype while I was seated one afternoon in my cube in the great Distribution Center. I was surrounded by work, endless work, immense piles of work I can never catch up on. I have all this work and I'm not being paid to do half of it. I'm working harder than ever and I'm making less and less money. It's all vegetation and no harvest of greenbacks. As they say in the warehouse, "*Mucho trabajo, poco dinero.*" If anything, I'm going in the opposite direction from wealth. I'm developing into a *poorer senex aeternus.*

I'm driving myself into an early grave—into an early pauper's grave. I certainly don't want to die on the job. It would be the ultimate shame and humiliation to be found by the cleaning lady stiff-as-a-board and lifeless. She's not even in the union.

I made up my mind. I don't want to stay a *poorer aeternus* forever. I want to be rich and live out my days like King Midas. I'll never make money on the job. I'll never make money in the job market. I'll never make money in the stock market. I'll never make money in the bond market. I'll never make money in the creative market. There's only one thing I can do. I'm going to pack up my bags and fly to the 'Ould Country and find a leprechaun and grab his pot of gold.

The alternative is to stand outside the post office and open the door for the customers. Recipients of good news may be inspired to drop their change in the Styrofoam coffee cup held under the sign posting the hours. Recipients of bad news will merely grunt as they pass, but that's all right—grunting is what I've mostly experienced on the job and off. Begging doesn't pay much, but the take is tax free and it's not hard work. I just have to get to the door handle quicker than the customers and I have to be able to keep my arm extended for the hours of operation.

I think I'll hang a sign around my neck. "Won't you help a *poorer aeternus* down on his luck?" "Please help the *poorer aeternus.*" "Please give some of your loose change to the *poorer aeternus.*" I might even print the truth on the sign. "Begging to bag a leprechaun." The college-educated customers will know what I'm referring to. Maybe they heard of Daddy-o Jung and maybe they'll take pity on me. The customers who've never been to college and who never heard of Daddy-o may ask what I'm referring to. If they ask I'll tell them about archetypes and about the *poorer aeternus* in particular. But I'll have to charge them for the information. After all, knowledge is power and time is money and I don't intend to stay broke forever.

200. I threw caution to the wind, along with most of my worldly possessions.

I cashed in my meager bank account. I closed out my meager retirement fund. I donated my clothing to a charity organization. I sold my car at a local dealership. I sold my books to a used bookstore. I gave two weeks notice to the Distribution Center. I was going to skip out and not give any notice, but they had always played fair with me. They needed time to hire five temps to replace me.

Once I gave notice there was no going back. I was buying a one-way ticket—I hoped it was to Paradise. I was going to find a leprechaun and his pot of gold or I was going to live on the road, desperate and homeless, like the despised Irish travelers of yore. I had positioned myself in a corner in the States. I intended to position myself in another corner when I reached Erin. It was going to be wealth or ruination.

I booked a night flight on Aer Lingus. I traveled coach on the way over—I was sure I was flying first-class on the return flight. The name of the plane painted below the cockpit was *St. Brendan*. That seemed an auspicious start to be riding in a plane named for the saint who blundered on his sea voyages onto The Blest Islands. When I arrived at Shannon Airport I took the jitney to the ferry port at Killimer. Once the ferry docked in Tarbert I hitched to Dooneen Point. It wasn't hard to get a ride. There are a lot of tourists in the vicinity bawling and wringing their handkerchiefs over the views of the Shannon River below the coast road and farmers frequently drive by as they haul livestock from the grazing fields to the chopping blocks. The tourists could easily mistake me for a local and the farmers, who aren't by nature a sentimental lot, want for company as they go about the onerous chore of delivering rump roast for the steak house crowd.

I reserved a room at a bed-and-breakfast on Carrig Island and immediately hiked to Dooneen Point. My North Kerry informant was standing at the same spot I left him on my previous visit. He reminded me of an ancient tree whose trunk was so mighty a grown man and a six-footer couldn't encircle it with arms spread wide. His hair was thicker and grayer than last time. His face was as rectangular as his body. The grizzle of unshaven cheeks deepened the ruddy shading on a heavy face the color of the great outdoors. He wore the same bronze-shaded coat, thick black sweater and black trousers. Despite the dark fabrics, the stitches looked frayed and threadbare. If this was the only suit he owned it had come time to visit a clothing store.

He stood at the edge of the road rather than on grass. He was encircled by a constellation of ruts poked in the soil by the rough cane he gripped in an embrowned hand.

When he saw me another rut punctured the soil. "You're back," he said in a gargly voice that didn't disguise the displeasure. He knew what I came to find.

"He's not here," he said, anticipating my question. "He's not been seen in many months."

"I'm going to find him nonetheless," I said optimistically. I'm sure my face betrayed the disappointment I tried to deny.

He made a sound like "Bah"—it could have been "Brrah"—and twisted the tip of the blackthorn deeper in the rut. He turned and looked away from me. It was the signal he didn't want to be bothered. I complied with the request.

I waited two days in the same field where I bagged the leprechaun. Like the North Kerry man said, there was no sign of the splattered elf. For that matter, there was no sign of any being supernatural or natural. I changed my tactic and rented a kayak from the Ballybunion Sportsman's Association. The leprechaun might be leaving the cave and taking a different route on his jaunts than the one I trapped him on. Like any creature, he learned from experience. He must have supposed I would be back and hiding in the field waiting for another attempt at his pot of gold.

The first two days bobbing in the blistered blue surf off the Kerry Coast were the worst of my life. They were worst, far worst, than the experience of my first hangover. I lost time and the contents of my stomach on that wretched sea. I hurled breakfast, lunch and dinner— the late night snack I had in the bed-and-breakfast got hurled, too. After I finished hurling food stuffing I started to hurl the mnemonic stuffing of my identity. Memories of my education went with one hurl. Memories of the Distribution Center went with another. Memories of my friends went next. My family followed. All that remained was the unquenchable wish to find that leprechaun and claim what he cheated me of. That wish could not be dislodged no matter how raucous the sea became.

The nausea stilled on the third day at sea. My memories stayed inside. I had given up food in the interim so there was nothing gastrointestinal to throw into the accommodating sea. I could never be seasick again.

I studied the seawall and scanned the innumerable openings on the deface of the cliffs. It looked as if some giant of yesteryear poked holes in the rocks with a mythological version of a blackthorn cane. A village of leprechauns may have lived inside the caves in former years. The place was empty now. If any leprechauns resided there, they were in hibernation. The only creatures that emerged were swallows and small gray birds I took for the Kerry version of American park pigeons. I tried to remember which opening I climbed into, but it had been a while and there were too many holes to count. I knew the opening was at shoulder level, but there were holes at shoulder level for the distance of a quarter mile.

After a few more days of tacking the surf I returned the kayak and headed inland. I carried a small duffel bag that held all my possessions. I found what I believed was the highest point in the vicinity of Kilconly Parish. It was a "fairy fort" located a few fields inland from the coast road. I hauled some blue stones to the middle of the fort and sat and watched and waited. I wasn't scared being in a "fairy fort". The locals said otherwise, but I knew the roughly circular declivity of bald soil in the midst of luxurious green had nothing to do with the "good people". There was nothing supernatural about the place. The sunken patch was the imprint of an enclosed Medieval homestead. The locals made up stories to attract tourist dollars the way American communities try to drum up business by claiming ghosts stroll the foyers of great old houses.

From my vantage I commanded a view for miles. The black rim of the coastal cliff was to the east. A line of trees was to the west. Ballybunion was to the south. The ponderous gray steeple of St. John's church laid like a scatter rug on the horizon. No other structures were visible of that bustling resort. The fields to the north were wild and unplowed. There were bare patches—fairy forts, probably—interspersed amid copses that had reverted to their original impassable states. The remnant of a cornfield ran along the coast road to the north. Like everything else in that direction it was well on the way to becoming feral.

Farmers inexplicably drove up and parked in the fields below me. They got out of their pickup trucks, walked around for a few minutes, and then left. They never did any farm work that I could see—I don't know what they were up to. Every now and then tiny red cars stopped on the coast road. The passengers emerged and pointed to fields and tried to match scenery with cartography. They were obviously family historians in search of the ancestral farms. I had performed a similar service in former years, so I recognized the look. An occasional parade of bicyclists rode by. They carried knapsacks and sleeping bags and were traveling Erin on the rough. Hikers, too, traipsed into view. Like the bikers they carried their accommodations on their shoulders. I sat at the center of the proverbial "forty shades of green" but the bearer of the particular shade I wanted to possess was nowhere in sight.

And then it started to rain. Heavy drenching rain. Pouring rain. White rain. Rain without surcease. Rain without an intermission. Rain on the verge of becoming hail. The Irish call this kind of rain "soft weather". I think this description must be a meteorological joke. The only "soft" thing about the weather was my epidermis that shrank as it grew soggy.

I reached in the duffel and retrieved the fold-up umbrella I took along for the trip. When I raised the umbrella the ribs on the left side cracked. Only the right side expanded. The left panels hung flat. It was typical of me. I bought an umbrella that didn't open. I felt very sorry for myself.

Maybe I made a mistake quitting my job in the Distribution Center. I had a comfy position there and could work till—well, that was the fate I traveled across the sea to avoid. Maybe I made a mistake returning to Erin. It seemed a good idea at the time, but I had impoverished myself trying to become rich. Chasing after leprechauns and their pots of gold didn't seem like such a good idea when I was standing in the rain under half an umbrella. What could I have been thinking? I must have been out of my mind. I must have gone off the deep end and become unhinged. I held the umbrella low over my head so the broken flap provided some minimal shelter. The sunken patch I stood in started to become a puddle. Soon I would have to step out of the fairy fort and stand on the grass. I became nervous and afraid. Maybe what the locals said of fairy forts was true.

It must be my fate to perish at my work station. Cows are put on this earth to grow fat on the way to slaughter. Drudge horses are put on this earth to haul drays till they're put out to pasture. Sheep are put on this earth to trim the grass and manicure lawns till their coats get sown as a peasant's mink stole. God must have put me on this earth to work without relent till I grew old and cold. I decided—I was going to buy a bottle of cognac with my last dollars and drink to the failure of a preposterous idea. I would have one last good night before I commenced my new career as a vagrant.

After half a day of incessant rain the sky began to clear. At first the sky was an indistinct white dome as colorless as the rain. Nimbostratus wisps of a slightly darker hue gradually emerged. I remembered Gustav Fechner and my psychophysics class in college. The difference between the dome and the clouds was *just noticeable*. And barely at that. The serrated edges of the small clouds turned definably gray—it looked as if they were making a get-away from the sky above. Rifts in the dome itself tore open and large clumps of storm clouds separated, exposing the palest blue of eternal space. It took a while for the clouds to scatter and for the sun to come into view. It took a while longer for the rain to stop. The last sheets of inclement weather dissipated beyond Ballybunion. Like a cosmic dog, the sun shook the wet off solar flares.

The sky was bright blue and cloudless. The air smelled clean—it smelled of flowers. Pellets of rain glistened on the rim of the fairy fort. I was surrounded by the beads of a watery rosary. I was no longer afraid. Courage returned with the clearing. A rainbow arched from the cliffs to the north. Below it a second and smaller rainbow commenced somewhere closer. My spirits soared and the sun glowed inside me. I knew exactly where the leprechaun was. This was my moment. I was sure of it.

A rainbow allows for one wish. A double rainbow allows for a second wish. In my case the wishes were the same.

I bounded from the fairy fort as rapidly as I could. I was quite a runner when I was young, but that was quite a while ago. The years had slowed me. St. Paul said otherwise, but this race was assuredly to the swift. The rainbows shone brightly, the seven rays of the spectrum shimmering vibrantly, but they wouldn't stay lit for long. The spume of the sky, the rainbows would dissipate in minutes.

The mud was thick and pasty. It grabbed my shoes, stifling my pace. The grass was easier-going, but slick and treacherous. In one spot I nearly lost my footing. My arms flung forward and I bent in half parallel to the turf. To keep from falling, my legs spun like the pedals of a cartoon character. Somehow I succeeded in staying on my feet. Gravity must work a little softer in this place.

I hurtled the rock border of the coast road. Despite the danger I stayed on the grass—it was faster going on grass than through the puddles in the grooves and potholes on the miry road. I passed my North Kerry informant—he was in the same position I left him several days previously. The ruts he cut in the road were filled with rain water. We didn't exchange greetings. There wasn't time for him to summon air into a grunt or wave the blackthorn in a hurrah and speaking would waste the precious air that was burning inside.

My lungs hurt. My legs hurt. My head hurt. My arms hurt and I wasn't using them. No matter the pain, I had to keep going. The rainbows held firm, but the rays blinked once or twice. There was less time than I thought.

I had seen many rainbows in my time, but until I reached the edge of the cornfield I had never seen the start of a rainbow or the place where it touched earth. The sight was stupendous. It was like seeing the ocean standing perpendicular to the shore. The sight was gorgeous. It was like seeing a sunset with the hues sorted and arranged in a vertical direction. The streams of vapor were much wider than I anticipated. They were as wide as a wall and as sturdy as wood, though made of water. I looked upward—the bow was so tall I couldn't see the place where the arch commenced. High over the smaller bow the belly of the second rainbow glistened. The bows didn't so much cross directly as on the oblique. For a moment I thought I saw the shadow of the taller bow fall over the smaller one. It could have been a leftover cloud caused the sunlight to blink.

The colors of the bow were in proper order, each ray a rippling plank, violet to the left and red to the right. Seen close up each ray held within it miniscule rainbows, as if they were liquid holograms. The vapor that formed the towers of light consisted of differing viscosities. In some places I could see desiccated cornstalks through a screen of water. In other places the vapor was dense, looking like floating chunks of ice.

Physicists claim the shortest distance between two points is not a straight line but the fold of space between the points. The rainbow was a natural arch. I couldn't fold it, but I might be able to use its elliptical shape to arrive at the opposite side. If I could climb the rainbow I could cut miles and minutes in half. I could avoid the pain of running altogether and I could avoid the cornfield.

The rainbow didn't look like it could support my weight, but I took a chance. Nothing ventured, no pot of gold gained. The red ray looked chunkier than the other rays. I touched the bow on that side—for a moment the ripple assumed the imprint of my hand. I grabbed the rainbow and simultaneously placed my feet in the orange and red rays. I boosted myself up and hauled myself off the grass with a jerk. I promptly fell through the rainbow and landed on my knees. Another preposterous idea. The rainbow couldn't support my weight. It was a ladder, but it was liquid. I could sooner walk on water. Gravity ruled in this spot.

I got up, wiped my face, scraped the green off my trousers, and charged into the cornfield. Running through the cornfield was surprisingly easy—it was no more difficult than running through a cloakroom. I was a human scythe of flailing arms, a sentient mower of dashing feet. The roots were strings loosely attached to the earth, the stalks were dry and hollow, the cobs shriveled and shrunken, the nibs rotting teeth in a botanical open-air crypt. The lifeless leaves and sheaths crumpled in a corrugated rain. Plants the height of a man tore easily as thread. Entire sections of the field disintegrated. I was proceeding at two miles an hour and I owned the destructive force of a gale.

I came to an abrupt knee-jarring halt when I reached the edge of the cornfield. One step more and I would have torn the second leg of the rainbow. The rays were rapidly dimming. Indigo and violet had blinked off for good. Orange and red weren't long for this world. I assuredly did not want to hasten their erasure by clumsily severing an anchor that had started to rust.

The taller rainbow ended in the woods about a quarter mile distant. It, too, was fading. I had reached my destination. The leprechaun would be where the double rainbows crossed. But there was no sign of him.

The field ahead of me resembled any field anywhere in Erin. The grass was uncut. Bald patches of yellow soil lay haphazardly amid the ripest green. Irregular rows of scraggly trees were in the distance. In Ireland trees are never nearby but always in the distance—I think the dearth of trees has something to do with the aristocrats cutting wood for fuel in the old days. Erratic clumps of bushes lay in front of the trees—with the diminished perspective it was difficult to tell how close or distant the clumps were. A small stream flowed in a westerly direction. The stream was silent and so narrow I could cross it without breaking stride. Blue-gray stones imprinted with lichen dotted the field in no particular order. The stones must have demarcated a farm in olden days, but traces of habitation and tillage had long been concealed under a green shroud. The snakes were gone, but there was precious little animal activity. No cows, no deer, no foxes, and no antelope such as St. Patrick changed into. Only a few birds, common robins and jays, their tails ringed blue, flitted about.

I heard a splash behind me and then a second and louder splash. The rainbows had come to earth.

It was getting onto evening and I started to despair. The Irish day is long, but there was no sign of the leprechaun. I didn't want to stay overnight in the field. I was soaked to the unmentionables and I didn't carry a change of clothes or a kit for starting a fire. I left the duffel in the fairy fort near the coast road. Before I returned to the bed-and-breakfast a vanquished man I looked very carefully at the field. I wanted a second and harder look around.

There were a lot more trees than I noticed at first glance. The bushes were thickly tangled and adorned with bell-shaped flowers whose yellow faces drooped toward the grass. Probably, the rain had bent them—they would recover in the next day's sun. The stream was making gurgling sounds and there was a man-made wall of stones three layers thick descending crookedly in a slope to the east. Something stirred in the grass to my left. I thought at first it was the leprechaun, so I lurched to grab it, but all I accomplished was to chase a rabbit back into its burrow.

With luck I saw it. There was a slight rise to the north. The base of the rise was pale earth and mud, the top a mop of grass and frail bushes stabbing upward. At first glance I took the spot to be another vacant section of soil, but I saw it was nothing of the sort. It was instead a cleverly concealed hovel that fit in perfectly with the rise and roll of the landscape. If I didn't study my surrounding with a squint I would have missed it.

I stepped closer. The exterior was packed turf and dried mud—strips of mud bubbled in the rainfall. A few boards and mauled logs pressed against the mud at ground level. A break in the wall served for a passageway. The break was no more than a foot wide and a few feet tall.

I had my man—my leprechaun. He was as good as cornered.

I crept to the side of the hovel and waited. One hour passed. Two hours passed. Three hours passed. As it neared the fourth hour—this was ten o'clock—I heard stirring inside the hovel and soft clicking sounds, as if one piece of metal dropped on another. I knew what that greedy little creature was doing. I understood his motivation—it was almost human to want to count your fortune over and over.

There was silence inside the hovel for a while. The leprechaun must have put his pot back into hiding. The only sounds were the occasional good-night chatter of the birds as they took their census and the slap of the stream as the water flowed over the corners of half-submerged stones. The stream sounded louder than previously—the tide must be up. Humming sounds soon emanated from the hovel. I couldn't identify the tune, but it sounded upbeat and cheery. It was the kind of tune I would expect from a man—a creature—of means.

Suddenly the leprechaun stepped from the hovel. As he emerged he sloppily struck a pipe against his thigh. Most of the ashes clung to the flannel of his trousers. A few ashes made it to the grass.

"Got you!" I yelled, pouncing.

I grabbed the leprechaun about the waist and swung him around so that he faced away from me. He was a little heavier than I remembered, but no great burden to hold. I had carried heavier in the Distribution Center. He dropped the pipe and his derby fell off. He had kinky black hair and he suffered from male pattern baldness. This was a sign he was in middle years. For leprechauns this was a few centuries old. His arms were secure in mine and the toes of his pointed shoes assaulted the air helplessly. The punches of his heels on my thighs didn't hurt at all.

"Got you for once and for good."

I tried to carry him inside the hovel, but the aperture was too narrow for both of us to fit at the same time. Without so much as a "look out below" I threw him inside and squeezed through the passageway bent and with shoulders sideways.

The only lights in the hovel were funnels that dropped from rends in the mesh of roots and vines that passed for a roof. If I were standing atop the hovel the sources of light would be called "holes".

The light was barely adequate, but it was enough to see that the leprechaun put the "ugh" in ugly. His flannel trousers had been bought off the rack as red cloth and had since migrated to a dark brown shade. A black coat was as dirty as the trousers. The coat was a little snug at the midsection and couldn't be buttoned. A white shirt was open at the collar and streaked with black marks. The marks looked like soot, but they were dark enough to have been drawn by a marker.

The leprechaun's face was the color and texture of a strawberry. Hirsute threads sprouted from fertile warts on both cheeks. Similar threads emerged from oversized ears that, curving round an oversized skull, extended his face in two side panels. Deep horizontal fissures started from beneath hairless eyelids and ended an inch above the jaw. The flaps of skin that carried his face an additional flight downward didn't hang loose like jowls ordinarily do. Instead they had the firm look of cellular cardboard. The same strict pattern of fissures extended above the eyes as well. I counted four grooves from brow to hairline. These fissures gave him the look of a frown. I was sure his emotional state at this moment went beyond simple annoyance.

His eyes were beady and black. They possessed a blank lifeless look and they barely moved. I wasn't fooled. There were dark thoughts and diabolical schemes lurking behind the unblinking blackness.

I couldn't tell if it was the same leprechaun—all leprechauns look alike to me. But then I noticed two dusty bottles of Hennessy Old Pale on a table in the right corner of the hovel.

He recognized me at the same moment. " 'Tis you, Yank," he said in a voice that was a mixture of roughest anger and the ripest surprise.

" 'Tis me, indeed."

The leprechaun became agitated, shivering from foot-to-foot and shaking his tiny fists at me. He skipped two steps forward and took a step backward. I was sure he wanted to accost me or cast some black art upon me, but he was powerless to act. It was against the rules to harm a person who captures a leprechaun on the fair and square.

"Who are ye in league with, Yank, that ye should find me twice? What occult power draws ye to me-self?"

"We must be joined by the mystic cords of covetousness," I conjectured.

The leprechaun shuddered when he heard he might be psychically connected to a human being. I was somewhat put out and offended that he loathed sharing mystic cords with me. I couldn't imagine that he thought his kind superior. I have an immortal soul and he doesn't and that puts me one up. I should be the insulted party. I kept my temper in check, however. I wasn't prepared to argue theology with an otherworldly being who was a few centuries old and I wanted to stay on task and not become distracted else he trick me.

"You know why I'm here."

"Isn't there wealth enough in Amerikay fo' ye to hurt a poor leprechaun who niver did ye hurm nor gave ye cause? The streets are paved wit' gold in Amerikay than fo' ye to travel all this way to take a leprechaun's pot. Why bother a harmless leprechaun and one in yer grandmuther's own parish?"

"Never mind the small talk. Where's the pot?"

"If ye want to hunt a leprechaun, why not one in anuther parish? There are more leprechauns in Ireland than me-self."

"Where did you hide the pot?"

"I'm one of the poorer leprechauns in these parts."

"Tell me, where's the pot?"

"I don't know. I don't have it anymore."

I ignored the pitiful lie and looked around the hovel or such of it as I could see in the receding light. He had come up in the world since last I saw him, but only by a little. The hovel wasn't much, but it beat living in a cave in a seawall. I walked over to the table that held the Hennessy bottles. I was going to poke my finger inside to be certain they were empty of gold coins, but a hairy spider the size of a marble sat on the rim of one of the bottles. I peeked inside instead. The bottles were empty.

An unpainted cabinet was beside the table. The edges of the shelves were splintered and stained. Shoemaker implements were on the shelves. A pile of shoes laid on the floor in front of the cabinet. The flaps of the shoes were spread and the tongues bent backward, as if someone had been trying them on. The smell of leather was strong. I kicked the shoes and sifted the pile with my foot. The pot of gold wasn't hidden in them.

"There be greater prizes than pots of gold in the 'Ould Countree," the leprechaun said, trying to distract me. "Do ye want to consort in the halls of power, eh? I can make that happen fo' ye. Or do ye want to consort in the halls of pleasure? I can make that happen too. I took ye fo' a man of action, but maybe yer the kind of easy-living fellow who likes his pleasures soft and sweet."

I stepped to the other side of the hovel—it was a walk of six short steps. A table stood on that side as well. A pile of clothes lay atop the table. A three-legged stool was in front. I didn't like touching the clothes, but I had no choice. I shook the rags with the bit tips of my fingers and flattened them with the side of my palms. The pot of gold was not under them.

'Do ye want a long life and a beautiful colleen fo' to marry?" the leprechaun continued. There was an edge to his voice—there weren't many places left to look. "A colleen who will bear ye a tribe of strong sons, eh? Do ye want a great house and a stocked cupboard to give you plenty to ate?"

The walls of the hovel were bare earth. I ran my hands over them in a broad sweeping pattern, but I found neither soft patches nor discolorations indicating a hiding place. I stepped to the hearth that was at floor level against the back wall in the center of the hovel—it was the last place to look. The turf fire had long been extinguished. The ash was inches thick behind a ring of small stones that once served to contain the fire. A large lidded pot, like the kind my sainted mother cooked beef stew in, sat on the ashes. I realized the leprechaun hadn't built the hovel. He was a squatter in a place some peasant family deserted in the long ago. From the looks of the disrepair, a very long ago.

I bent over the pot. The leprechaun shouted "Yank!" Mentally I added the word he left out, "No!"

I turned and looked at him. "Lep," I said with a smile. I'm sure he added mentally what he left unsaid, "You found me pot of gold."

I opened the lid and saw the glint of the top row of coins. Even in the bad light they were dazzling to behold. It took all my strength to lift the pot. I risked a hernia and a double hernia raising the pot to waist level, but that was all right. I could afford the finest medical care.

The leprechaun let loose a torrent of words at the top of his brogue. I wasn't sure of the sound or of the syllables. I wasn't sure of the language, whether English, Irish, or an elf dialect not commonly heard above ground. Whatever the language, the cry loosened a rain of soil from the roof. I couldn't raise a hand to cover my head in protection—it took both hands to hold the gold. The pebbly pelting continued for so long I was sure the earthen roof was going to bury me in my moment of victory. But my luck ran strong this day—maybe my luck changed because of what I held. The soil stayed in place over me and the pot stayed in my arms.

"The woe is me, the woe is me," the leprechaun said in a voice broken with the hiccups of grief. He took out a handkerchief from a jacket pocket—to my surprise the handkerchief was spanking white— and blew his nose. It sounded like something cracked inside. "Me poor pot," he mourned, returning the handkerchief to the jacket, "what's to become of me poor pot?"

"It'll find a good home in Amerikay—America."

"And what's to become of a poor leprechaun? Wit-out me pot I have nothing in the world."

I felt a tinge of regret taking his gold. He held the gold coins for centuries, after all, and had grown fond of them. I'm sure he took individual care of each coin, counting and shining them breaths to cuffs. Maybe he knew the coins by the dates he procured them. Maybe he named them and made up stories about their origins. I'm sure he never spent a single coin. The look of his clothing and habitation showed he was rather tight with his fortune. I almost felt sorry for him, but he was a leprechaun, soulless and shifty, and beyond ordinary pity.

"I claimed the gold fairly."

"Ye did, aye, and it was ably done. There be few men in the barony of Munster, the poor law union of Iraghticonnor, the county of Kerry, and the parish of Kilconly, who could find a leprechaun twice." He paused and his voice deepened in affliction. "The same leprechaun."

"I wasn't looking for you in particular. Any leprechaun would have sufficed."

"It grieves me that no born man of Kilconly parish found their leprechaun, but a man from beyond the sea. If there be such men as ye in exile from Muther Erin, it was only a matter of time before another came for me pot. If I must give me gold up, I give it to the man who found me not one time but twice."

I knew the leprechaun was up to his tricks, altering his tune from a fervid rage to a feigned conciliation. He must have accumulated centuries of tricks to regain his pot of gold.

"But I am surprised that a wurthy man such as ye-self should come into riches wit-out praising the Lord."

Maybe he didn't have as many tricks as I anticipated. He had pulled this one on me before. I was onto him.

"A fine Catholic lad taking a leprechaun's pot wit-out giving a word of tanks to the Man Above who showers his generosity so abundantly. 'Tis a crying shame ye harven't learned yer religion."

"You're right, I have been remiss." The corners of the leprechaun's packed cheeks pinched in a malicious grin. His fingers opened and closed in rapid succession. He was counting the coins in imagination in anticipation of getting them back. He thought he was pulling a fast one reminding me of my religious obligations—I had already decided to donate a handful of coins to the Salesian order.

"Good Lord, thank you for making me rich," I said to his chuckle of a response. I reached in my pants pocket and pulled out a tacky eyeglass gag I bought in a novelty store for a dollar. It was the kind of gag glasses where the eyes roll around in the frames and never close. I bent and put the glasses on without spilling a single coin. I could continue my prayer in proper fashion and all the while keep my plastic eyes on the leprechaun. With these glasses I could never take my eyes off him no matter where I looked.

When the leprechaun realized how he had been tricked he uttered another shriek, shorter in duration and with less vehemence than the first, and jerked backward in a violent startle that gripped his entire body. If boards hadn't been pressed to the exterior of the hovel, he would have propelled himself clear through the wall, like a character in the final reel of a cartoon short. He remained upright against the wall for a few seconds and then slowly slid till he reached the floor. He sat with his spine straight and with his legs extended like a fairy check mark. He made no attempt to conceal the tears that rode the convolutions of his face. If he didn't stop crying he would soon be seated in a mud puddle.

I never had any money till I won the leprechaun's pot, so I don't know what it feels like to go broke in an instant. But I do know what it feels like to be poor. I took pity on him. Truly, it was a tragic sight to see so ancient and weird a creature reduced to such a moan-worthy state. I couldn't leave him in total poverty. I wiped the soil his second cry had showered on the pot and placed a few coins on the table next to the Hennessy bottles. He gasped when he saw what I did. I was sure he would not have done the same if our places were reversed.

I became obscenely wealthy in that hovel, but I'm not an ostentatious person. I lived poor in my adult life, but I had the modest habits of the old moneyed class. My attitude was never show it, never flaunt it. Getting listed in magazines and on the Internet as among the world's wealthiest men was not my style. I preferred to live quietly and to keep the wealth hidden. I was like the leprechaun in that regard.

My single extravagant purchase was a 98-foot five-deck yacht built to specification by the Dixie Boat Company in Hampton Roads, Virginia. I live on the yacht a part of the year and sail the Mediterranean. Occasionally I venture through the Suez and into the Indian Ocean. My crew consists of four skinny Italian women. They have green eyes and black hair that stops where their hips start. They don't speak English and I don't understand a word of Italian, but we get along fabulously. As you can tell, I'm quite preoccupied and will be for a long time to come. If you need me for anything, for anything at all, find someone else.

EXCELLENT GROANERS

Dear Reader:

Here in no particular order is a collection of puns, jokes, and witty observations. I thought them up myself, every last one. No one helped me. You can tell that by reading them.

The learning psychologist Edward Tolman once wrote that the kindly experimenter looks after his lab rats in the same way God looks after his creation. In a similar manner the kindly author looks after his readers. I urge you to read *Excellent Groaners* while seated in a comfortable chair with broad armrests. You might want to read it in bed—make sure it's a bed that's not too high off the floor. You might want to raise the sidebars and lock them to be on the safe side. If you insist on reading *Excellent Groaners* while standing be sure to place fluffy pillows on all sides on the floor around you. I'd hate for you to fall and hurt yourself laughing. I want you to groan for the right reasons.

Regards,

The Author

~ When Satan goes to the toilet he has a Baal movement.

~ Malism is the philosophical belief that the world is a bad and evil place. Minimalism is the belief that the world is a slightly bad and evil place.

~ A fight broke out at the magic show. Two magicians were having a mep-fist fight.

~ Human beings hold staff meeting. Germ beings hold staph meetings.

~ Did you hear what happened in the high school? The vice principal discovered card games were going on in the boys' locker room. It was jocks and better to open.

~ Island hopping takes a toll on travelers.

~ Truckers provide a bill of lading when they arrive at the loading dock. Viking truckers provided a bill of raiding when they arrived at the loading dock.

~ Sometimes when we look in a hole in a wall we see a wall in the hole.

~ We know there was a Kemo Sabe in the Old West. Was there a Bingo Sabe in the Old West?

~ A woman is sometimes called a "broad". This makes an oversized woman a broad broad.

~ The Episcopal Church is allowing gay marriage, but only between homosexuals.

~ The bookseller stopped for a shave on his way to work. He was lather-bound.

~ Oystermen speak in tongs.

~ What the sun administers—a tan. What the salon administers—a charlatan.

~ What does a pastry chef have in common with a major league umpire? They both holler, "Batter up."

~ The Mensa room is the place where male geniuses go to pee.

~ Is there a firefighter's hall of flame?

~ Hemogoblin is demon blood.

~ Do they say swearwords in a cursory review?

~ "Young man" as in "her young man" is often a suitornym for "boyfriend".

~ The maid knocked herself dizzy doing housework. She punched herself in the chore.

~ The whale shark can grow to a length of forty feet. It is the largest fish in the world. This makes it an auspisces species.

~ A classmate of mine has the disease "Mono". That's no reason to brag. I once had the disease "Stereo".

~ A crook was caught stealing Big Macs at the local McDonald's. He was a hamburgler.

~ Pollen is the wheezin' for sneezin'.

~ The sheriff was strung out on amphetamines. His name was Wired Earp.

~ A human uses carpet cleaner to get the stains out. A jinn uses magic carpet cleaner to get the stains out.

~ A gig is a musical performance. A gig that goes bad when the performer chokes is a gag.

~ Neurons are microscopic. This invites the question how many neurons can fit on the tip of a pin. The answer depends on how wide the tip of the pin is.

~ Ghoulash is the grub ghouls relish.

~ The bishop gave the errant clergyman a rap on the taberknuckles.

~ If bees could talk their buzzword would be "Ouch."

~ We frequently use the phrase "new-born baby". We never say "old-born baby", not even if the delivery took a whole afternoon.

~ There was a district attorney who was also a cannibal. His favorite part of the trial was when he grilled a witness.

~ Guys date chicks. Cannibal guys date Chicklets.

~ The executives in the department held a staff meeting. If their wives held a meeting it would be a distaff meeting.

~ My sensei's name is Joe. When I pay him for the weekly lessons in karate I say, "Here's your dough, Joe."

~ A private conversation in a tavern is a bar side sidebar.

~ Profits in the brewery overflowed expectations. The brewmaster was very hoppy.

~ The father tumor said to his disrespectful offspring, "Don't give me any polyp."
~ And Lucy Riccardo frequently disrespected her husband. It was a desicration.

~ This was overheard when the Dublin bookstore opened for business, "The top of the bookcase to you." "The rest of the shelves to you."

~ In crime lore "The game's afoot." Detectives who suffer a particular fetish say, "The foot's a game."

~ If the president of Russia was a short man and deprived of height, we can call him a "lilliputin".

~ Some people say, "The world is our oyster." Microscopic organisms who reside inside oysters can rightfully claim, "The oyster is our world."

~ Locustard—a pudding-like snack much favored by flying insects.

~ A flatitude is a platitude that didn't quite make it.

~ His awful-fitting toupee was the centerhairpiece of conversation.

~ The poet Richard Eberhart claimed that poetry is a "natural energy resource." Richard, if that's the case, fill my tank up with unlettered.

~ Identical twins have this in common with a wall phone that doesn't work—they're both dead ringers.

~ There's a County Down in Ireland. There's no County Up in Ireland.

~ "Once more into the breeches." This was said by a courageous tailor preparing to do battle with an unruly customer.

~ To the judge's chagrin the sex offender got off.

~ What Rhett Butler suffered from—Scarlet Fever.

~ What Scarlet O'Hara would have majored in if the women of her time were allowed to attend college—Rhettoric.

~ What Santa Claus said in the sandwich shop—"Ho, ho, hoagie."

~ Logistics is the art of moving freight. Logjamistics is the art of not moving freight.

~ The kind of tree you can eat is an entree.

~ A henpecked husband is a wusband.

~ Children of morticians play formaldehyhe-and-seek.

~ The Japanese rabbi wore a yarmulkaze.

~ We tried to locate a relative's grave in Ever Rest Cemetery, but we couldn't find it. The groundskeeper's directions were too cryptic to follow.

~ Do gnomes have genomes?

~ A girl pins flowers in her hair for decoration. She has a case of the cuties.

~ A man who thinks he's a Casanova and flirts with every skirt is called a "womanizer". It follows that a woman who flirts with every pants can be called a "manizer".

~ Physicists who advance string theory are trying to pull the wool over our eyes.

~ I feel flu-ish. I have a fever. I have the sniffles. I have an upset stomach. A virus must have kecked in.

~ The woman was on the chunky side. Her behind was so huge it was a preposterior.
~ The bookstore sells *Hooters Cookbook*. Every dish in the book comes with buns.

~ A Thai restaurant opened in town. So many people rushed to dine there the first day it became a Thai-phoon restaurant.

~ A man suffered from hay fever for many years. He was recently cured of this mallergy. Miracles never sneeze.

~ Alfred Hitchcock once said that "Murder belongs in the home." That's why it's called home-icide.

~ For real. There was once a publishing company that made a mistake on an errata slip. To correct the correction they inserted an era-errata slip into the book.

~ The levee broke. It was a case of bankrupture.

~ If a husband is called "hubby" informally, it follows that a wife can be called "wifey" informally.

~ Is a person who flies "stand-by" allowed to sit?

~ Did you hear about the hypocritical priest who got knocked off his sacriledge?

~ If plants need to have sap drawn for medical purposes, they go to a phlebotanist.

~ Scottish people call girls "lassies". Scottish people call dimwitted girls "molassies".

~ What does an exit on the New Jersey Turnpike have in common with a bra? They're both jughandles.

~ Two barflies couldn't come to agree which was the best beer on tap. They were at lagerheads on the issue.
~ He was so dumb he couldn't answer the question, "Where was the battle of Gettysburg fought?"

~ He was so dumb he asked if he could surf the Sea of Tranquility.

~ The first cowboy out on a cattle drive serves as a cattlelyst.

~ I visited Sheriff Taylor in Mayberry. The furniture was classic Americana, rustic looking and heavy on the wood. The artwork consisted of Normal Rockwell prints of small-town America. Overall the aunt-bee-ance was homely.

~ I knew a girl who suffered half the eating disorder bulimia nervosa—the binge half.

~ The prisoner got stabbed. He died so quickly he didn't have time to say "Shank you" to his murderer.

~ After clearing the sidewalk of snow, the groundskeeper looked disshoveled.

~ The weather the day of the funeral was embalmy.

~ There was a bomb in Gilead. It was a terrorist attack.

~ Coffee is so expensive nowadays they are raffling off cups. The raffle is called a lattery.

~ Queerulous—a gay person given to a bad temper and frequent outbursts.

~ A hoolijinn is a genie gangster.

~ A cucumber is a pickle that hasn't gone to college yet. A pickle is a cucumber on Social Security.

~ Filmflam—a movie that did not live up to the price of admission.
~ To nosh is to munch on snacks and chat. To gnosh is to munch on snacks and argue.

~ The crook's partner double crossed him. Actually, it was the first time this happened, so it was a single cross.

~ Mick is an Irishman. Gim-mick is a stage Irishman.

~ People of normal height have kin. Short people have munchkin.

~ The pitcher was in the throws of a horrible slump.

~ There are dogwood trees, but there are no catwood trees. That's because catwood trees don't have bark.

~ The argument came to a head in the toilet. The janitor didn't know what happened. What goes on in the toilet stays in the toilet. It's privyledged information.

~ A masochist was fit to be tied—and he was annoyed, too.

~ What every criminal masochist desires—to be slapped in jail.

~ The parts of speech formed a criminal conspiracy and dangled a participle. The grammar police raided the rulebook, arrested the parts, and insisted they assume the preposition.

~ Exasperatu—a frustrated vampire.

~ The cross-dresser stopped wearing women's clothing when the experience turned into a drag.

~ A man bought a hot dog on Halloween. It turned out to be a trick rather than a treat. The roll was empty. It was a hollow weener.

~ Cars are so sophisticated we no longer say, "Drivers, start your engines." Instead we say, "Engines, start your drivers."

~ A recent boxing match in Bayonne was fixed. When it came to the outcome, the boxer who won got the benefit of the bout.

~ There's a new reality show on television. It's the search for the laziest man in America. The name of the show is *American Idle.*

~ Apocalypso—the music playing when the world comes to an end.

~ When a family has to take out a loan to go on a cruise we wish them, "Bum voyage".

~ To a cannibal a murdered body is a corpus delectable.

~ There was a tribe in South America called the Incas. If one of them got thrown out and ostracized he joined the Outcas tribe.

~ When they turn bad Roman Catholics get excommunicated. When they turn good witches get hexcommunicated.

~ A poet was able to write in a number of genres and meters. He was very verse-atile.

~ The voyeur couldn't control his lust. He got in trouble over a fit of peek. The cop who arrested him couldn't control his anger. It was a peak of fit.

~ A man was drowning in the ocean at Asbury Park. A dolphin immediately swam to his rescue. The dolphin didn't show the least hesi-cetacian.

~ When Arab horsemen meet in the desert they exchange greetings with, "How you been douin?"

~ There is such a thing as well water. Is there such a thing as sick water?

~ New York City cab drivers sing that they live in the "sweet land of livery." They do not sing it in English.

~ The linguist overdosed on morpheme.

~ I inquired whether I could ask my physician a question. He said he'd put himself at my indisposal.

~ Atheists live in penthouses. Theists live in repent houses.

~ Are satellite dishes microwavable?

~ The children of terrorists study this in high school—jihagraphy.

~ What termites take on the job—a coffee table break.

~ Do termites saw wood when they sleep?

~ I didn't have an appointment. I called the podiatrist and asked if he takes a walk in.

~ She was attached to me, which explains why I have trouble walking.

~ A dillusion is a false belief about pickles.

~ A student who is chronically absent from class and who refuses to mend his errant ways can be described as recalcitruant.

~ During High Mass the sermon went on for so long the thurifer became incensed.

~ If rocks could talk, their voices would sound gravelly.

~ We call a warm and kindhearted father "Pop". We call a cruel and coldhearted father "Popsicle".

~ In Old Rome a vomitorium was a place where gluttons deposited their binges. In the Old West a varmitorium was a place where rustlers hung out.

~ An alp-habit of mine is solving anagrams.

~ When an ink pen runs out of ink it becomes an inkless pen.

~ Prison guards have this in common with children's electronic games— they're both pokeymen.

~ A person who uses flowery words in ordinary speech ostenstates his case.

~ The Dalai Lama is a man of peace. The Amygdalai Lama is not.

~ She was on a Swiss cheese diet. She ate the cheese in the holes.

~ A sweet-talking imposter is an euphony.

~ When he's well the rock star plays the guitar. When he's sick and has an inflammation of the musicosa the rock star plays the catarrh.

~ She had an affair with her eye doctor. It was an optometryst.

~ A height-deprived monk can be called an erudite ere-mite.

~ And a learned spider—the kind that scrolls across a short monk's books—can be called an erudite mite.

~ A bad thing about going overseas and visiting different countries is that so many foreigners live in those places.

~ Not all, but some spirits are well spooken of.

~ When a railroad man drinks to excess, he ties one on.

~ A friendly hick of a farmer exhibits the virtue of socialhillbility.

~ Asking an alcoholic if he wants another round is an exercise in pintlessness.

~ A father used his strap so frequently it singed the air. It became a cauter-o'-nine tail.

~ The building where they manufacture fragrances is an olfactory.

~ A doxology is a prayerful expression of gratitude to one's god. A doxyology is a prayerful expression of gratitude to one's mistress.

~ When people who committed sexual sins die, they have to be reborn and pay for those sins in another life. I'm not making this up. I read it in the Karma Sutra.

~ Being reincarnated in order to pay for your sins amounts to corporeal punishment.

~ This was overheard in the cafeteria. "She threw her eye at me." "She fell for you romantically?" "No, she threw her eye at me. It was a glass eye."

~ Permit me to ad-duce Mussolini as an example of a failed dictator.

~ The religious station on cable television now offers pray-per-view programming.

~ A blurb is a short endorsement on the back of a book or album. A blarb is a lengthy endorsement on the back of a book or album.

~ An Eskimo who studies esoterica can be said to deal in reklondike matters.

~ To save money a plumber cut costs. It was a drainconian measure.

~ The timbre of the singer's voice was wooden.

~ Can you swear in American sign?

~ A nuance is a carefully reasoned subtlety in an argument. When a nuance becomes stale and overly referenced, it becomes an old-uance.

~ I have no musical ability, but I dreamed I was a concert pianist. Call me an utopianist.

~ Sick birds fly in search of tweetment.

~ If the Blessed Mother was losing her eyesight in her old age, we could say she suffered from immacular degeneration.

~ There's a new perfume on the block. You can buy it cheap in the supermarket. It's called *Fascia* and advertised as "The perfume you wear close to the skin."

~ Investment bankers who exhibit sanitary habits in the corporate rest room can be said to exhibit doo diligence.

~ There was a proctologist in town who either cured his patients or wrecked them.

~ When Fijians exchange greetings in Suva they say "Bula". When Fijians exchange greetings in Outer Space, they say, "Nebula."

~ The sweets were so stale they weren't so much chocolates as chockolates.

~ A chocolatte is hot chocolate made with steamed milk. It is sold in coffee houses at astronomical prices.

~ A teenager from the ghetto was insulted by his peers so frequently he died of dis-entery.

~ We say that a person who walks around on the job engages in legwork. It follows that a writer engages in armwork.

~ Satan on a toot is on a hell-bender.

~ I called and asked if I could hold the meeting at the public library. They said I couldn't. The place was all booked up.

~ Give a hateful person enough misanthrope, he'll hang himself.

~ If I get sentenced and condemned to death at the gallows, I'll make like St. Peter and say, "I am not worthy to be hanged in an upright position. I demand to be hanged upside down."

~ Lazy workers in the shoe store can be called "loafers". Ditto for lazy workers in the bakery.

~ In sociology meme are called, but few are chosen.

~ The optometrist made a spectacle of himself.

~ Are you allowed to walk around in a stationery store?

~ There was an old lady who swallowed a frog. Perhaps she'll croak.

~ A moo-cher is a cow that borrows hay and never returns it.

~ In the Jewish faith God is omnipotent. It's Yahweh or no way.

~ There was an Irishman named MacGillycuddy who smelled badly. They said of him "MacGillycuddy reeks."

~ Actively psychotic schizoidal demons suffer hellucinations.

~ If the angel of death was named Jack, he would be Jack the Reaper.

~ A narcissist who teaches the basics in grammar school is a primer-donner.

~ An acrobat who drinks out of a thermos is a tumbler drinking out of a tumbler.

~ It's World War One and the Allies have mounted an offensive. The doughty British charged across No Man's Land, the brave Americans followed, the French went next, and the Belgiums waffled.

~ Some orders of monks have a pen-chant for singing hymns.

~ Other orders of monks fling their missals around the chapel. This is slinging hymns.

~ Lugrubrious—the untidy situation of being sad and soiled.

~ The barista added too much milk to the latte. It's downright creaminal what she did.

~ If you drink too much you play jaun-dice with your liver.

~ He was so dumb he thought the musical *My Pal Joey* was about a baby kangaroo.

~ The timely correcting of a chronic mistake is the end of an error.

~ Simulachrymose—a state of fake grief known as "crocodile tears."

~ Why do they call film "footage"? It should be called "eyeage".

~ Divvynation is the art of sorting things out ahead of time.

~ People who die at advanced ages are said to show longevity. It follows that people who die young show shortevity.

~ A detachable chapter in a dissertation can be called a pros-thesis. If the chapter is well done it can be called the Ph D' resistance.

~ A giant of limited abilities is a mediogre.

~ An apprentice barber who works in his father's shop and who will inherit the business some day is the hair apparent.

~ The king's food-taster liked the job at first, but then it got to be too much of a chaw.

~ What Jewish people do when they see a loaf of bread—they *challah*.

~ The sailor stole the boat. It was a case of pilferry.

~ A host asked at a Christmas party, "May I wassail you?" The guest replied, "I'm sorry, I don't sing that way."

~ The algebra teacher was light on her feet and a swell ballroom dancer. She had algorhythm.

~ Unions often refer to their members as " the rank and file." In former years unions were so corrupt they referred to their members as "the rank and rank".

~ The milkman was a cranky old man. We called him a curdmurgeon.

~ In matters marital the dutiful German wife toed the frauline.

~ A West Point cadet got caught cheating on the armaments quiz. He tried to plebe bargain for leniency, but every request was shot down.

~ Homargarine—buttering up the boss.

~ The relationship between a hooker and her john can be described as sin-biotic.

~ Couples say "breaking up is hard to do", unless you're on a cell phone.

~ We are creatures of habit. J.R. Tolkien was a creature of hobbit.

~ Heard in a biker's club, "Don't be a pillion, get on the motorcycle."

~ Basil was so full of himself and of his importance people renamed him "Basilica".

~ Muggy. This word describes the weather. It also describes a sea of faces. But "a sea of faces"? Are they human or piscine?

~ We made an excellent choice of wine at dinner. It went down magently.

~ We describe a deaf person as "hard of hearing". Similarly, we can describe a blind person as "hard of seeing".

~ Seated high in the chair, the infant made a mess of bib-lical proportions.

~ The chef had a long lean face—his appearance wasn't helped by the two-foot tall toque he wore. You might say he had a culinear look.

~ A brawl broke out in the restaurant. The chef of police had to be called.

~ Spanish people say "Ola" as a greeting. When they greet someone they don't like they say "Crap-ola."

~ Boring people are jejune. Boring gastroenterologists are jejunum.

~ The billionaire gave so much money to charity the president gave him a philantrophy.

~ The porn film went on for so long they needed an intromission between sex acts.

~ The man was so ugly he wasn't a throwback. He was a throw up.

~ The fortune teller broke her crystal ball. She started to scry.

~ I have a first edition Charlie Chan novel from the 1930s. The covers have held up well. As befits the characters the pages are turning yellow.

~ If Hamlet was a barber and not an unemployed prince, the line would be "Toupee or not toupee."

~ "Toupee or not toupee" is also heard outside rest rooms.

~ A florist can be called a la-vendor.

~ A clairvagrant is an itinerant psychic.

~ A prophet who overeats is on a harbinge.

~ I had a large meal, a really large meal. When I opened my belt afterward, creaking noises came from my stomach regions. They sounded like a ship was moored inside and the tide was up. I visited the doctor out of concern. He said that it was quite possible a ship was inside. The ship may have docked at a sheltered cove on the Islet of Langerhans.

~ Skin walkers are supernatural entities that change shape from human to animal and back again. They do this by carrying pelts of the animal they transform into. To stay fresh they change pelts every now and then. If a skin walker is too cheap to change pelts he's a skinflint walker.

~ I hate these new cell phones. They have so many functions I don't know if I'm dialing a number, taking a picture, or summoning the Internet. The other day I got so hung up figuring out what to do I couldn't make the call.

~ A clammy broth has this in common with an Italian farewell. They are both caioder.

~ An author was asked when the short version of his book would appear in print. He answered, "We'll cross that abridge when we come to it."

~ In grade school we frequently put things over on Sister Magdalina, like when we copied homework or cheated on tests. She never found out what we were up to. You might say she was nun the wiser.

~ If I die before you, does that make me an ante-decedent?

~ Chef Bee exclaimed, pointing with his rolling pin, "Rather than kneading dough the baker is standing like a Sconewall."

~ Travelers who visit places are sightseers. When psychics visit places in the astral plane they are second sightseers.

~ The greedy banker suffered from avaricose veins.

~ What farmers say in parting, "Untill we meet again."

~ The trombone player's horn was bugle-rized. When he found out it was gone, he remarked, "That blows."

~ There was a rumble in Gondwanaland. A Giganotosaurus knocked a T-Rex on its jur-ass.

~ An oghamic alphabet that's edible—macarunes.

~ My financial advisor is heavyset. We describe him as "stocky".

~ A "knucklehead" is a dumb person who makes mistakes frequently. A "Ca-knucklehead" is a dumb Canadian who makes mistakes frequently.

~ He made a joke about his sexual prowess or the lack thereof. It was an ad-libido.

~ The beautiful Arabian woman was paid a houri wage.

~ A creamatory is a place where spoiled milk is poured down the drain.

~ The barista graduated magna cum latte from coffee college.

~ Booth camp—a training ground for assassins.

~ An African American who happens to be an brilliant intellectual is a cere-Bro.

~ We know we can beat a retreat if we have to. Can we beat up a retreat?

~ Di-agnostics—the informed practice of cataloging people as believers or as atheists.

~ The artilleryman had a premunition that a battle was imminent.

~ A pair of dice—a gambler's heaven.

~ Some people clam up when they get nervous and uneasy. Not my pal Harley. He starts to run off at the mouth when he gets nervous and uneasy. If he gets loud I tell him to shudder up.

~ The skeet shooters were having a blast. They didn't take anything seriously, not even their misses.

~ A chink was found in the armor. The question was how he managed to squeeze in.

~ I shutter to think how many unfocused pictures the photographer took.

~ The lonely boy had a stack of *Playboy* centerfolds hidden in the closet. It was a pin-utopia.

~ After dinner the ladies were talking about pregnancy. I told them to stop and not to talk about pregnancy when I just ate.

~ Kohler Beer was named for a German psychologist who demonstrated that chimps think like people—or is it the other way around? People who drink Kohler Beer think it's teneriffic.

~ Kohler once saw an ape climb on a table and change a light bulb. The ape climbed back down and started grinning and hooting as only apes can. The ape was pongiddy with success.

~ There are Method actors. In church on Sundays there are Methodist actors.

~ Scatterbrained—this describes the mind-set of the riot squad as they disperse a crowd.

~ Aichmophobia is the fear of sharp objects. People who suffer this phobia are cutlery of silverware.

~ Dendrology is a branch of learning.

~ A new species of tree was observed in the rain forest. The arborist was stumped what to name it. He refused to go out on a limn and offer a suggestion.

~ If you copy the party line and then have to recant, you can be said to eat parrot.
~ A debutante is a person who makes an entrance into polite society. A debt-utante is a person who makes an entrance into the poorhouse.

~ The witch doctor was caught selling purple box sarsaparilla instead of the real thing—for shamen, for shamen.

~ A dive is a filthy and disordered apartment, store, or bar. It follows that an apartment, store, or bar that is cleaned up, rearranged, and put in good order is a dove.

~ Hotmail.com is a common e-mail site used by ordinary people. The beautiful people use hottiemail.com.

~ A connoisseur is a person who enjoys the finer things in life. A connoisewer is a person who enjoys the trash-filled side of life.

~ Criminals who commit major crimes get sentenced at trial. Criminals who commit misdemeanors get claused at trial.

~ Hokey is a winter sport played on ice by people who don't know how to skate.

~ A porta-john is a precious commode-ity when you're stranded in the woods.

~ There was a lady named Mable. She had a fierce and uncontrollable temper. People called her Flammable. But only behind her back.

~ Wiccanpedia—an on-line encyclopedia of paganism.

~ Latino men palm gel in their hair. If they overdo the palming they become Gelatino men.

~ "Flapper" is an obsolete term for a socially active party woman who enjoyed hanging out with the fellows. If a flapper went insane—and this could happen—she became a "flipper".

~ Soldiers sometimes receive medals for valor after they die. They receive the medals posthumously. If solders receive medals before they die they can be said to receive the medals anthumously.

~ But posthumorously? This is when a person gets the meaning of a joke long after its telling.

~ If a baby-sitter gets up does that make her a baby-stander?

~ There is nothing funny about a brouhaha.

~ The husband and wife took a walk in the park. They found a waif hiding in the bushes. The cannibal husband and wife took a walk in the park. They found a waifer hiding in the bushes.

~ Fin—what a fish has in common with this, the final entry in *Excellent Groaners*.

PROF. FAWCETT'S NOTORIOUS LECTURE ON TEST-IRRELEVANT THOUGHTS

This is the mostly verbatim transcript of the notorious lecture Prof. Phil Fawcett of Umatilla University delivered on the topic of test anxiety. The lecture was delivered in Room 107 of Hobart Hall as part of the Advanced Personality seminar. The course number was 240, the section number was eight.

Prof. Fawcett was in his late 40s. He was a short man, probably 5'8 in height. He was on the stocky side and carried his weight in his midsection. He had a full head of black hair that was turning gray at the ears and thick eyebrows that looked like mustaches growing in the wrong places. He had the trace of a five o'clock shadow—he probably shaved between classes. He was the assistant chair of the psychology department and a full professor. He was an authority on personality structure and functioning and the author of so many books, articles, and monographs he was a reference section of the library all to himself.

Prof. Fawcett wore his regulation white shirt and gray trousers. He had worn the same colored shirt and trousers for every lecture. A square blue tie was half-knotted at the neckline. The tie concluded two buttons short of his belt. As he walked into the classroom he carried a sheath of worn notes in manila folders and a large-sized Styrofoam cup of coffee. He never once opened the notes throughout the lecture. He frequently opened the lid of the container and sipped the coffee. He must have nuked the coffee—the fumes clouded the front of his face.

I sat midway in the room and in the center aisle so I could see the blackboard unobstructed by the heads of my classmates. Prof. Fawcett's lecture could get phlegmbouyant, so it was safer not to sit in the front rows. And it wasn't good to sit in the rear of the room, as he did a lot of board work. He never used the computer or optical equipment available for professors tuned into the electronic age. He wrote the important points the old-fashioned way—in white chalk. We came out of class with pages of notes. Fortunately for everyone, he was fond of acronyms.

It's 3:00 PM and time to start, Prof. Fawcett commenced, closing the lid of the coffee container. Do you know where your psychology class is? From the looks of the room it appears a few people do not. I note several empty seats. But that's all right. You're here. More importantly, I'm here.

As you will note from the syllabus today's topic is *test anxiety*—he wrote T and A in capital letters and broke the chalk when he put a period after the A. I don't have to tell you that test anxiety can be a serious issue in the world of education. If test anxiety is conceptualized as a variant of evaluation anxiety it can be a serious issue in the world outside education. The number of the student population affected by test anxiety is hard to pin down. Estimates vary from 10% - 20%. A smaller percentage of students are affected by test anxiety to such a severe degree they can be described as clinically anxious. Test anxiety affects students at every grade level from kindergarten to graduate school. Numbers are believed to be on the rise in the lower grades given the emphasis educators have placed on performance on state-mandated tests.

Students dislike tests and for good reason. Tests play a major role in moving students through the education system. In grade school students have to pass tests to get promoted. In high school students have to take the Scholastic Aptitude Test to get into college. In college students have to take the Graduate Records Exam to get into graduate school. In graduate school students have to take comprehensive exams to get to the doctoral level. Once students get their graduate degrees they have to take board exams and licensing tests. Never mind these "big tests". Along the way and in every course students face innumerable small tests and quizzes. It never ends. It's raining tests big and small and the weather does not promise to clear up anytime soon.

Tests play an important role in our lives and test anxiety plays an important role in sabotaging performance. Tests make us or break us and anxiety may be the reason tests break a fair number of students. It is a fact that an elevated level of test anxiety is negatively correlated with poor performance on a test. As anxiety increases, performance decreases. Students get left back. They need to repeat grades. They don't get into the college of their choice. They don't get advanced degrees. They are dismissed from graduate school. They go broke hiring coaches to pass qualifying exams. No wonder students detest tests.

I'd like to review two older conceptualizations of anxiety and then move onto the current conceptualization of test anxiety. Before I do that I'd like to describe the vignette of Doris—he wrote a capital D on the board and broke another piece of chalk. I'm not going to say Doris's last name in the event you know her. I don't know who you know and it's not proper to use former students as examples of concepts. In any event Doris was a psychology student here in Umatilla University some years ago. She was about the most learned student I had ever known. She knew more psychology than any professor. She knew more psychology than I did. That may not be saying much—the class groaned at that and a brownnoser in the front row blurted, "That can't be."

Doris was absolutely brilliant in the classroom and she didn't have trouble with course tests, as they didn't carry important implications for her career. But she suffered the most horrible test anxiety and she bombed three times on the Graduate Records Exam. The first time she took the test her mind went blank. She was, I assure you, a walking, breathing, note-collecting encyclopedia of psychology. She got sick the second time she took the exam and had to leave the room. The third time she took the exam she stayed out to the wee hours and drank too much red wine. She arrived at the test exhausted and hung over. Obviously, her score was atrocious and in no way indicative of her vast knowledge. She engaged in a self-defeating strategy of carousing the night before the exam in order to explain and to explain away her poor performance. She was tired and hung over, but it was not exhaustion and alcohol consumption that sabotaged her performance. It was test anxiety.

Doris's story ends somewhat happily. She never got into graduate school in psychology. Our discipline is the worse for her absence. She did get into graduate school in public health, however. The standards may be lower in that field than in psychology.

Any questions?—Prof. Fawcett pointed to the class and waited, but no one asked a question. No one ever did.

Let's move on to the first conceptualization of anxiety. This was the one offered by Uncle Sigmund Freud. Uncle divided personality into three contentious components—he wrote the words "id", "superego", and "ego" on the board and took a sip of coffee. A cloud passed in front of his face, but I didn't know whether it was coffee fumes or chalk dust. The id is the depository of instincts, notably those always reliable motives of love affairs and fisticuffs. The superego is the primitive voice of conscience. Mostly, it is the voice of father and mother scolding and punishing the child. And the ego is the executive part of personality that must deal with the id, with the superego, and with reality, as these forces emerge and play out in the individual's life.

The ego is assailed on all sides by anxiety. Uncle used the word "anxiety" exactly as anyone in this room uses the word. Anxiety is that uneasy, nervous, shuddery feeling we get at times. Anxiety is that feeling we have that things are getting worse. Anxiety feels much like fear. Anxiety is the comprehension that things are getting out of sorts and that we're losing control. Anxiety is that feeling that our self-esteem is being challenged and is in question.

According to Uncle, anxiety arises from three sources—he wrote the capital letters ICE on the board. Anxiety arises from the instincts—he pointed to the letter I. We get nervous when we feel the onslaught of sex and aggression. Think how you feel when the stirrings of lust set you on edge. Will she like you? Will he like you? Will he be able to get it up? Will she be able to fake it convincingly? And think about the aggressive instinct. How do you feel when a person challenges you to a fight? Will you hold your own? Will you get hurt? Will you turn into a man or will you stay a mouse and run away?

Anxiety also arises from conscience—he pointed to the letter C. We find the thoughts of sex disturbing. We are encumbered with modesty. We are loaded with social mores and cultural standards how to behave sexually. In a basic way we find sex dangerous. We find the sex act disgusting. When it comes to aggression we were all raised in a moral way. We were told to love our enemies and to do good to those who threaten to beat us up. We can get in trouble for fighting. We don't want to hurt another person. We don't want to get hurt. And we don't want to be arrested and spend the night with the lowlifes in the county lockup.

Anxiety also arises from the environment—he didn't bother to point to the letter E. The ego needs to take the environment into account. There are religious and political rules that need to be adhered to. There are powerful forces and powerful people who need to be placated. There is a physical structure to reality that we need to respect. Wood hurts when we run into it. Nails hurt when they cut into us. There are little things called germs lurking in the sexual organs of our partners. And there are brutes who know how to kick box and who carry concealed weapons. We have to be careful in satisfying the instincts. We have to be thorough in mollifying conscience.

Uncle conjectured that the ego is not totally defenseless in handling these sources of anxiety. The ego is able to use defense mechanisms to control anxiety and to continue to function. The defense mechanisms operate in an unconscious manner to minimize anxiety. They include such famous and controversial processes as repression, projection, reaction formation, intellectualization, and sublimation, to name five of many.

Any questions?—he didn't wait long before continuing.

Let's move on to the second conceptualization of anxiety. This was posited by such 1940s learning psychologists as Neal Miller and Hobart Mowrer and it derived from experimental studies of lower organisms. The operative concepts are classical and operant conditioning and the two-factor theory of active avoidance.

Here is the prototypical experiment. A rat is placed in a box. A barrier a few inches high divides the box into two chambers. A tone sounds for a few seconds and then shuts off. A second or two after the tone ends the floor is electrified. The rat is surprised, to say the least. It scurries about and scrambles to find a safe place. We would do the same if the floor to this classroom was suddenly electrified. By accident, the rat climbs up and over the wall. That side of the box is not electrified. The rat tumbles to safety. We can imagine the rat rubbing its stinging paws and thinking to the effect "That was a close call."

After a few pairings—a very few pairings—the rat gets better at fleeing the shock. The rat leaps to the other side as soon as the shock comes on. Technically, this is called "escape conditioning" and can be understood as negative reinforcement. As you certainly recall from your undergraduate courses, negative reinforcement is the operant conditioning procedure in which a response successfully reduces an unpleasant or aversive stimulus, in this case shock. Whatever terminates an aversive stimulus increases in rate. The response of flight to shock increases and becomes more frequent.

Our rat isn't stupid. It must be a rat from Volusia County. The rat learns to leap to the safe side as soon as it hears the tone. The rat learns to avoid shock altogether. This is called "avoidance learning". It's analogous to what we would do if we heard a warning siren. We would run for safety before the bombs start dropping.

Escape and avoidance conditioning constitute the first factor in the two-factor theory. The first factor involves operant conditioning. The second factor involves classical conditioning—Fawcett wrote the letters US and UR on the board joined by a thick dash of chalk. He wrote the letters CS and CR below them, slightly to the left and joined by another dash.

The unlearned or unconditioned stimulus of shock leads to the unlearned or unconditioned response of discomfort and pain—Prof. Fawcett pointed to the letters US and UR. No rat has to learn to feel pain to shock. Not even the rats from Lake County have to learn this. Heck, we wouldn't have to learn this unconditioned response and we're what you call "human beings"—running his hand above the dash he pointed to the CS and the CR. The conditioned stimulus is the tone and the conditioned response is? Wait a moment, what is the conditioned response? The tone comes on and shuts off before the shock comes on. The conditioned response cannot be pain, since there is no shock present when the tone is on or when the tone shuts off.

We easily understand why the rate of flight in escape conditioning increases. Flight terminates pain. With a little thought and a little empathy we might be able to understand why the rate of response in avoidance conditioning increases.

Think carefully about the procedure. A tone comes on and shuts off. A second or two later shock comes on. Suddenly, the rat is in pain. The rat goes through the procedure a few times. A tone continues to sound just before the shock comes on. What would the rat feel when the tone comes on?

A young lady in the front row with curly blond hair and a clingy blue blouse raised her hand. Fawcett pointed to her. "The rat would feel nervous," she said.

"Precisely. Anyone else?" Fawcett pointed to the short lady in the right row near the door.

"The rat would feel fear."

"Precisely."

I knew where this was going, but the heavyset guy next to the window said the answer before Prof. Fawcett called on him. "The rat would feel anxious."

Just so. The rat feels fear and anxiety—Prof. Fawcett circled the letters CR and underlined them. The conditioned response is fear and anxiety. The conditioned response is the anticipation of pain.

Avoidance conditioning is a powerful form of learning that persists for extended periods. It is difficult to re-condition because it is so awfully effective. The fear and anxiety are reduced by a particular behavior. The response is not allowed to extinguish. That is, the response is not allowed to occur in the absence of reinforcement. The rat never stays around long enough to find out if shock is coming. Maybe conditions have changed. Maybe the experimenter has joined a humane society. Maybe there's a short in the wiring. Maybe there's been a blackout at the power plant. The rat doesn't know that shock will not follow the next sounding of the tone. At the first sound of the tone it leaps to safety up and over the barrier.

Learning psychologists like Mowrer and Miller immediately noticed the correspondence of their concepts to those of Uncle Sigmund. They believed they had defined in the clear light of an experimental setting what Uncle left undeveloped in the cigar smoke of the consulting room. For Uncle anxiety was reduced through defense mechanisms. For Mowrer and Miller anxiety was a conditioned response reduced through avoidance learning. Treatment with Uncle meant reviewing dreams and defensive maneuvers. Treatment with the learning psychologists involved practicing incompatible responses, such as is done in desensitization and in exposure therapy. In a manner of speaking what is done is to facilitate extinction. The rat or the person must not be allowed to avoid experiencing the conditioned stimulus when it is not followed by an aversive unconditioned stimulus.

Of course there are major differences between psychoanalytic theory and learning theory. Two-factor theory stressed the environment as the origin of anxiety and not the instincts or the conscience—Prof. Fawcett pointed to the E in the acronym ICE. I noticed that the shirt under his arm was stained black with sweat.

Anxiety has been conceptualized in other influential ways in the history of psychology. The latter-day Gestalt psychologists led by Fritz Perls suggested that anxiety occurred when the person left the present tense and started thinking about what is going to happen in the future. In this regard the noted gangster and "man of honor" Joe Bonnano defined fear in his autobiography in as solid a way as any psychologist worth the letters following their names. Bonnano wrote, "Fear is when you think ahead about what may happen to you." No statement about fear is as decisive as this one.

We've been using fear and anxiety as synonyms, but they may not be. The interpersonal psychiatrist Harry Stack Sullivan suggested we needed to demarcate fear and anxiety. According to Sullivan fear follows biological threats. This view is compatible with the learning approach. Sullivan suggested that anxiety derived from an interpersonal source and involved no biological threat. Rather, anxiety was a drop in self-respect or self-esteem—Prof. Fawcett wrote the letters SE on the board. This view is not compatible with the learning approach. We can assume the rat is unconcerned with issues of self-respect or self-esteem. If it is, we don't know how. We'll never know how.

Let me offer an example that may highlight the difference Sullivan posited between fear and anxiety. Say you're in a tavern. Maybe you've gone there to unwind after class. In any event while you're unwinding a man walks in and flashes a gun. You immediately feel fear. After robbing the register the bandit instructs all the men to lower their trousers so he can make an escape unimpeded by heroics. Lowering your trousers you immediately feel anxiety.

Sullivan conjectured that self-esteem is restored through the use of "security operations"—he wrote SO and drew an arrow between them and the letters SE. Security operations are analogous to Uncle's defense mechanisms. To restore self-esteem they must work unconsciously. Sullivan preferred the term "outside awareness". If they operate inside awareness the person continues to feel reduced self-respect. No one wants to experience reduced self-respect, not even the people who live in the Ocala forest. Sullivan provided a different list of defensive maneuvers to handle anxiety than Uncle. Sullivan's list includes selective inattention, anger, and disparagement.

Prof. Fawcett paused and took a sip of coffee. There was only the slightest wisp of fumes from inside the container.

Let's move on to test anxiety—he underlined T and A and put a check mark to the right of the A. The initial studies and conceptualizations of test anxiety arose in learning laboratories and in experimental psychology. Unlike many topics in psychology test anxiety had a rich experimental history before clinicians started to treat it. The initial conceptualization was by George Mandler and Seymour Sarason in 1952—for some reason he wrote the initials GM and SS on the board.

Since that time conceptualizations of test anxiety have evolved into social learning theory and the information processing perspective. Perhaps the main researcher in the 1970s and 1980s was Irwin Sarason—for the sake of consistency he wrote the initials IS. Sarason developed what became the most widely used questionnaire to assess test anxiety. This is the Test Anxiety Scale, a questionnaire filled out over the years by thousands of students. Test anxiety has become the most studied topical anxiety and the one most rooted in psychometrics and in controlled experimental research.

I'd like to examine test anxiety using the person-by-situation interactional approach developed by Norman Endler and others—he didn't write NE on the blackboard. In understanding personality we must consider both psychological factors and situational or environmental factors. People differ in the extent to which they experience test anxiety. Some people are not bothered by it and other people, like Doris, are devastated by it. There are situations that elicit and maximize the occurrence of test anxiety in people predisposed to experience it. For test anxiety to remain at manageable levels the individuals must not be predisposed to experience anxiety and the situations must carry no potent implications. For test anxiety to become psychologically disruptive the individuals must be predisposed to experience it and the situations they're in must carry potent implications.

Personality variables include the following. The person is unprepared for the test. The person is aware that he or she lacks the competencies to succeed. The person feels challenged in ways that cannot be surmounted. The person has flunked previous tests. The person has failed in past or similar tasks. The person has unrealistic expectations of success and failure. The person comes from a history of excessive punishment. The person has experienced disapprobation for success in past tasks.

Situation variables include the following. The test is difficult or ambiguous. The test has stringent time constraints. The test is unexpected. In this regard you might think back to high school and to the dread students felt in classes where the teachers were fond of giving "pop" quizzes. The test is especially important. Think of the difference between a lowly quiz in an elective and a make-or-break test like the Graduate Records Exam.

Prof. Fawcett paused and sipped the coffee. No fumes emerged. He had talked so much the coffee had grown cold.

Freud and Sullivan saw anxiety as an unpleasant experience that is handled by psychological processes outside awareness or at the fringe of awareness. Dealing with rats learning psychologists could hardly consider the concept of awareness. Nevertheless, they saw anxiety as an unpleasant experience that instigates escape and avoidance responses. The modern view of anxiety concurs with these interpretations. Anxiety is most definitely an unpleasant experience. But the modern view suggests that the experience of anxiety involves heightened awareness and self-consciousness. The heightened awareness is of negative self-evaluations that are clearly and uncomfortably inside awareness. The evaluations involve self-criticism, disparaging comparisons to others, anticipations of failure, feelings of inadequacy, and the motivation to end the task and to get out of the situation as expeditiously as possible. The person believes that he or she will not succeed in the test or at the task. These thoughts do not habituate. We never get used to thinking badly of ourselves.

This circle is the totality of thoughts that we can devote to the task of taking a test—Prof. Fawcett drew a large circle on the board. This circle represents the total attention we can devote to the test. It is the total energy directed toward taking the test.

If you are devoted to the task and not distracted the entire interior is filled with task-relevant or task-appropriate thoughts—he wrote the acronym *tats* in the center of the circle. But let's say you've grown distracted while taking a test. You're thinking about a movie or television show you watched or a book you read. Maybe your mind wanders to a different class. Maybe you start thinking about what you're doing after class. Maybe you're thinking about the incident in the tavern after class and about what a good mother you had for telling you to always wear clean underwear. Each of these thoughts detracts from the totality—he drew four boxes inside the circle and scratched their interiors white with chalk. See how you've reduced the totality of available thoughts, the totality of available energy. See how you've sabotaged yourself by falling prey to these distractions and daydreams.

He erased the interior of the circle and grabbed the coffee cup. He immediately set it down. He must have remembered that the coffee had grown cold.

Okay, let's consider how test anxiety enters into this circle. Let's say you are predisposed to experience a little test anxiety and the situation involves no potent implications—he drew a curved line near the left border of the circle. See how you've cut into the totality of task-appropriate thoughts—I wrote *tats*. Let's say you're predisposed to a greater amount of test anxiety and the situation includes somewhat potent implications—he erased the first line and drew a curved line a few inches into the circle. See all the *tats* you've lost. Now let's say you're like Doris. You're a person who gets devastated by test anxiety and you're taking a really important exam—he erased the previous line and drew a straight line in the center of the circle.

As it grows intense anxiety reduces performance on tests. You can see why. Anxiety detracts from the totality of thoughts we can bring to bear on what we're doing. Anxiety detracts from attention. Anxiety detracts from motivation. We start thinking about something other than the test and these thoughts are not pleasant. The circle has been cut in half. On one side we have test-appropriate thoughts—he rewrote *tats* in the left half of the circle. On the other side we have test-inappropriate or test-irrelevant thoughts. I couldn't believe what he wrote in the right half of the circle or that I copied it letter-by-letter, but *tits* sure beat writing "test-irrelevant thoughts" repeatedly.

Some of these *tits*—he pronounced it "test-irrelevant thoughts", but I used the acronym—are going to involve heightened awareness of physiological processes. The test anxious person becomes aware of bodily processes that usually remain at the fringe of awareness. The person not afflicted by test anxiety notes these processes and pays scant attention to them. The test anxious person notes these processes and magnifies them out of all proportion. As they get magnified *tits* distract from thoughts we might otherwise devote to performing the task. Taking a test the anxious person uses half the circle rather than the full circle.

Such physiological *tits* include the following. My head hurts. My stomach hurts. My nose is stuffed. My mouth is dry. I have palpitations of the heart. I feel warm. I feel queasy. My foot fell asleep. My writing hand is cramping up. I have to go to the toilet. I'm itchy. Is the mole on my wrist cancerous? I'm going to be sick.

Some *tits* include the assessment of performance on the test. The assessment is never positive. These *tits* include the following. I'm not doing well. I'm flunking. I don't think I can finish. I should have studied more. How much time is left? There's not enough time left. What if I fail the course? Maybe I can get extra credit. What does the question really mean? This test is tricky. The instructor has it in for me. I don't think the answer's on the page. I can't continue. I have to get out of here. My memory's failing me. I'm making mistakes. I don't care how I do.

Other *tits* include persistent negative self-evaluations. These are global, stable, and generalized judgments you make about yourself. They are not flattering. Think of the rat jumping over the barrier. The rat thinks that shock will always follow the tone. The test anxious person thinks he or she will always fail. Such thoughts make failure likely.

Negative self-evaluation *tits* include the following. I always make mistakes. What's the matter with me? Why is everyone in the class so much brighter? Why is everyone so much better? Why can't I be like other people? I'm a failure. I'm no good. I never do anything right. I never succeed at anything. I never seem to get started in life. I shouldn't be in this class. I'm not college material. My future is bleak. I don't have a future. I'm all messed up. I'm stupid. I'm a loser. I never get anything right. I always let other people down. I'm shaming my father and mother. I'm such a disappointment to my family. I hate myself and everything I stand for.

Prof. Fawcett paused. He looked at the coffee container, but he didn't reach for it.

I could continue this litany of negative self-evaluations, but that would be too depressing. We'd leave class in glum moods. We'd hurry to the tavern to drink ourselves back into brighter moods. I think I've made my point. *Tits* are potent and influential thoughts. *Tits* have potent consequences. People become preoccupied with *tits*. But becoming preoccupied with *tits* detracts from succeeding at the test. Students sabotage themselves thinking *tits* rather than *tats* and they fail the test or they get lower grades than they should have.

When you think *tits* it becomes difficult to think about anything else. When you think *tits* you can't think about the test. We may think we can, but we cannot successfully think about two things at the same time. We cannot think simultaneously *tats* and *tits*. Jesus Christ said, "A house divided against itself cannot stand." The Irish peasants of yesteryear had a saying, "You can't whistle and chew at the same time." In the context of test anxiety a student divided between *tats* and *tits* cannot get a good grade. A student can't whistle answers and chew on *tits* at the same time. Instead of thinking about the answers to the questions test anxious students are thinking *tits*. And *tits* ruin them.

Tits make class an unhappy experience. *Tits* make class a place test anxious students do not enjoy coming to. Just like with the lab rats in the chamber, *tits* make students want to escape the class as soon as possible. Just like with the rats, anxious students avoid the classroom at the first thought of *tits*. Students preoccupied with *tits* are complex and self-divided people. They think of *tits*, they try not to think of *tits*, they try to think of *tats*, but they can't. People not preoccupied with *tits* think only of *tats* and they get good grades. They graduate and go onto careers proud and self-confident of their abilities rather than becoming ashamed of themselves and of their *tits*.

As they grow intrusive *tits* are associated with lowered academic performance. As they become prominent *tits* are associated with reduced happiness and with elevated levels of stress. *Tits* are associated with doubts and with second guessing and with self-defeating thoughts. *Tits* are themselves self-defeating thoughts. The inner dialogue of anxious students afflicted with *tits* involves flagelallation. Rather than praising oneself and flooding oneself with cheery upbeat thoughts, test anxious students lash themselves with thoughts of failure, defeat, and inferiority. Instead of thinking about success, test anxious students think *tits*. And they are not particularly happy thoughts.

The key to avoiding anxiety and its consequences is to stop thinking *tits* and to keep thinking *tats*. The only way to stop thinking *tits* is to stop thinking about them. This sounds like an onerous task, but it is not difficult. It requires students to become aware of the thought process and it requires students to differentiate between thoughts that are test relevant and thoughts that are not. The solution to reducing anxiety is to shift awareness from *tits* to the task at hand. Students should pay attention to the test and not to the sources of anxiety. Thomas

"Stonewall" Jackson once said, "Never take counsel of your fears." We can rephrase Stonewall's advice, "Never take counsel of your anxieties."

Becoming aware of the thinking process has been a fundamental part of philosophy and religion from the olden times. In the West becoming aware of one's thoughts is called "reflection", "contemplation", and "introspection". In the East becoming aware of the thought process is a vital part of the Buddhist and Zen meditative traditions. Regardless of the orientations students prefer—philosophical or religious—it is critical to make the attempt to take back the mind and gain control of awareness. It is time for students to take charge of consciousness and to shepherd the wandering minstrel of thoughts back into fertile fields. Students should become masters of their minds rather than permit their minds to master them.

As students become aware of their thoughts during a test they can ask themselves, "Is the thought I'm having relevant to answering the question?" "Is the thought I'm having irrelevant to answering the question?" Simpler questions can't be found. If the thought is relevant and if it helps to answer a question on the test, the student can leave it alone. Better still, the student can express a word of private encouragement and reinforcement. "Good job, well done," you can tell yourself. "Mind, you've done right. Mind, you're all right." Lord knows, even if we have to give it to ourselves, all of us can use a bit more positive reinforcement.

If students determine that the thoughts they are having as they take a test are irrelevant and that they are physiological *tits*, or performance *tits*, or negative self-evaluative *tits*, or the old-fashioned daydream variety of *tits*, they can gently shift attention back to the test. There's plenty of time for *tits* when the test is over.

Prof. Fawcett raised the coffee cup and dropped it in the garbage receptable near the door. That was a sure sign—it was a conditioned stimulus—that the lecture was nearly over.

An advanced technique developed by the best minds in cognitive-behavioral therapy is the "rubber band" technique. In this technique students wear a rubber band around their wrists. Be sure to wear a rubber band tight enough to snap sharply against the skin but not so tight to cut the circulation off. Whenever students find their thoughts wandering from the material they snap the rubber band and mentally direct themselves to shift attention from those devilish *tits* to productive *tats*. After this happens a number of times the snap of the rubber band serves as a cue to remind students to keep their thoughts on task, which is where they belong.

Prof. Fawcett hesitated and then asked, "The rubber band technique is analogous to what element of classical conditioning?"

After a long pause a student in the front row answered, "The unconditioned response."

"No." Prof. Fawcett pointed to the letters on the board. "Anyone else?"

The nerdish guy sitting to my left answered, "The unconditioned stimulus."

"Not quite. Anyone else?"

A third student answered, "The conditioned stimulus?"

Prof. Fawcett shook his head. Apparently, the class had engaged in *tits* during the lecture. There was one choice left, but it seemed rather pointless to say it. Fawcett beat the class to the answer.

The rubber band technique is analogous to the conditioned response. Conditioned rats habitually jump over the barrier at the first sound of the tone that precedes shock. By snapping the rubber band, students habitually shift attention to thoughts that are task-relevant.

Prof. Fawcett picked the eraser up. With broad sweeps of the hand he cleaned the board from left to right. When he was done he returned the eraser to the runner and clapped his hands clean of chalk dust.

I'd like to offer a few hints how to minimize test anxiety. We can never avoid anxiety altogether, but we can reduce it. Try to keep a sensible perspective on the implications of the test. Course exams are rarely make-or-break in the total education process and even major tests can be retaken. Try not to compare yourself to your classmates. You're not in competition with them, you're in competition with the pirate anxiety that's looking to steal your grade. Try not to generalize your performance. Maybe you did poorly on a test. That doesn't mean you're going to perform poorly on the next test. Maybe you did superlatively on the test. That doesn't mean you're always going to perform superlatively. Every test is different, every situation is different.

Make sure you prepare for the test. Study to the best of your ability and don't cram. Cramming is a very inefficient and very stressful way to prepare. Cramming practically guarantees failure. Knowing the material that's going to be on the test reduces the fears and worries about taking the test. Be like an athlete coming into the stadium of the classroom. An athlete can't predict the score of the game before it starts. An athlete can't predict the quality of his or her performance. But an athlete can prepare to the maximum extent possible. Doing one's homework doesn't guarantee passing grades, but it makes passing grades more likely. Preparation makes it more likely that students will do well once the test commences and they engage with their mortal opponents, the questions on the test.

Know the type of test you're taking. There are recall or essay tests and there are recognition or multiple-choice tests. Don't turn one type of test into the other. Commonly, students turn multiple-choice tests into recall tests. This is a major mistake. Students start to think about the questions—what do they really mean?—and about the choices—what do they really mean? Before they know it, students sabotage themselves and start thinking *tits*.

In tests of recognition memory the answer is not in your head. The answer is on the paper looking up at you. The answer is practically screaming, "Hey, student, here I am! Pick me! Pick me!"—Prof. Fawcett laughed at what he thought was a joke, but no one else joined in. The student's task is to recognize and select the correct answer. The task is not to mull over what the answer means. Thinking can get even the brightest, best-prepared, students into trouble.

Try to arrive early for the test and to put yourself in a restful mood. Rushing in late is going to add to the stress. Try to sit in the same seat you ordinarily studied in during the course. The seat serves as?—Prof. Fawcett waited, but no one answered. The seat serves as a conditioned stimulus—he turned to point to the acronym, but remembered he erased the board. The seat will help slide prepared students into the right frame of mind. Of course, sitting in the same place can backfire if you've been a goof-off all semester and used the seat for *tits*.

I'd like to remind you that the final exam is in two weeks—Prof. Fawcett picked the folders up. Even as I'm speaking the exam is being typed in an apartment on the south side of Route 19. Second floor left. Maybe you know the place. It's above the Dollar General Store and across the road from Chandler's Farm Antiques. I'd like you to put the information we covered today to good use in preparing for the exam. We'll put this lecture to the test and learn just how anxious you are.

I thank you for your attention and hope to see you next week. As you can note from the syllabus, next week's lecture is on Albert Bandura's concepts of reciprocal determinism and self-efficacy—he wrote the letters AB on the board. No one copied them.

I closed my notebook, clicked the pen shut, and slipped it in my shirt pocket. I watched the students leave the room in single file. Prof. Fawcett stood behind the desk and wished the students well. He told the students to make sure they studied in the intervening week and not to waste time with frivolous activities. For a moment I thought to stay behind and review the lecture notes while they were fresh in my mind, but I caught sight of the young lady with the curly blond hair and the clingy blue blouse as she walked out of the classroom. I wondered whether she was a psychology major. I wondered what kind of person she was. And I wondered what she was doing after class. I looked at my, thus far, unscarred wrists. I became aware of the process of thinking, but didn't see a need to wear a rubber band and snap myself bloody. I couldn't make up my mind whether these thoughts were relevant or irrelevant to the situation and it didn't seem to matter very much.

I slipped my notebook in my briefcase, got up, and walked one flight down for the evening seminar on Systems and Theories. I didn't want to be late for Prof. Finaghty's lecture on the continuing relevance of Heinz Kohut.